I0752923

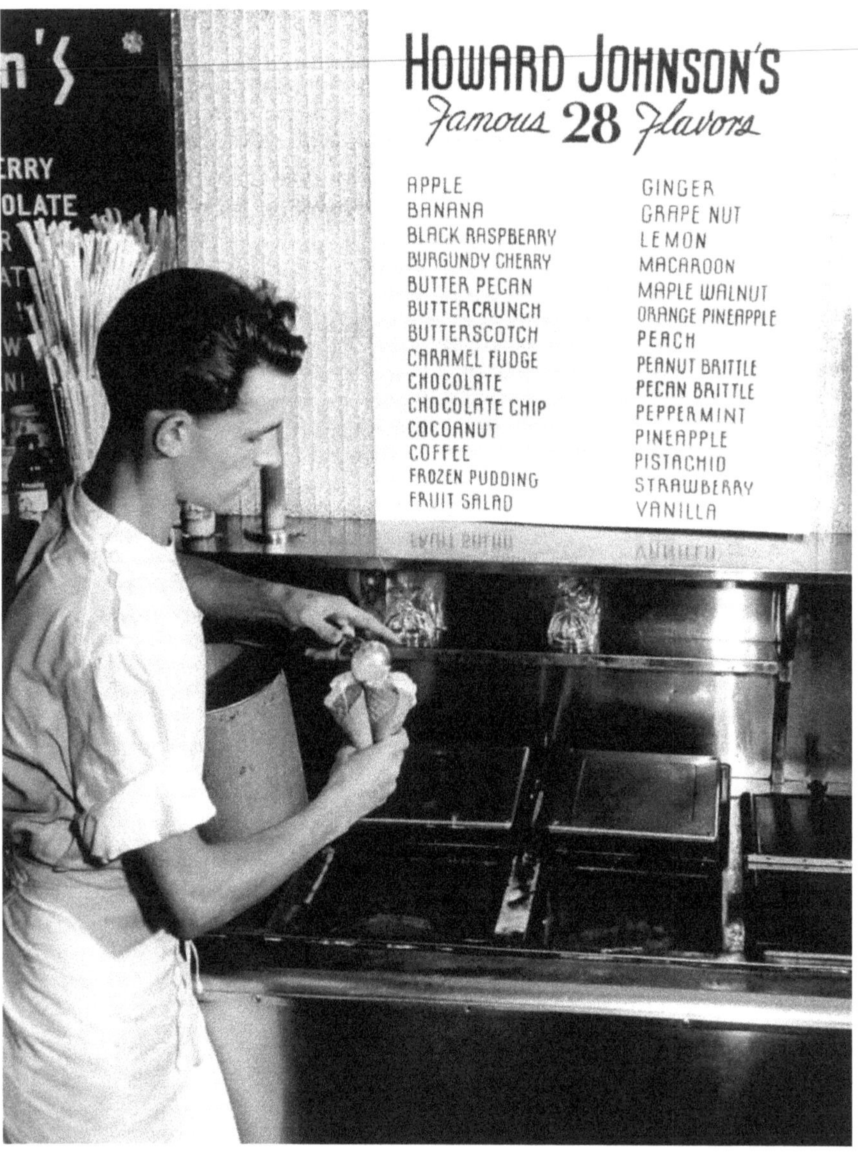

A white-dressed server scoops ice cream from the freezer with his left hand, with four waffle cones nestled in his right hand. As the wall sign reads, these are "Howard Johnson's Famous 28 Flavors," which are listed alphabetically. Although these premium ice cream flavors sometimes changed regionally, it was said that vanilla was by far the most popular choice.

A History of

HOWARD JOHNSON'S

How a Massachusetts Soda Fountain Became an American Icon

ANTHONY MITCHELL SAMMARCO

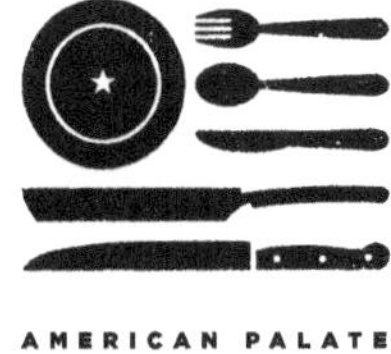

Published by American Palate
A Division of The History Press
Charleston, SC 29403
www.historypress.net

All photographs, unless otherwise noted, are from the Sammarco Collection, Archives and Special Collections, Joseph P. Healey Library, University of Massachusetts–Boston.

First published 2013

Manufactured in the United States

ISBN 978.1.60949.428.5

Library of Congress Cataloging-in-Publication Data

Sammarco, Anthony Mitchell.
A history of Howard Johnson's : how a Massachusetts soda fountain became an American icon / Anthony Mitchell Sammarco.
pages cm
Includes bibliographical references.
ISBN 978-1-60949-428-5 (paperback)
1. Howard Johnson (Firm)--History. 2. Johnson, Howard Deering, 1897-1972. 3. Restaurants--United States--History. 4. Restaurants--East (U.S.)--History. 5. Motels--United States--History. 6. Motels--East (U.S.)--History. I. Title.
TX945.5.H595S25 2013
647.9573--dc23
2013029385

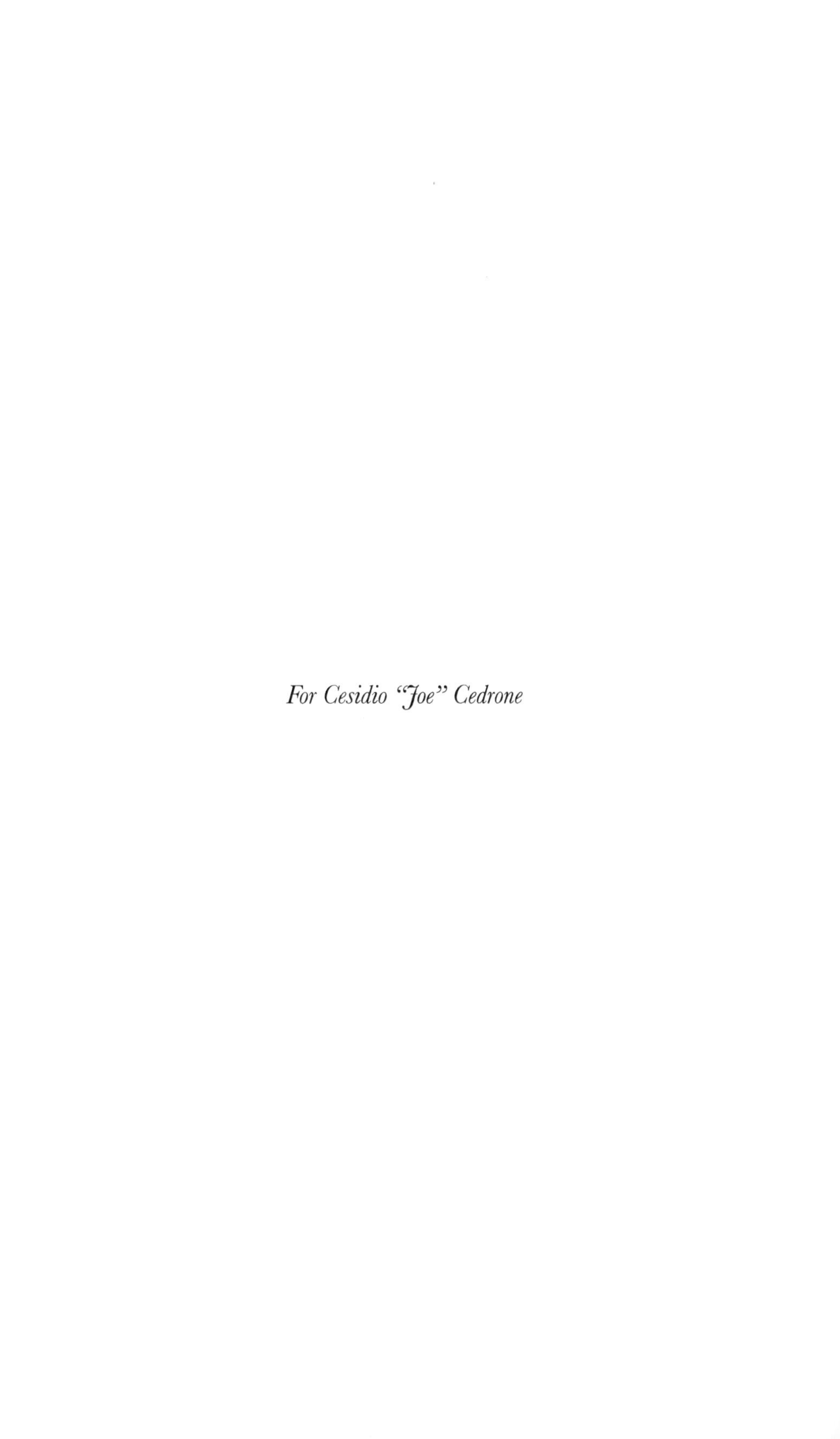

For Cesidio "Joe" Cedrone

Nunquam non paratus *("Never unprepared")*
—*Clan Johnstone*

Contents

Acknowledgements

There's many a king on a gilded throne
But there's only one king on an ice-cream cone.
So we crown him today with friendly acclaim,
All over the country we'll blazen his name.
With hot dogs barking in approbation,
He's the man who believes he can feed the nation.
—Howard Johnson's, 1940

I would like to extend my sincere thanks and deep appreciation to the following friends, acquaintances and kind interested people who offered assistance, shared their reminiscences of Howard Johnson's or loaned photographs:

The late John Eagles Alcott; Kai Bridge Armstrong; Leslie Rappaport-Atlas; Steve and Christine Alcott Baptiste, for loaning family photographs; Harris Beals; Boston Public Library, Henry Scannell; the women at the Brighton Tops; Ronald J. Brodeur; Sue Anne Brogan; Jennifer Brooks; Helen Graham Buchanan; John Burrows; Robert Burrows; Carol Campanelli; Jamie Carter; Cesidio "Joe" Cedrone; Elise Ciregna and Stephen Lo Piccolo; Edie Clifford; Regina K. Clifton; Katherine Coleman; Colortek of Boston, Jackie Anderson and Girolamo Grassa; Matthew Hallowell Crocker; Elizabeth Curtiss and Lynne Matthews; Patricia Desmond, publisher of the *Milton Times*; Paul J. Durgin, for the loan of annual reports and Durgin family papers; Olivia

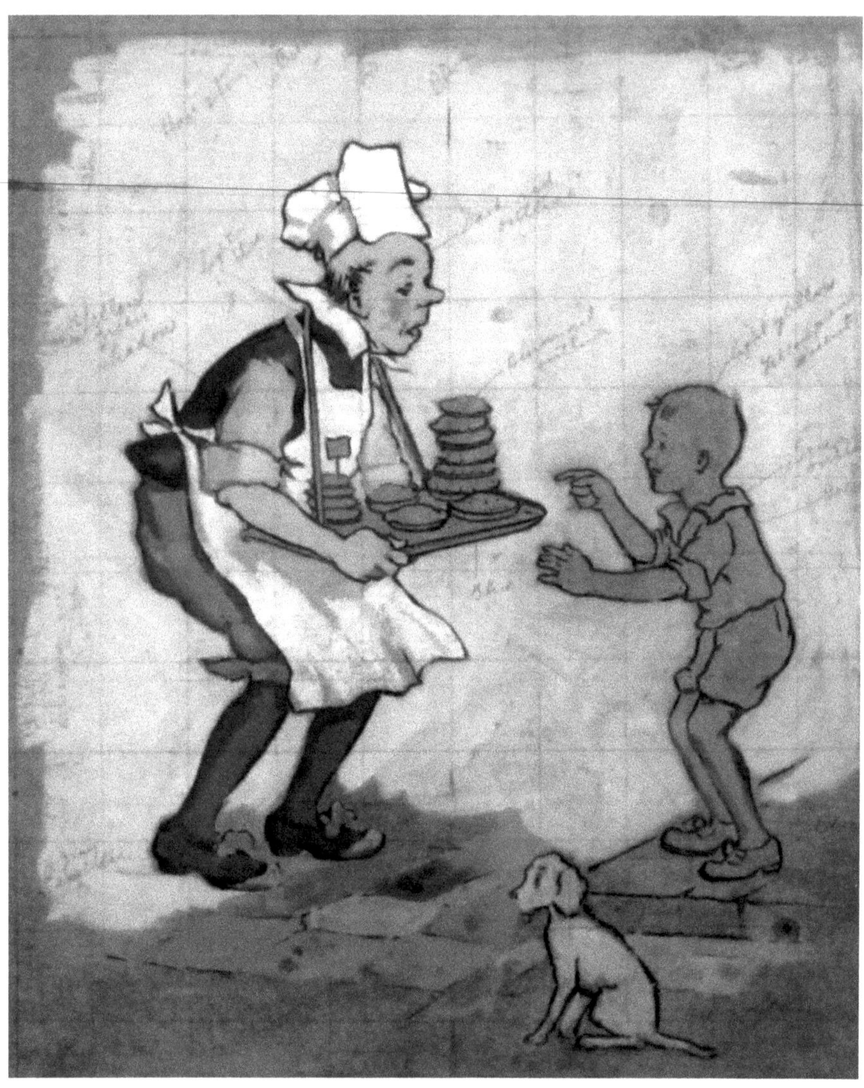

The first sketch for the proposed logo of Howard Johnson's company was drawn by John Eagles Alcott (1899–1978) in 1935: "Simple Simon and the Pieman at the Fair," complete with a drooling dog, with pencil notes on colors, design and details. As the brand that was to be used on advertising, dinnerware, swizzle sticks, napkins and roadside marquees that stood in front of the restaurants. *Courtesy of Steve and Christine Alcott Baptiste.*

Grant Dybing; eBay; Larry and Betsy Edsall; Frances Pierce Field; Dale H. Freeman, digital resource archivist, University of Massachusetts; Jean Goldman and Vincent Da Forno; Edward W. Gordon; Gretchen Grozier; Daniel Haacker, assistant director, Milton Public Library; Joan Halpert and

Peter Hanson; Ronald and Donna Lee Hanlon; Helen Hannon, with thanks for her assistance in research on the Johnson family; Dorothy Verne Johnson Weeks Henry; Historic New England, Lorna Condon; Jon Robert Hogan and Gaveston Nguyen; Muriel Cicco Holmes; Hutchinson; Barbara Kerr; Stephen Kharfen; the late Kathleen Kingston Lawlor; Paul Leo; Michael Lonardelli; Chris Lovett; Caroline Stewart Macon; Brenda Murphy Madden; Reverend Karen Maleri; Martin Manning; Massachusetts Historical Society, Andrea Cronin; Dr. John McConville; David McGinness; Milton Cemetery, Therese Desmond, superintendent; Town of Milton, Mary Fitzgerald and Rena McDermott; Elizabeth Mock; Hilda M. Morrill; Allan R. Morris; Mount Wollaston Cemetery in Quincy, Massachusetts, Jeanne Flaherty; Eddie Mulkern; Fran Murphy; New England Historic and Genealogical Society, Alice Kane, for her genealogy on the Johnson and Wright families; Bruce Nord; Frank Norton; Orleans Historical Society, Tamsen George; James Pardy; Pasqualina; Mary E. Paul; William H. Pear II; Scott Piatov; Steve and Linda Mason Pirie; Harold Irving Pratt Jr.; Providence Public Library; the Quincy Historical Society, Dr. Edward Fitzgerald, director, as well as Corinne Waite and Robert Bloomberg; the Quincy Public Schools, Mary McDonald; Lilian M.C. Randall; Kita and Chris Reece; Louise Richardson; Joanne Riley, University of Massachusetts, archivist; Patricia Rissmeyer; Matt Rocheleau, Boston.com; Charlie Rosenberg and Fran Perkins; Jeffrey Saraceno, my ever patient commissioning editor; Carolyn S. Savage; Andy Sawicky; Schlesinger Library, Radcliffe Institute, Harvard University, Diana Carey; Bonnie Snow; Snow Library, Orleans, Tavi Prugno; Peter Soffron, for loaning family photographs; Steve Soffron; Ernest C. Sofis; Kelly Spalding; Jean Sprague Stewart; Jeanne and Bill Sutton; Robin Tetley; Thomas Crane Public Library, Megan Allen, director, and Linda Beeler, head of reference; Jean and Joseph Troccoli; Ken Turino and Chris Mathias; University of Massachusetts, Archives and Special Collections, Joseph P. Healey Library, Boston, Joanne Riley; the Urban College of Boston, Michael Taylor, president; the Victorian Society, New England Chapter; Steven Walker, South End Photo Lab; Ann and Tom Walsh; WBZ Radio 1030, Jennifer Brien; Richard E. Weber, the Sprague Project; Ellen and Tom White; Wikipedia; Jennifer Morgan Williams; James Preston Wysong; Andrea Young and George A. Soffron; Jack and Marie Zinkus.

Introduction

The consumption of ice cream among Yankees varies inversely with the velocity of the east wind.
—Fortune *magazine, September 1940*

Howard Johnson created an orange-roofed empire of ice cream stands and restaurants that, following World War II, stretched from Maine to Florida and from the East Coast to the West Coast. Popularly known as the "Father of the Franchise Industry," he revolutionized the restaurant industry in the United States and thereby ensured the continual existence of delicious foods and quality prices that brought appreciative customers back for more.

Howard Deering Johnson (1897–1972) lived as a young man on Belmont Street in Wollaston, a neighborhood of Quincy, Massachusetts, and was the son of John Hayes Johnson and Olive Belle Wright Johnson. John owned a small cigar store and manufacturing company in downtown Boston, and Howard would leave the Wollaston Elementary School in the eighth grade to work with his father. He entered World War I, serving in the American Expeditionary Force in France, popularly known as the Yankee Infantry, and returned following Armistice Day to resume work with his father as a cigar salesman. His father's untimely and unexpected death in 1921 left his cigar business heavily in debt, and Howard Johnson assumed the responsibility for it without question.

With a $500 loan from his widowed mother and another loan of $2,000 from Dr. George Dalton, a well-known internist and a close family friend,

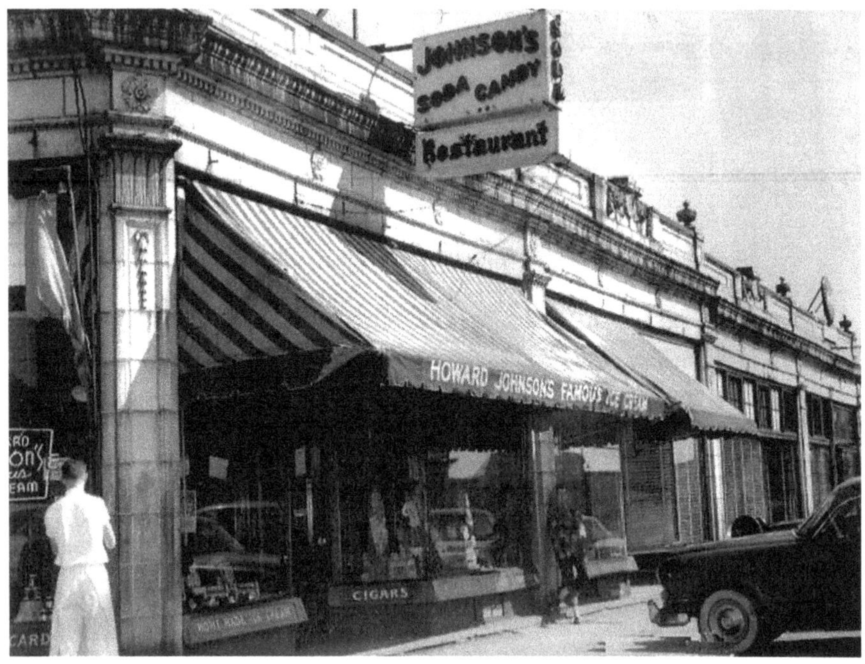

The original Howard Johnson store was at 89 Beale Street in Wollaston, a neighborhood of Quincy, Massachusetts, near the Wollaston Depot of the Granite Branch of the Old Colony Railroad. Selling everything from newspapers to magazines, cigars, sodas and candy, Johnson began to offer in 1925 naturally flavored premium ice cream with a double butterfat content that was as decadently delicious as it was likely to ensure repeat customers (after tasting, that is).

Howard Johnson purchased from Dick Simmons in 1925 the Walker-Barlow drugstore at 89 Beale Street in Wollaston, where he had been working. The store had a marble soda fountain and sold newspapers, magazines, cigars and three standard flavors of ice cream: vanilla, chocolate and strawberry. In the mid-1920s, Johnson began producing a rich, creamy ice cream that had a doubled butterfat and was flavored with all-natural ingredients, with the important fact that the quality and taste of the ice cream never varied. This ice cream brought a steady stream of loyal customers to the store, later augmented by grilled frankforts and fried clams. His ice cream stand on Wollaston Beach in Quincy, a small stand attached to a house that he leased for $300 for the summer, proved so successful that the next summer he was able to open an ice cream stand at Nantasket Beach in Hull, Massachusetts, and at Revere Beach in Revere, Massachusetts. It was said that Howard Johnson "sold $60,000 worth of ice-cream cones that [first] summer—14,000 cones on one Sunday—and there's good reason to suppose that when the summer visitors went home they kept up the argument about the flavors." Thus, a word-of-mouth publicity spread compliments about his business.

In 1929, he opened his first restaurant in Quincy Square's Granite Trust Building, the only high-rise building in the city at that time, strategically located at the busy intersection that faced Quincy City Hall and the famous Church of the Presidents. Here, he opened an elegantly appointed restaurant that served traditional New England fare throughout the day, with daily specials that attracted business people at lunchtime and diners in the evening, as well as families. Howard Johnson's restaurant was strategically placed and well located at the junction of Chestnut, Granite and Hancock Streets in the thriving shopping and business district of Quincy Square.

In 1929, Eugene O'Neill's infamous play *Strange Interlude* was banned in the city of Boston by Malcolm Nichols, the mayor, and the no-nonsense New England Watch & Ward Society, and it was moved by the Theatre Guild to Quincy, in the Quincy Theatre on Hancock Street, directly opposite Howard Johnson's new restaurant. As the play was extremely long, averaging just over five hours, there was a scheduled dinner break that allowed the hungry theatergoers to flock across the street to Howard Johnson's restaurant, where dinners were served at one dollar per plate.

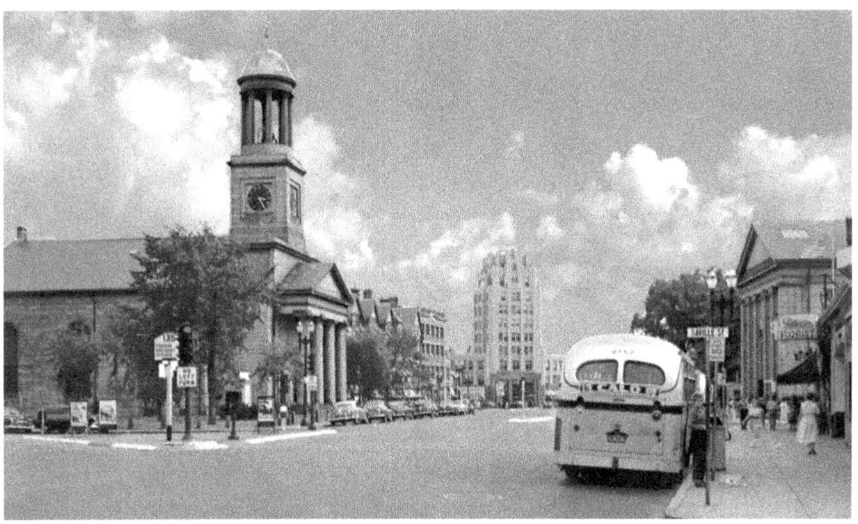

Quincy Square, seen in 1950, shows the United First Parish Church Unitarian (often referred to as the Church of the Presidents) on the left and Quincy City Hall on the right. In the center is the Art Deco Granite Trust Company, Quincy's first skyscraper, designed by J. Williams Beal Sons of Boston and built in 1929. Howard Johnson opened his first restaurant to the left of the bank entrance.

The restaurant was immediately a great success, with thousands of people from Boston coming to see the play that season, but the impact of the Great Depression in the fall of 1929 caused severe problems with both patronage and the credit line his business depended on, which was severely restricted by his bank. The concept of franchising his name was a fairly new business idea, but Johnson reasoned that if he let a franchisee use the now recognizable Howard Johnson name, and it purchased all food and supplies from him provided from a central supply commissary, he could charge a fee in exchange of the use of his brand or the logo "Simple Simon and the Pieman." The franchise concept was immediately successful, and Johnson has been justifiably thought of as the "Father of the Modern Restaurant Franchise" in the United States.

Howard Johnson's restaurants—in attractive Colonial Revival buildings sporting colorful and eye-catching orange porcelain tile roofs, projecting dormers, illuminated cupolas and turquoise blue shutters—were said in *Reader's Digest* in 1949 to be the epitome of "eating places that look like New England town meeting houses dressed up for Sunday." They soon began to be franchised throughout the New England area. The aspect of franchising was a sort of licensing in which the franchiser agrees to provide to the franchisee with the use of the name, logo, standardization of the operation and products for a sum of money or a percentage of the net profits. Johnson franchised not only restaurants but also ice cream stands, which were opened throughout the metropolitan Boston area.

By the late 1930s, Howard Johnson had come to recognize the ascendency of the automobile and the ability of the public to travel longer distances for both pleasure and business, and these newly franchised restaurants and ice cream stands began to be opened on major roads—preferably at major intersections—and interstate highways, where the traveling public would be assured of consistently high-quality foods that was the same served locally or in Maine or Florida. These franchised restaurants sprang up as if by magic along the eastern seaboard, serving the same delicious Ipswich fried clams, butter-grilled frankforts, grilled chops and steaks and the now standardized twenty-eight flavors of his famous ice cream.

In 1949, *Reader's Digest* published an article entitled "Who Is Howard Johnson?"—so well known had his name actually become through his successful franchise concept. Yet people really knew nothing of his accomplishments. The public had come to expect quality service, affordable prices and family-friendly service, and the rapidly multiplying restaurants became known as the "Landmark for Hungry Americans."

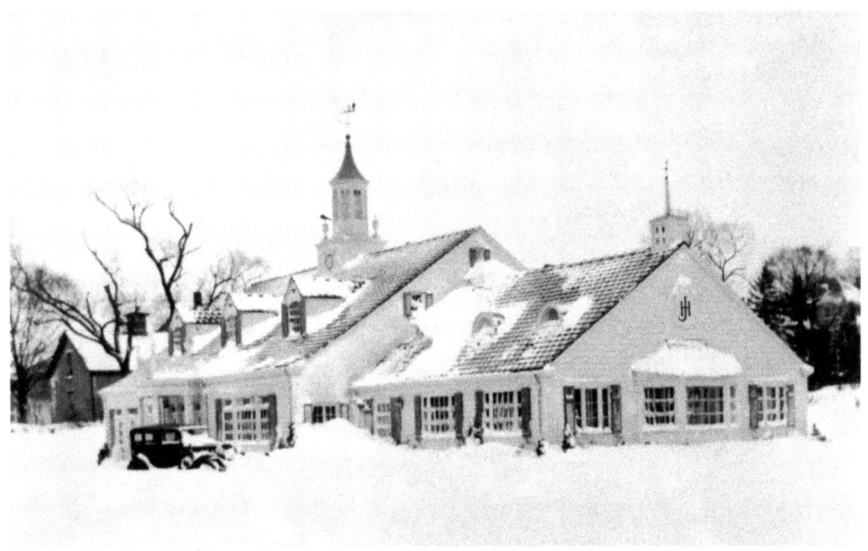

The Providence, Rhode Island Howard Johnson's restaurant, seen in 1938, was the epitome of the Colonial Revival roadside restaurant that had been designed with white clapboards and orange tile roof, and the turquoise blue shutters could not fail to attract the attention of the public with the bold color combination, but it was the delicious foods and ice cream that brought them back.

Opened in the summer of 1935, the restaurant in Orleans on Cape Cod was the first of the franchises and was opened by Reginald Heber Sprague, a lifelong friend, former school chum and confidant of Howard Deering Johnson. This franchise was strategically located at the prominent intersection of Route 6A and Route 28 on a portion of the Sprague estate and was seen by the traveling public using either road as they passed; the opening of this franchise was almost immediately followed in the next few weeks by the restaurant that opened in Dorchester. Located on the Old Colony Parkway (now known as the William T. Morrissey Boulevard) at the foot of Pope's Hill near Neponset Circle, those traveling south from Boston in the two decades before the Southeast Expressway was built in the mid-1950s passed the orange porcelain tile-roofed restaurant, and with ample parking spaces and a solid tradition of quality foods, ice cream and family-friendly service, it was a major attraction for the public. These restaurants were said to have "roomy table stalls of natural wood matching knotty-pine walls, [where] the travelers eat inexpensive Yankee-style meals and one or more of 28 flavors of ice cream," according to a 1938 Howard Johnson's brochure.

By the end of 1935, Johnson had franchised twenty-five roadside restaurants and ice cream stands throughout eastern Massachusetts, and by 1940, he had opened the first toll road restaurant on the Pennsylvania Turnpike and was to see further expansion so that he had the majority of turnpike restaurants in the country, all of which catered to America's increased highway travelers, who sought good food at all hours of the day, clean facilities and a reliable standard of quality. Howard Johnson was quoted as saying as he reviewed potential franchisee applications, "This is what I like to do best—help a good man to make a go of it himself."

Howard Johnson's business had expanded tremendously over the decade since he opened his first restaurant in Quincy Square in 1929, as it was reported that "[t]hirty-nine new agents opened stores in 1936 alone. In addition Howard Johnson owned 13 roadside and beach stands himself. In all, 61 establishments bore his name." However, World War II would be a severe trial for his business. With the implementation by the federal government of gas rationing, the driving public was forced to curtail all unnecessary automobile travel, and as a result, his restaurants and ice cream stands suffered an immediate setback in a dramatic decrease in patronage. Second, a labor shortage of chefs and line cooks who had been drafted into the war

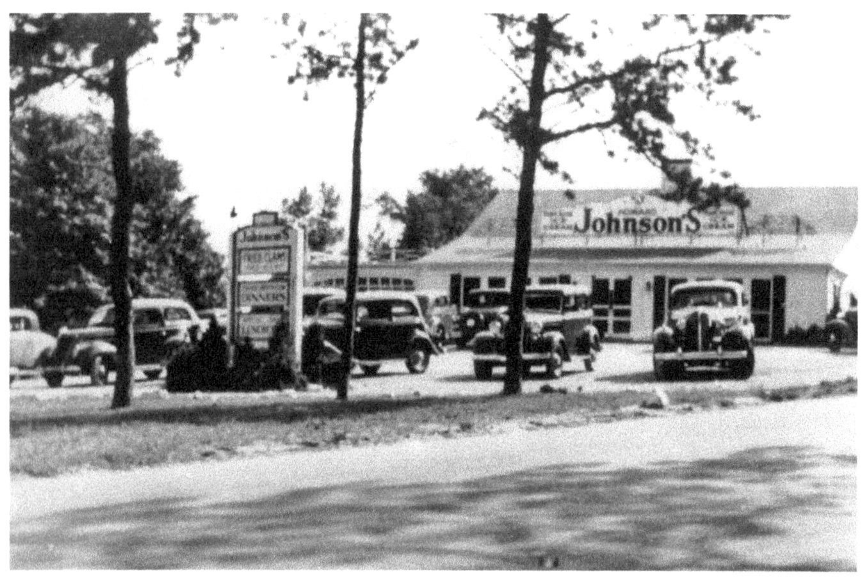

The first restaurant franchise offered by Howard Johnson was opened in May 1935 by Reginald Sprague in Orleans, Massachusetts. The restaurant was located at the junction of Routes 6A and 28, a major intersection on Cape Cod. *Courtesy of Caroline Stewart Macon.*

service meant that he had to radically change his daily operation; he became a leading "pioneer in the development of the fast food industry, shipping standardized and pre-portioned food from company-operated central plants to restaurants for final preparation, ensuring consistent quality throughout the chain," noted Johnson's *New York Times* obituary. Although it was said that 90 percent of the restaurants and ice cream stands closed directly due to gas rationing, Howard Johnson was able to survive these business reversals by cementing contacts that supplied prepared foods for government workers in large industrial plants, as well as for universities training student officers.

Following World War II, Howard Johnson was able to regroup. He began at once by planning expansions and by opening new restaurants and ice cream stands so rapidly that his business was perceived as the world's largest food chain, with hundreds of restaurants serving standardized but highly delicious fare such as fresh roast turkey, grilled steaks, chops and chicken, the newfangled clam strips known as "Tendersweet," whole-bellied clams and twenty-eight flavors of delicious ice cream that the public had come to love.

With identical menus, ice cream containers, doilies and napkins, it lent uniformity of appearance throughout the Howard Johnson's chain. The diligent and impressive business acumen of this astute and savvy man was incredible, and he was once quoted as saying that "I think that [building my business] was my only form of recreation. I never played golf. I never played tennis. I never did anything after I left school. I ate, slept, and thought of nothing but the business." Howard Johnson was to retire as president of his far-flung and successful company in 1959, becoming chairman of the board and treasurer, and his son, Howard Brennan Johnson, assumed his father's position with a nationwide company that had 675 restaurants, 175 motor lodges and annual sales of $127 million. When the company went public in 1961, it had a proven track record of success and was consistently well received by the public, and the sale of Howard Johnson's stock on the New York Stock Exchange was brisk and inclusive of both major investors as well as the customers who purchased just one share of stock.

Having franchised motor lodges as early as 1954, the first being in Savannah, Georgia, the restaurants were now often paired with motor lodges that had comfortable rooms, private telephones and a pool. It was said by historian Chester Liebs that "Howard Johnson's was the first [chain] to fully package motels, tying exterior and interior motifs into a total design concept launched in the 1950s; the rooms were at once decorative and easily duplicated, leading to prefabricated construction, which revolutionized the motel-chain industry." Operating close to one thousand restaurants and five hundred motor lodges throughout the United States, "Howard Johnson's did more business than McDonald's, Burger King and Kentucky Fried Chicken combined." The company was successful with the Red Coach Grill restaurants that expanded in the 1960s, with a red stagecoach in front of its charmingly rustic, red-roofed restaurants, and in 1969, it created the popular Ground Round chain, which appealed to the younger public with its hip, modern interior décor and delicious foods.

However, the founder of this very American restaurant empire never really retired, as he "continued to monitor his restaurants for cleanliness and proper food preparation. He would be chauffeured in a black Cadillac bearing the license plate HJ-28 [his initials and the standardized twenty-eight flavors of ice cream] while performing unannounced and thorough inspections of the restaurants," according to a *Reader's Digest* article. He created an orange-roofed empire that attracted the public to dine at the restaurants on a daily basis and thereby would ensure repeat business. "His contribution to the restaurant industry was the idea of centralized buying and a commissary system to prepare menu items for distribution to his restaurants. This helped to insure a uniform consistency and quality, as well as lower costs," according to Liebs. The American public would repay

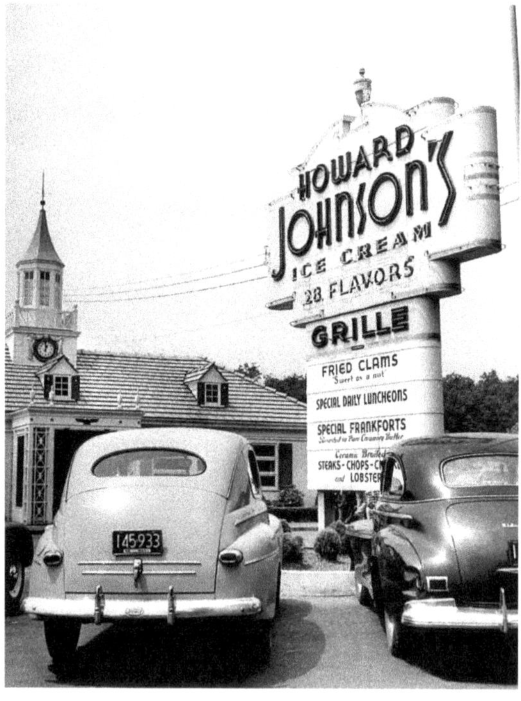

Howard Johnson's restaurants always had tall roadside marquees, often with neon lights for nighttime illumination that could be seen by those traveling in automobiles. This is the Canton, Massachusetts restaurant at 2786 Washington Street (Route 138) advertising in 1949 the famous twenty-eight flavors of ice cream, as well as fried clams, special frankforts and ceramic broiled steaks, chops, chicken and lobster.

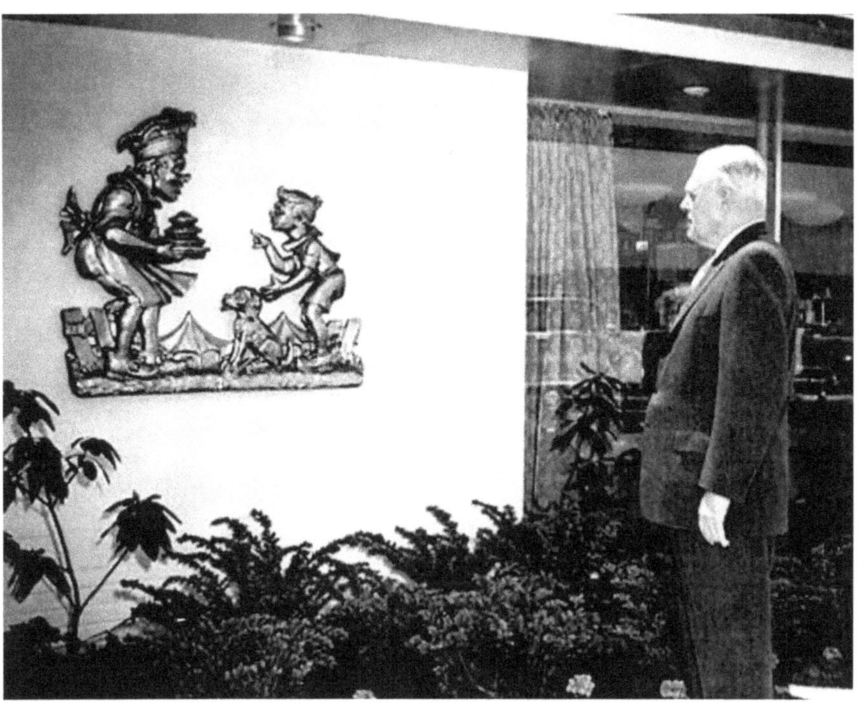

Howard Deering Johnson retired as president of his company in 1959, becoming chairman of the board and treasurer, and his son, Howard Brennan Johnson, assumed the presidency. Since 1925, when he served his first customers in Wollaston, Johnson had become one of the most successful and well-known businessmen in the United States. One wonders if he could have realized how influential his restaurants would be on the public's appreciation of his traditional New England fare and twenty-eight flavors of ice cream.

him in kind, as the Howard Johnson name will forever be remembered by referring to him and his restaurants as the uncontested "King of the Road."

In 1979, the Imperial Group Limited bought the Howard Johnson's restaurant chain. Known as a highly successful British food conglomerate that had thousands of pubs and hotels in the United Kingdom, it was well aware of the chain's popularity throughout the United States, but it was said to have "squeezed it for profits" and sold it to Marriott Corporation just five years later. Marriott Corporation tried to stem the tide of intensely competitive fast-food restaurants and sold off the motels and lodges to Prime Motor Inns while remodeling the restaurants to adhere to the standardized design concept of Marriott restaurants. The franchisees of the Howard Johnson's chain strongly reacted to the changes taking place and incorporated themselves as the Franchise Associates, continuing the use of

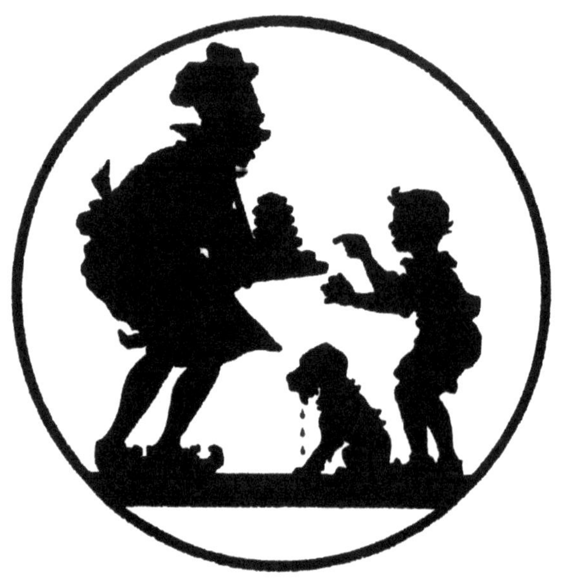

The logo of Howard Johnson's, seen in an encircled silhouette, has become one of the most readily recognizable brands in the food industry. Designed by John Eagles Alcott, it captured that age-old nursery rhyme "Simple Simon met a pieman going to the fair; says Simple Simon to the pieman: 'Let me taste your ware.'"

the long-respected name as well as the original twenty-eight flavors of ice cream as standardized by the founder.

Today, only two Howard Johnson's restaurants survive—in Lake Placid, New York, and Bangor, Maine—but occasionally, one still comes across prepackaged frozen foods and ice cream in larger grocery stores.

As Howard Johnson said in a brochure he published in 1939, "The success of the Howard Johnson's Ice Cream Shops and Restaurants has been built upon high standards…in food, in cleanliness and in service. I appreciate your patronage and pledge myself and my entire organization to a continuation of these same standards." And so he did!

This work on Howard Johnson's deals primarily with the early history of the company, from its founding in 1925 with the incredible business drive and acumen of Howard Deering Johnson to its sale to Imperial Group Limited in 1979. Although the company continued to expand with motor lodges, the Red Coach Grill and the Ground Round restaurants after he relinquished the presidency in 1959 to his son, the Johnson's restaurant business, ever since the first restaurant opened in 1929 in Quincy Square, had come to represent the "Home for Hungry Americans."

CHAPTER 1
The Johnson Family

In the early days, the company was a lovely place to work because it was a small outfit with closeness between the people. Everyone worked together.
—Jack Hipson

Howard Deering Johnson, the son of John Hayes Johnson and Olive Belle Wright Johnson, was born on February 2, 1897, in Dorchester, Massachusetts. The Johnson family lived at 4 Franklin Street in Port Norfolk, a neighborhood today referred to as Neponset. In 1899, the family moved to Quincy, Massachusetts, and lived at 309 Belmont Street in Wollaston (it has been listed as both 34 and 241 Belmont Street, but the house was renumbered when the street was extended toward Squantum Street). His father, John H. Johnson, was a cigar manufacturer for many years, first doing business under his own name and conducting a retail store at 69 High Street and, later, at 15 Court Square in Boston, in addition to manufacturing cigars. He was referred to as a "shrewd business trader." He later served as the treasurer and general manager of the United Retailers Company, a cigar manufactory on Summer Street in downtown Boston.

It was said that the "senior Johnson believed in facing facts squarely with courage and conviction and reared his son…under rigid disciplinary methods. As a result Mr. Johnson's strong determination and phenomenal memory were products of early training and discipline and were to prove invaluable in the years to come." The Johnson family, like most aspiring middle-class families moving at the turn of the twentieth century to Quincy, set down roots in the community, and they joined the Wollaston Unitarian Church, a shingle-style church designed by noted Dorchester architect Edwin J. Lewis Jr. and built in 1888 at 155 Beale Street in Wollaston. In 1960, the congregation merged with the First Parish Church in Quincy, and the church was sold to St. Catherine's Greek Orthodox Church. John H. Johnson also became a member of the Neighborhood Club, the Granite City Club, the Quincy lodge of Elks and the Community Club in Quincy.

Howard Johnson and his sisters attended the Wollaston Grammar School, then a small wood-frame stick-style school that was located on Beale Street between Prospect and Winthrop Avenues, but he left school in the eighth grade to begin working with his father. According to an article in *Pageant*, "When he was 12 years old he went to work in a Boston drugstore. For $5 a week he washed windows, scrubbed the floor and sold cigars. At 16 he became a salesman for his father, a cigar wholesaler." The grit and determination manifested by the young Howard Johnson toward work was obvious when his father imported a large order of cigars from the American West Indies Trading Company in Puerto Rico on a prepaid basis to receive a steep discount. However, they arrived damaged and could not be sold or returned, as the company had subsequently folded. According to an article in the *Saturday Evening Post*:

> *When Howard was only three months away from grade-school graduation, a financial storm gathered over the Johnson family. A big shipment of Puerto Rican cigars turned out to be not only substandard but infested with worms. Johnson senior, having signed a sight draft for the shipment, had no legal recourse against the supplier. Hearing the news, Howard announced that he was quitting school and going to work in his father's store. The elder Johnson roared disapproval, but Howard stood his ground and won a compromise. If he got his diploma he could work in the store that summer, and if, in the fall, he still didn't want to continue his schooling, he could stay on. September came, Howard hadn't budged, and his father grudgingly kept his part of the bargain.*

Without Howard Johnson's determination to leave school, in opposition to the wishes of his parents, the family would have been in a precarious position, and he and his father doubled their efforts to try and recoup their losses.

With the advent of war in Europe in 1914, the aggression of Germany provoked strong opposition from Allied countries; they thought that the war would be over in a matter of weeks, but it extended so much that thousands were killed in the trenches, and the lives of civilians were imperiled as well. On April 6, 1917, following the sinking of seven United States merchant ships by German submarines, President Woodrow Wilson called for war on Germany, which was formally declared by the United States Congress.

Like most of the young men of his generation, Howard Johnson entered World War I, serving in France in the American Expeditionary Force, known as the Twenty-sixth Infantry Division, before returning after the armistice to rejoin his father. This division was formed on July 18, 1917, and activated a month later at Camp Edwards, Massachusetts, consisting of units from the New England area. General Clarence Ransom Edwards, the division's commander, chose the nickname of the "Yankee Division" to highlight the division's two brigades comprising national guard units from the six states of Massachusetts, Connecticut, Rhode Island, Maine, Vermont and New Hampshire.

Sent to Europe during World War I as part of the American Expeditionary Force, the division saw extensive combat in France. During World War I, it was said that "the division spent 210 days in combat, and suffered 1,587 killed in action and 12,077 wounded in action." The division returned to the United States and was demobilized on May 3, 1919, at Camp Devens in Ayer, Massachusetts. Following World War I, Route 128, which is a major highway that encircles the city of Boston, was called the "Yankee Division Highway" in honor of the Twenty-sixth Infantry Division and its heroism during the war. Upon his return, Howard Johnson resumed his job working with his father, with "a determination to place a cigar in every male mouth in New England."

In 1919, John Hayes Johnson began to market the "Yankee Division Brand" cigar that was named for the division in which his son had served in World War I. Volume 28, issue 12 of the *National Association of Retail Druggists* noted that "John H. Johnson, a former president of the T.M.A. of the Massachusetts Pharmacists Association has placed on the market a new cigar which is becoming popular." Father and son continued to sell cigars, during a new age when cigarettes were becoming more prevalent in society, to an aging male customer base. One thing Howard credited his father for was his mnemonic skill, which is a memory system developed by the ancient Greek scholars and orators to help remember long passages and speeches. Howard Johnson said, "When I was a young punk out on the road selling cigars, my father asked me if I had addressed the customers by name. I told him no, that I just couldn't remember 50 to 100 names. He told me to train my memory by will power. So I made a business of training it, just like he said." However, no amount of customer-relations skills could stem the flow, as the cigar business continued to lose money and would never regain its once profitable base.

When John Hayes Johnson died of pneumonia in 1921, he left his family heavily in debt, with $30,000 owed by the company. Howard Johnson, who had been successfully selling cigars on commission for the company since his return from the war, continued alone after his father's death for three years until he realized that it was an unsustainable business. He signed a personal note assuming the debt. Realizing that he needed to provide for his widowed mother and unmarried sisters, he began "working at a small patent medicine store with a soda fountain and newsstand that was losing money in Quincy, Massachusetts…Johnson borrowed $500 to purchase the store from the [late] proprietor's son and began his journey to gain access to the prosperity that was being generated by many entrepreneurs in America."

On September 3, 1925, he open the newly purchased store at 89 Beale Street, the former Walker-Barlow drugstore in Wollaston, where he had a marble soda fountain and sold newspapers, cigars and three flavors of ice cream. Within a short time, Howard Johnson "soon had the [corner store] bringing in $30,000 a year, with 75 boys delivering papers for him." Conveniently located near the Wollaston Depot that was on the Granite Branch of the Old Colony Railroad, it had commuters traveling daily to Boston for business, shopping and pleasure throughout the day, so the store was well placed for business.

Here follows a brief four-generation Johnson-Wright family genealogy:

> *John and Charlotte Johnson were born and died in Sweden and were the paternal great-grandparents of Howard Deering Johnson.*
>
> *John Matheson (1785–1868) was born in Lochalsh, Scotland, and died in Boston, Massachusetts. Flora McQueen Matheson (circa 1793–1874) was born in Scotland and died in Boston, Massachusetts. They were the maternal great-grandparents of Howard Deering Johnson.*
>
> *Joseph Johnson (1827–1895) was born in Stockholm, Sweden. He was married in 1858 to Catherine McQueen Matheson (died in 1911), who was born in Arichat, Richmond, Nova Scotia, Canada. He worked as a mariner and sea captain. He was naturalized as a United States citizen*

in 1854 in Boston, Massachusetts, indicating an immigration year of about 1848.

Charles Wright (circa 1830–1870) was born in Pennsylvania and is presumed to have died in Butte, Montana. In 1856, he married Anna Wright (born circa 1834). He worked as a railroad agent in Montana for several years. Following her husband's death, Anna worked for a time as a keeper of a boardinghouse in Butte, Montana, and possibly remarried, as her daughters were said to be raised in Salt Lake City, Utah. Their daughter Olive Belle Wright had come east to study at the New England Conservatory of Music.

John Hayes Johnson (1865–1921) married Olive Belle Wright (1867–1939).

Howard Deering Johnson (1897–1972) was born in Dorchester, Massachusetts, to John Hayes and Olive Belle Wright Johnson and died in Milton, Massachusetts.

Howard Deering Johnson married four times, and his wives were as follows:

Pauline H. Long, married in 1921. She divorced Johnson in 1927 for desertion.

Dorothy E. Smith of Quincy, married in 1929, died in 1930. She was the daughter of Robert D. and Jessie A. Wood Smith, mother of Dorothy Verne Johnson.

Bernice Louise Johnson of Methuen, married in New York City in 1931, divorced in 1938, mother of Howard Brennan Johnson. She later married Reginald J. White of Providence, Rhode Island, president of J.J. White & Company.

Marjorie C. Smith Burgin, married in 1949. She was divorced from Thomas Skudder Burgin, a former mayor of Quincy, Massachusetts

John Hayes and Olive Belle Wright Johnson also had four daughters:

Barbara Johnson married Dr. David D. Montgomery, and their daughter was Peggy Montgomery.

Margaret Johnson married Dr. L. Starrett White, and their children were Sally White and Nancy White.

Katherine M. Johnson

Olive K. Johnson

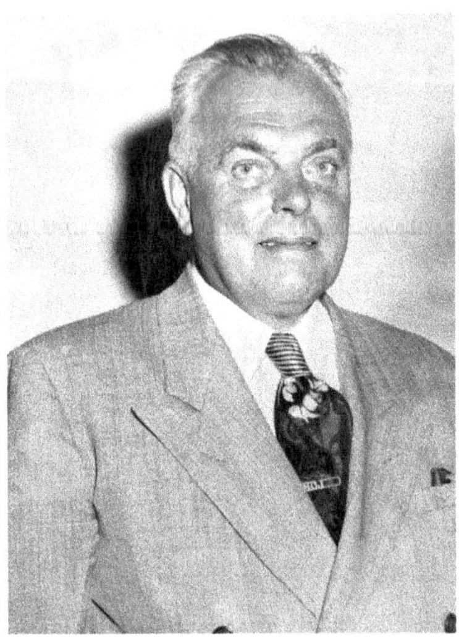

Howard Deering Johnson (1897–1972) was photographed in 1949, nattily attired in a suit complete with a "HDJ" gold tie clip.

Howard Deering Johnson had done well enough in business that in 1929 he was able to purchase 114 Summit Avenue in Wollaston, a neighborhood of Quincy, Massachusetts. The street surmounted the crest of Forbes Hill, which had been developed in the late nineteenth century by the Wollaston Land Associates. The house was designed by noted architect John F. Kelly and built by Pearson & Anderson, well-known local builders. The house was designed as a Colonial Revival three-bay house, with a large dormer in the attic, and it is set so high on a terrace at the crest of the hill that the panoramic views of North Quincy, Boston and the harbor are superb. This house would be the Johnson home for the next decade, after which Johnson's phenomenal success motivated him to seek a larger and even more prestigious property.

By the late 1930s, Johnson was doing very well in business thanks to the numerous restaurant and ice cream stand franchises, and he was looking to move to a more affluent and socially prominent town. He gravitated toward Milton, Massachusetts, a town adjacent to Quincy but which retained much of its bucolic rural aspect well into the mid-twentieth century. In his book *Who Killed Society?*, Cleveland Amory (1917–1998)—an acerbic wit whose once wealthy family lived on Brush Hill Road in Milton in their former summer house after having sold their Back Bay townhouse following the Great Depression—described in detail the negotiations concerning the purchase of a house between Howard Deering Johnson and Norwood Penrose Hallowell at their large Brush Hill Road mansion.

The Hallowell family hailed from West Medford, Massachusetts, where their estate, Noddebo, had been home to the family since the mid-nineteenth century. In the early twentieth century, three sons of Norwood Penrose and Sarah Haydock Hallowell moved to homes on Brush Hill Road in Milton, Massachusetts, and created, in essence, a Hallowell enclave on the prestigious semirural road. Robert Haydock Hallowell lived at 1336 Brush Hill Road, John White Hallowell lived at 1425 Brush Hill Road and N. Penrose Hallowell lived at 1372 Brush Hill Road, which was in 1939 on the real estate market and being advertised by Marsh & Rice of Dedham, as he and his family had decided to move to Park Avenue in New York City.

In what was considered by Cleveland Amory to be a "textbook story of the warfare of celebrity and Aristocracy," the tale concerns the sale of their Brush Hill Road home by Mr. and Mrs. N. Penrose Hallowell. One more in a long line of old Boston family houses to see the change to a new day, the house was sold, after some deliberation, to none other than Mr. Howard Johnson, of roadside restaurant fame. Mrs. Hallowell, a gentle person, thought it would be nice for the Hallowells to have some personal contact with the Johnsons in the course of the signing of the papers. At first, not knowing quite how to do this—she could not, of course, invite the Johnsons to a meal since she didn't know them—she decided at length to have them to tea.

Mr. Johnson arrived, bringing with him young Master Howard Johnson Jr., at that time a young gentleman not quite ten. Everything went extremely

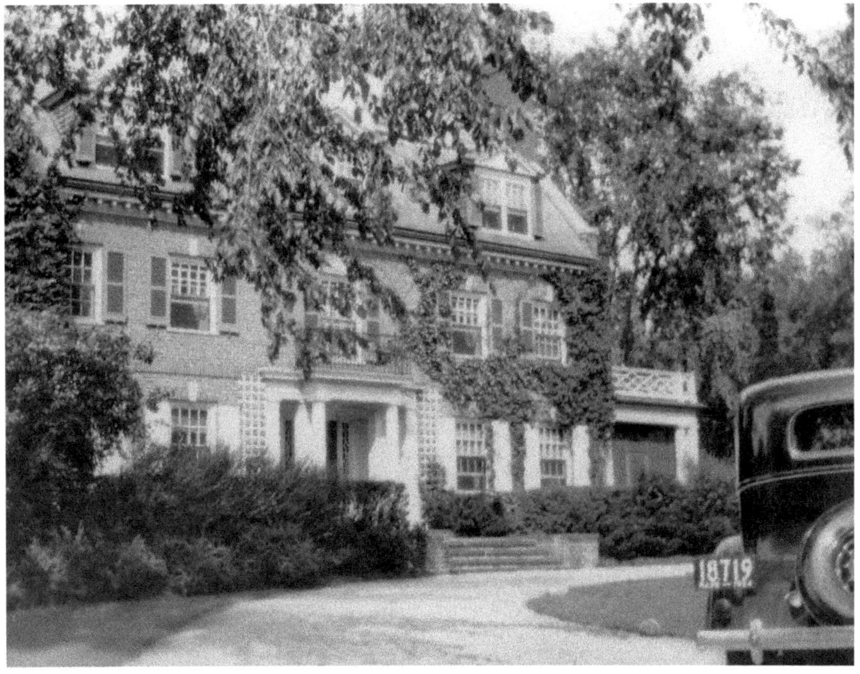

The Hallowell-Johnson House was located at 1372 Brush Hill Road in Milton, Massachusetts. The stately Georgian Revival house was purchased by Howard Johnson in 1939 and was described as having twenty rooms, with seven master bedrooms and five baths. The mansion was demolished in 2004 for Fuller Village at Brush Hill, a senior living community. *Courtesy of Harold I. Pratt Jr.*

smoothly. Mrs. Hallowell poured the tea from her customary position on the sofa. Mr. Hallowell sat in his old chair by the fire. The Johnsons, father and son, sat across the room, and the papers were signed. The tea, English muffins and S.S. Pierce marmalade were satisfactorily consumed. Suddenly, however, a wave of sentiment overcame Mrs. Hallowell. She looked around the room at everything she loved—the portraits, the tapestries and the books—and then she looked back at Mr. Johnson. "Oh, Mr. Johnson," she sighed, "I do hope that you and Mrs. Johnson will be as happy here in all the years to come as Mr. Hallowell and I have been in all the years that have passed."

There was a silence. Furthermore, it was soon apparent that it was a silence that was not going to be broken by Mr. Howard Johnson Sr. Finally, however, it was broken by Master Howard Johnson Jr. "There isn't any Mrs.

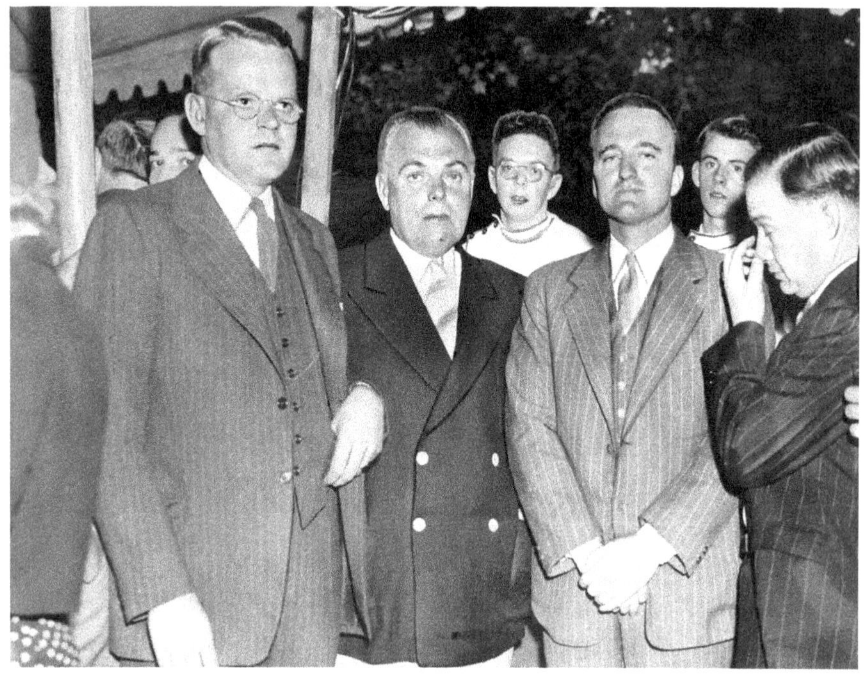

At a "Frankfort Roast" held in June 1940 at his Brush Hill Road estate in Milton, Howard Johnson entertained more than five hundred guests and served one of his most popular restaurant foods. *Left to right*: Irving R. Carter of Fairfield, Connecticut, who had two Howard Johnson's restaurant franchises in Connecticut (Fairfield, opened in 1935, and Milford, opened in 1936); Howard Deering Johnson; and George Larsen of Boston, Massachusetts, who was the owner of the Pillar House restaurant, opened in 1952 in Newton.

Johnson," he said, obviously trying to be helpful. "One's dead and one's divorced, but Daddy's got a girl friend." He had said the latter in such a hopeful spirit that everyone was by now stunned. And there was another silence—this time an ear-splitting one. In many other societies, the breaking point might have been reached, but not in Boston society. Boston society has a way of coming through in the pinches, and now, surely, the pinch was on. Out of the old Hallowell chair by the fire jumped Mr. Hallowell. Without a word, he drew himself up, strode briskly across the room and smote Mr. Johnson Sr. a smart blow on the back. Then, for the first time, he spoke. "Bully for you, Johnson," he said.

The mansion was described in the *Milton Record* as having "twenty rooms, with seven master bedrooms and five baths and is of Georgian Colonial type. There is a stable, four car garage, greenhouse and tennis court and 16½ acres of high land." In 1940, according to the Milton Residents Street

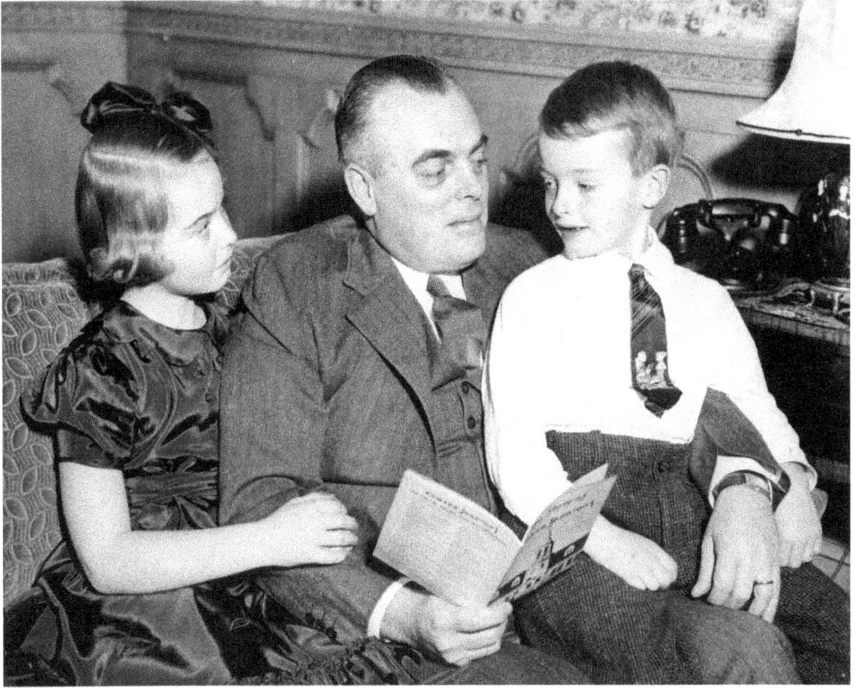

Howard Deering Johnson—with his daughter, Dorothy, and son, Howard, seated on either side—are seen in December 1938 relaxing on a sofa in the parlor of the family home on Summit Avenue in Wollaston as he reads to them from *The Story of Howard Johnson's*, a small paperbound booklet published by the company in 1938.

Listing, the Johnson mansion was staffed by a butler, a housekeeper and two live-in maids. The house was on a section of Brush Hill Road, an estate area in the foothills of the Blue Hills, between Milton Street and Blue Hill Avenue. Johnson lived here in elegant splendor until 1947, when he sold the mansion to the St. Columban's Foreign Mission Society and purchased 1063 Metropolitan Avenue in Milton, a mansion built at the turn of the century by industrialist Eben Sumner Draper of the George Draper & Sons Company just half a mile east of the first house.

Metropolitan Avenue had been laid out in the 1840s by the Twenty Associates, a consortium of real estate investors headed by Alpheus Perley Blake that purchased farmland in Milton and created a new neighborhood that attracted middle-class residents, with the proximity of the railroad being a major feature. Known as "Fairmount," the neighborhood was eventually ceded by the town of Milton in 1868 when the new town of Hyde Park, Massachusetts, was incorporated. However, the streets, such as Fairmount,

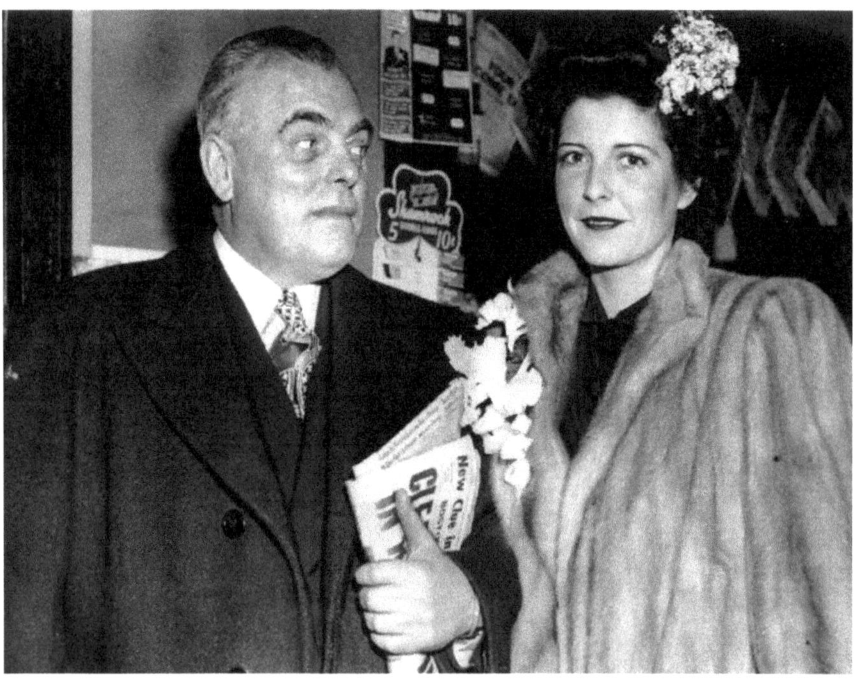

Newlywed couple Howard and Marjorie Smith Burgin Johnson pose for their photograph at the Back Bay Station in Boston following their wedding on January 23, 1949, in the parish house of the First Parish Church in Milton by the Reverend Vivien T. Pomeroy. Following the ceremony, the couple left by train that afternoon for a honeymoon in Florida.

Williams and Metropolitan Avenues closest to Brush Hill Road, would remain in Milton. In 1947, Howard Johnson remodeled the mansion and garage, which was set on a large estate, and in 1954, the entire upper floor of the mansion was removed and a modified Mansard roof built by Leard Brothers, which gave the mansion a quasi-French architectural look.

In addition to the houses in Milton, Howard Johnson also had a place in Miami Beach, Florida, an apartment on Sutton Place in New York City and, later, a seven-room apartment at 812 Fifth Avenue facing Central Park.

Howard Deering Johnson died in 1972 in New York City, and following a well-attended funeral service conducted by Reverend Prescott B. Wintersteen, DD, at the First Parish Church in Milton, Unitarian, the oldest place of worship in the town and where he and his fourth wife were married, he was buried in his lot at the Milton Cemetery. His large granite monument was engraved on the rear with the motto *Semper Paratus* ("Always Prepared"), which is the also the motto of the United States Coast Guard. He truly was always prepared, and he will forever be known as the "Host of the Highway."

CHAPTER 2

Quincy in the Age of Howard Johnson

I love Wollaston. Wollaston has been good to me.
—Howard Deering Johnson

Quincy is a city just south of Boston and is often referred to as the "City of Presidents," as both John Adams and his son John Quincy Adams, the second and sixth presidents of the United States, respectively, were residents. Settled in 1625 by Thomas Morton, who referred to the area as "Merrymount," it was initially and successively a part of both the towns of Dorchester and Boston, Massachusetts, until 1640, when it was separated and became part of a new town called Braintree. In 1792, the North Precinct of Braintree separated and officially became the town of Quincy, and in 1888, the town was incorporated as the city of Quincy. Steeped in historical tradition, the city was named for Colonel John Quincy, a respected early resident and grandfather of Abigail Smith Adams, the wife of John Adams and the mother of John Quincy Adams, for whom she named her son.

The American Indians who inhabited the area just prior to the settlement by English colonists in the seventeenth century were led by Sachem (Chief) Chickatawbut, whose seat was at Squantum near the headwaters of the Neponset River and referred to as Moswetuset Hummock. The surrounding lands were fertile, and the early settlers found the area suitable for farming, as Chickatawbut and his people had cleared much of the land of trees and brush by slash-and-burn agriculture. The settlement was named Mount Wollaston in honor of the leader, Captain Richard Wollaston, who soon after

1625 left the area and settled in Virginia. Today, the Wollaston neighborhood in Quincy still retains Captain Wollaston's name.

Another prominent early resident of the area was Thomas Morton, a lawyer, writer and social reformer who took over leadership of the post. The settlement proceeded to gain an ill reputation for relations with American Indian women and public drunkenness. Morton renamed the settlement "Merrymount" (literally meaning "Hill by the Sea") and later wrote the following in reference to the conservative Pilgrims, known as separatists, of Plymouth Colony to the south, who disapproved of his practices: "[They were] threatening to make it a woefull mount and not a merry mount." The neighborhood of Quincy, now called Merrymount, is located on the site of the original English settlement of 1625 and takes its name from the punning joke by Morton.

Retaining many of its farms well into the nineteenth century, Quincy saw tremendous development beginning in 1844, when Nathan Carruth, president of the Old Colony Railroad, laid a railroad line from Kneeland Street in downtown Boston through Quincy to the South Shore towns of Massachusetts, terminating in Plymouth. The Old Colony Railroad was said to be "the beginning of a trend toward suburbanization" and allowed people to live in Quincy and other South Shore towns while commuting to the city for business, shopping and pleasure. Quincy became easily accessible to Boston with the railroad, which was served by two railroad lines by the late nineteenth century. The first suburban land company, the Bellevue Land Company, was organized in northern Quincy in 1870, and the Wollaston Land Company laid out house lots in the 1880s. Quincy's population grew dramatically, as a direct result of both the ease of transportation and the massive residential land development, by more than 50 percent during the 1920s, bringing people of all walks of life to live in Quincy, Massachusetts.

Among the city's several "firsts" in history was the Granite Railway, the first commercial railroad in the United States. The railway was the work of Gridley Bryant, who as engineer and planner began in 1826 to direct the transportation of granite from the Bunker Hill Quarry in Quincy to Railway Village (now East Milton, Massachusetts), where the granite was dressed and then transported by the railway to the Neponset River in Milton, where the granite was then loaded onto flat barges. The granite was transported to Charlestown, where it was to be used to erect the Bunker Hill monument, a large obelisk designed by Solomon Willard and dedicated in 1843 marking the site of the Battle of Bunker Hill in 1775. Granite would become famous throughout the country as the building material of choice for churches, municipal buildings and hospitals, as well as street curbstones. Stonecutting and funeral monuments became two of Quincy's principal economic activities.

Quincy was equally important as a shipbuilding center. Sailing ships had been built in Quincy for many years, including the only seven-masted schooner ever built, the *Thomas W. Larson*. The Fore River area, near the Quincy- Braintree town line, was developed as a major shipbuilding center after the Civil War and continued for more than a century as the largest employer on the South Shore of Massachusetts. At the Fore River Shipyard, many famous warships were built, among them the aircraft carrier USS *Lexington*, the battleship USS *Massachusetts*, the USS *Nevada* and the USS *Salem*. Quincy also had early attempts at aeronautics, with the Squantum section of town being the location of one of the world's first airports, the airfield being used by many early aviators, among them Amelia Earhart. In 1910, the Squantum Airfield was the site of the Harvard Aero Meet, the second air show in America.

By the early twentieth century, Quincy, Massachusetts, was a thriving city with a burgeoning population that had increased tremendously since the turn of the century. Howard Johnson's family was typical of the aspiring middle-class, choosing Quincy as their home, and although the family had disappointments, they represented the stalwart citizens of the day. Johnson was said to be surprised to find it easy to pay back the money lent to him by Dr. Dalton and a family friend after discovering that his recently repaired marble soda fountain had become the busiest part of his drugstore.

Eager to ensure that his drugstore would remain successful, Johnson decided to come up with a new ice cream recipe—being a "stickler for quality, Mr. Johnson was dissatisfied with the ice cream served in his newly acquired enterprise and he set out to manufacture his own." Some sources say that the new recipe was based on his mother's homemade ice cream, while others say that the new recipe was from William Hallbauer, a German immigrant whose ice cream shop in Nahant, Massachusetts, served a delicious, creamy and smooth ice cream; perhaps Hallbauer was induced by a large check to share his secrets with Howard Johnson. The newly acquired recipe made the ice cream creamier due to an increased content of butterfat. Asked by a customer how he could produce such a delicious ice cream, he proudly said, "The smoothness that you noted is brought about by the rich cream that is used and the fact that we have a special freezer that freezes the cream in the French way. I designed the freezer." Eventually, Johnson came up with twenty-eight flavors of ice cream. He is quoted as saying, "I thought I had every flavor in the world. That '28' [flavors] became my trademark."

Howard Johnson's new business was officially opened on September 3, 1925. As a newly minted businessman, Johnson fondly noted that his mother

> *really started me out. She really financed the Wollaston store, which was the nucleus of the system. Although she was not actually active in the direction of the business, her sage counsel gave me in the privacy of our home, I believe, was largely responsible for the development of the industry. Her woman's intuition and her mother's interest in my affairs brought countless little suggestions that would probably not have occurred to a man—and I relied on her advice to a larger extent than sometimes I realized.*

Olive Belle Johnson (1867–1939) was beloved by not just her family but also her many friends, and on a bronze memorial tablet for her, it was noted that "[h]er noble character and loving sympathy will remain a guiding influence in the lives of all who knew her."

From then on, the Howard Johnson name increasingly became a recognizable part of American culture. So popular had his ice cream become that people were said to have caused traffic jams in Wollaston. A September 1940 *Fortune* magazine article noted that in the late summer of 1925, customers said to the

> *young man behind the fountain that they wanted chocolate ice-cream sodas. Not vanilla or tutti-frutti, neither strawberry nor raspberry. But chocolate…It will be noted that the first band at the bottom of the glass is a mark for the sirup, the second is for the cream, the rest for the soda water. The ice cream itself is laid athwart the top of the glass, an innovation among Yankee soda makers. It was not a neat, penny-pinching scoop, but a homey gob with an "edge" to it—soda fountain argot for that extra portion that seems to have been scooped out by mistake. That edge gave the soda a definite "more-than-my-moneys-worth" aspect. This was not carelessness by the lad toiling alone behind the counter. It was a precise movement of a skilled hand, a hand that went faster and faster as the perishing Yankees cried: "For Pete's sake Howard, hurry up!" In fact the design of the soda was one of Howard Johnson's first triumphs as a manager, although marked glasses had long been in use at Thompson's Spa in Boston. The other triumphs were the chocolate sirup and the chocolate ice cream. He made them himself.*

Throughout the summers of the late 1920s, Howard Johnson opened concession stands on beachfront property along the coast of Massachusetts. The stands sold ice-cold soft drinks, grilled frankforts and, of course, his famous ice cream, and each stand proved to be successful. The first stand was opened in 1926 on Quincy Shore Drive facing Wollaston Beach, where he paid "$300 to be allowed to sell ice cream from a twenty two foot stand attached to a house at Wollaston Beach." The first Sunday in operation, the little stand took in $200. By the end of the summer, it had done more ice cream business than the drugstore had done in two years:

> *On the night before a Sunday that promised to be good ice-cream weather, he moved in. He also painted a beautiful sign, which, in addition to the first public appearance of his name, also announced that the ice cream to be vended in the stately structure of boards was "the most famous in New England." The state was put to the expense of rushing twelve policemen to the stand to hold off the mob. He sold $60,000 worth of ice-cream cones that summer—14,000 cones on one Sunday—and there's good reason to suppose that when the summer visitors went home they kept up the argument about the flavors.*

The next year, Howard Johnson added soda pop and frankforts and opened a similar place at Nantasket Beach in Hull and Revere Beach in Revere, and they were "a success due not only to the quality of the ice cream but to the fact that this quality never varied."

The chocolate soda at Nantasket Beach was precisely the same as the first one served at the store in Wollaston. Johnson also opened a small ice cream shop in the Uptown Theatre building in Boston. The theater was located on Huntington Avenue, next to Horticultural Hall, just off Massachusetts Avenue, and was a popular movie theater in the 1930s. "This is the principle of management that supports the present structure: the clam sold in Portland, Maine, varies not at all from the clam sold in Miami." Within three years, his father's $30,000 debt had been paid off, which was not only remarkable but also a credit to this honorable man.

Howard Johnson's success in just a few short years, as well as having paid off his father's debt, had given him the confidence to not just dream but dream big—opening a restaurant in Quincy Square would do. He said in 1938, "I figured that America really preferred good food, nicely served," and he knew that if he made "it as attractive as I knew how, easy to look at and hard to forget," it would be bound to be a success. Quincy Square, which

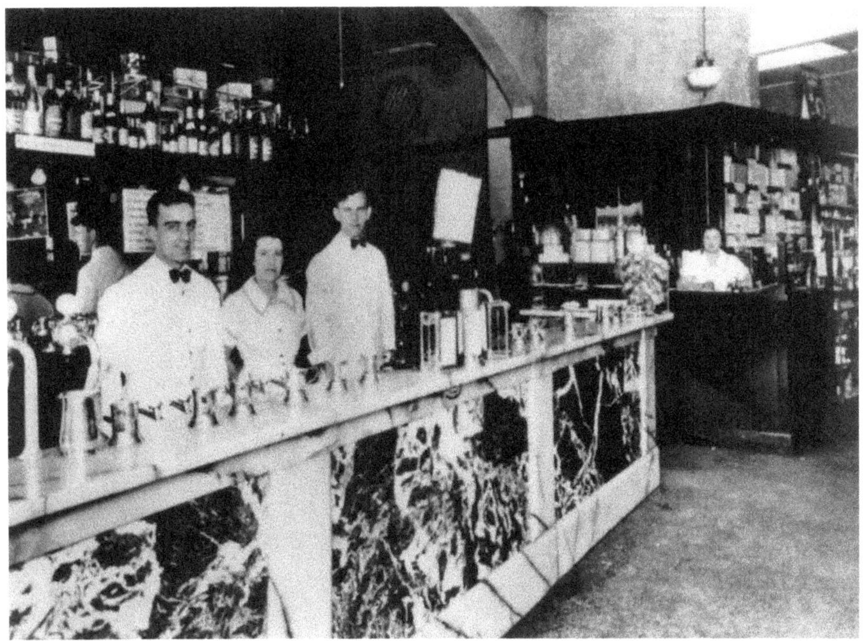

Workers pose for a photograph behind the marble counter at Howard Johnson's corner store at 89 Beale Street in Wollaston. The fountain sodas, ice cream and delicious foods were served to a growing customer base that patronized Howard Johnson's and his famous twenty-eight flavors of ice cream.

had the First Parish Church and Quincy City Hall, was the geographical as well as business center of the city.

Rising in the center of the square was the ten-story Granite Trust Company Building, which was founded in 1836 as the Stone Bank and had the shrewd Theophilus King (1844–1935) as president. King lived at 270 Adams Street in Quincy and was one of the city's biggest champions, as well as a generous benefactor to many local charities. When he wanted to build his new bank, he wanted it at the southern end of Quincy Square, at the junction of Chestnut, Granite and Hancock Streets, so that it was not just the tallest building in the city but also among the most prominent. However, the site he chose was that of the Bethany Congregational Church, of which he and his wife, Helen Baxter King, were members. His bank purchased the church property and helped the congregation to move to Spear Street, just east of the old site, where a new church was designed in 1927 by J. Williams Beal Sons as an impressive random ashlar stone church adjacent to the Thomas Crane Public Library. Now unencumbered, he commissioned the noted architectural firm of J. Williams Beal Sons of Boston to design the modernistic Art Deco skyscraper, built of local Quincy granite and limestone, which created a distinctly urbane and imposing aspect to the square. King and his son, Delcevare King (1874–1964), were said to have provided extraordinary banking leadership to Quincy between World War I and World War II, and it was to them that Howard Johnson approached for a loan to open a restaurant.

In early 1929, Howard Johnson began negotiations with Theophilus King to open a sit-down restaurant on the ground floor of the new Granite Trust Bank Building, just to the left of the bank's main entrance. The Granite Trust Bank gave him a loan of $50,000 to open the restaurant, and a lease was agreed on, after which Johnson hired workers, who began to transform the space into an elegant restaurant, with the basement being used as the kitchens, an office and for storage space. This, the very first Howard Johnson's restaurant, opened to the public in June 1929 with traditional New England foods, including roast turkey, steaks and chops, chicken pot pies, baked macaroni and cheese, baked beans and, of course, his delicious twenty-eight flavors of ice cream. He said, "I figured that America really preferred good food, nicely served," and he was right. That summer, local residents and those shopping in Quincy Square found not only that the restaurant served

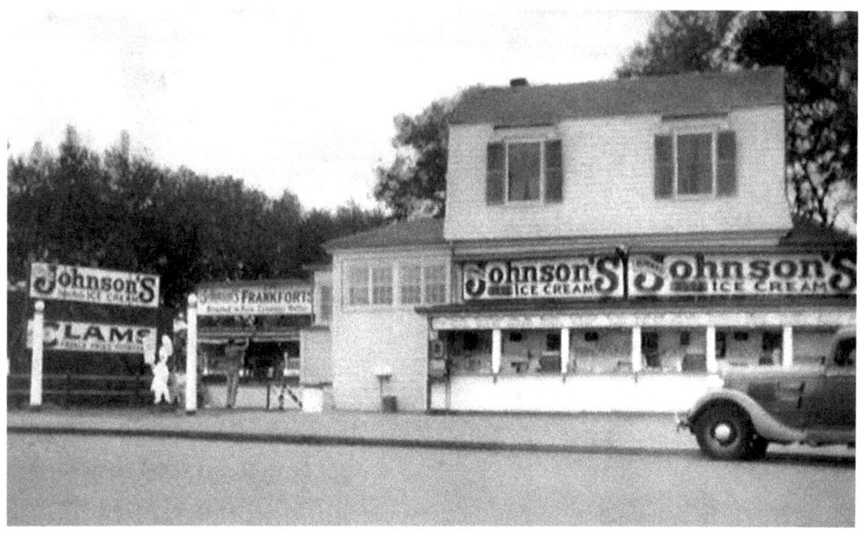

The Wollaston Beach Howard Johnson's ice cream stand was opened in 1926. Renting the stand for $300, the ice cream sales that summer were staggering, and its success ensured that the next summer ice cream stands were opened at Nantasket Beach and Revere Beach, leading to ice cream shops throughout the Boston area.

delicious food, but also that they were pleased with the pleasant atmosphere of the dining room.

In the *Patriot Ledger*, an article appeared on "New Devices at Johnson's" that described the electric kitchen of the new restaurant. It noted, "Through the room flowed a sweet warm breath of air like one finds on a pleasant day in spring. No super chef in the modern sense concocted the pastry and pies, but recipes of the good old New England cooks, tried and true combinations like one gets at home. Mr. Johnson insisted from the start that there were people enough in Greater Boston who would appreciate the cooking like mother did. To do this on a large scale required thought and attention to eliminate the machine taste of the cookery. The installation of an all-electric bakery is a big step toward that accomplishment."

In 1929, the first Howard Johnson's restaurant received an incredibly fortunate break due to an unusual set of circumstances. The mayor of Boston, Malcolm E. Nichols, at the recommendation of the New England Watch & Ward Society, prohibited the planned production of Eugene O'Neill's play *Strange Interlude* from performing in his city. Rather than fight the mayor and the somewhat high-handed tactics of the society, the Theatre Guild decided to move the stage production to suburban Quincy at the Quincy Theatre, which was on Hancock Street in Quincy Square, and it opened to great publicity there in September. At five hours, the play was so long that it had to be presented in two parts, with a dinner break rather than a short intermission. The new Howard Johnson's restaurant, only open a matter of months, happened to be across the street from the theater, and during the play's scheduled break, hundreds of influential Bostonians flocked to the restaurant over the next few weeks. Through this fortuitous occurrence and by word of mouth regarding the delicious foods, more residents of Quincy and Boston became familiar with Howard Johnson's.

As strange, dark and immoral as the play was thought to be by critics and the public, less than two weeks before the New York company was scheduled to travel from the John Golden Theatre in New York for its first scheduled out-of-town performance, to be held in Boston in September 1929, the Theatre Guild was confronted with censorship demands that dwarfed the earlier difficulties in New York. Boston's well-respected mayor Malcolm Nichols, who also happened to be the chairman of the city's theatrical licensing board, determined that *Strange Interlude* was "not a fit spectacle for the public to witness" and had Boston's theatrical censor John Casey warn the Theatre Guild that the play would be banned in Boston. Although Mayor Nichols was unfamiliar with O'Neill's play as a whole,

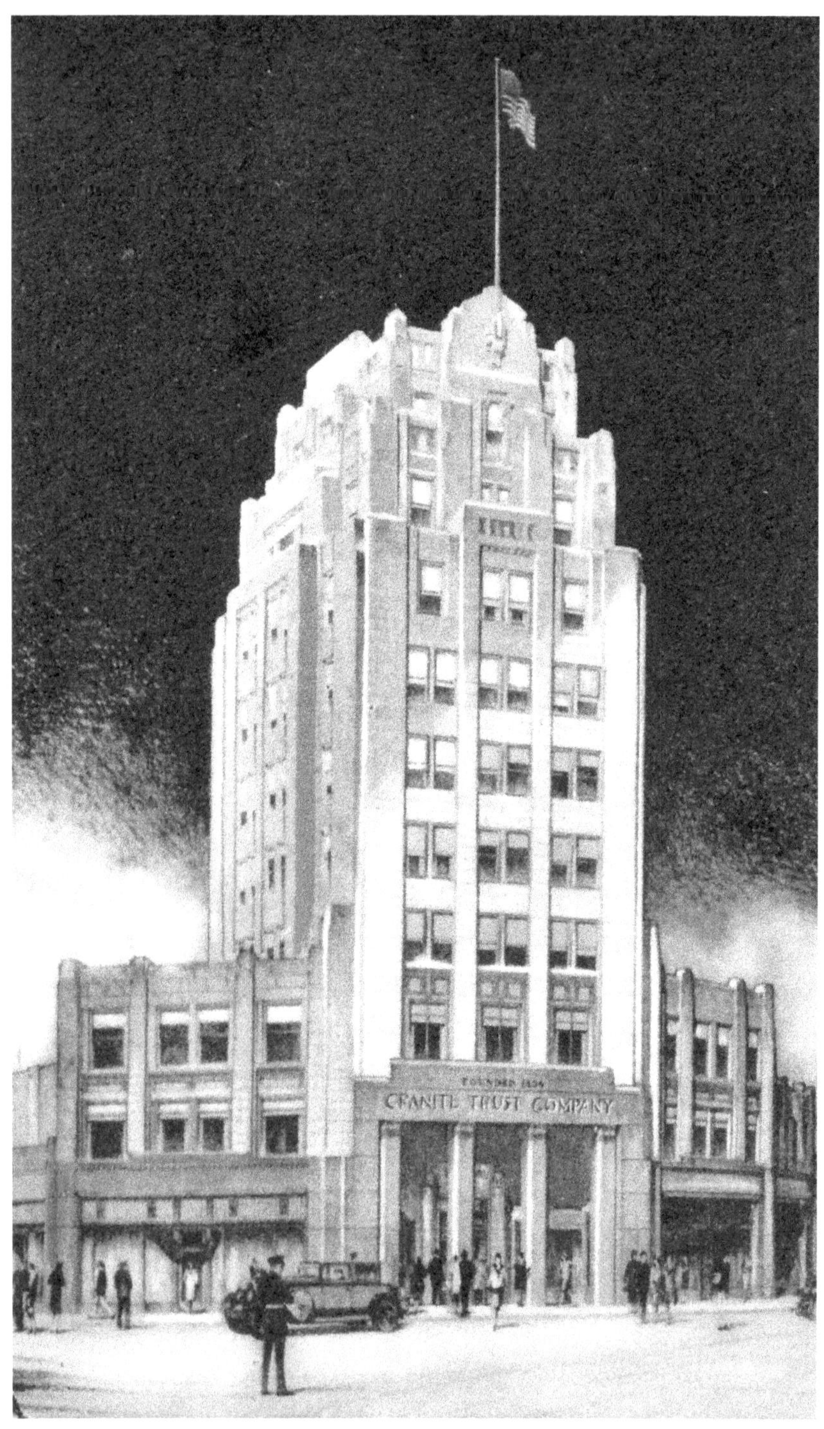
GRANITE TRUST COMPANY

he had read excerpts of the more comprehensive published version and called *Strange Interlude* "a disgusting spectacle of immorality, an advocacy of atheism, of domestic infidelity and the destruction of unborn human life." These damning words placed the play squarely in the public eye and gave it free and invaluable publicity.

The Theatre Guild producers, who believed in the artistic value of *Strange Interlude* and who had already sold $40,000 worth of advance tickets for the Boston showing after advertising it for months, were determined to fight the threatened ban. With the help of Walter Prichard Eaton, who was a member of the jury that awarded *Strange Interlude* the Pulitzer, a "citizens' committee of protest" was organized and the matter discussed on the radio. Eaton commented, "The forces behind censorship in Boston are afraid not of obscenity, for there is plenty of that about, but of modernism and speculation." The producers contemplated taking legal action against the mayor but stated they would prefer to work out a compromise so that *Strange Interlude* could be presented in Boston as planned. Eager to demonstrate that many of the passages that the Boston authorities found objectionable were not contained in the "acting version" of *Strange Interlude*, Mayor Nichols was presented with a "blue-penciled" copy of the more elaborate published edition, and he was encouraged to recommend further cuts. Lawrence Langner told the *Boston Post*, "The deletion of a few pages from a great play cannot destroy the whole," and Theresa Helburn commented, "The play does not depend upon mere words for its effect, and we can easily cut out every one of the words that the Mayor wishes deleted."

However, Nichols had already said that he was not interested in suggesting deletions and considered a "collaboration" with the Theatre Guild "of doubtful value" because he fundamentally "objected to both text and theme" of *Strange Interlude*. It is likely that his attitude prompted the producers to make additional cuts to the play before they submitted it to him. As Eaton noted, on September 20, writers "spent several hours…deleting passages in the published version of the play, so it would correspond to the actual script used in the production." Yet the text that emerged from these efforts, to which the guild referred as the "acting version," was not

Opposite: The Granite Trust Bank is an Art Deco skyscraper in Quincy Square. Designed by J. Williams Beal Sons, it was built in 1929. Howard Johnson opened his first restaurant in 1929 to the left of the bank entrance, serving traditional New England fare and his delicious ice cream. The bank was known as the "Friendly Bank," and engraved above its entrance was the motto "as solid as our granite hills."

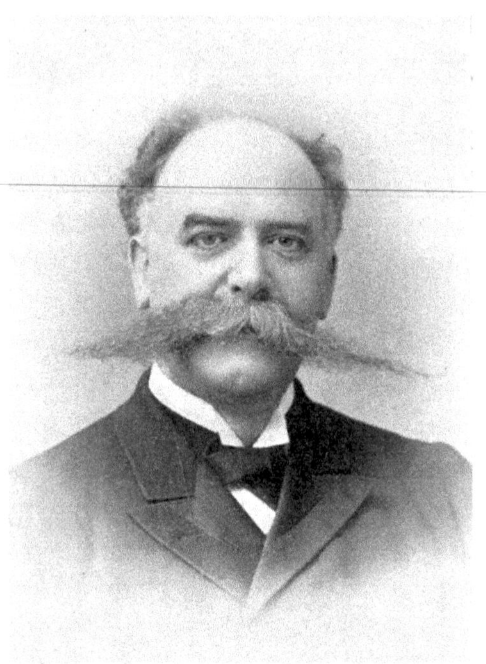

Theophilus King (1844–1935) was the president of the Granite Trust Bank and arranged in 1929 the loan of $50,000 for Howard Johnson to open his first restaurant on the ground floor of the bank. King was a well-respected banker and served as a trustee and receiver of estates.

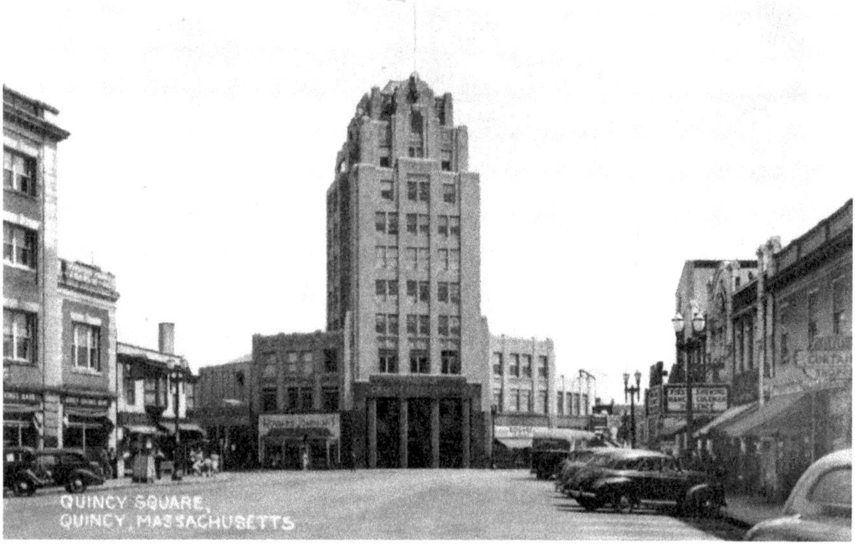

The Art Deco Granite Trust Bank dominates Quincy Square, and to the left of the bank entrance, with its polished granite columns, can be seen the first Howard Johnson's restaurant, which opened in June 1929. On the right is the Quincy Theatre on Hancock Street, where Eugene O'Neill's play *Strange Interlude* was performed after the New England Watch & Ward Society banned its performance in Boston.

the New York promptbook but rather a substantially condensed version of *Strange Interlude* that anticipated a broad range of objections by the censor. "What upset the censors particularly, we were told, was the reference to an abortion in act 3."

The severely censored script of *Strange Interlude* was a skeletal version of the performance text that was used on Broadway and seriously undermined O'Neill's plot, characterizations and themes. However, anxious to placate the mayor and to improve the chances for a Boston production, the play was edited and eliminated nearly all references to sexuality, religion and science in the play and even severely reduced indications of physical contact between the characters. They made these cuts without consulting Eugene O'Neill, who by this time was living in Europe and who only found out through a newspaper article that *Strange Interlude* had encountered restrictive censorship problems in Boston. "Can't the Guild do anything to force this issue, I wonder?" O'Neill was said to have asked his agent, Richard Madden, in a letter written the very day that the censored play manuscript was sent to Mayor Nichols. It is unknown whether Eugene O'Neill ever really found out to what extent the Theatre Guild had gone to make his outré play acceptable to the New England Watch & Ward authorities.

With *Strange Interlude* officially banned in Boston, the Theatre Guild producers considered offers to stage the play—in its now severely censored form—from several Boston suburbs that welcomed the business a Theatre Guild production would bring to town. In the end, *Strange Interlude* was performed in Quincy, despite some opposition from local religious leaders. In what seems like an attempt to appease critics of the play, Quincy's mayor, Thomas McGrath, selected a citizens' play jury, which was supposed to pass judgment on *Strange Interlude* after attending the opening-night performance on September 30, 1929. The fact that several newspapers immediately reported Mayor McGrath's favorable reaction to the play, which he expressed even before hearing from all members of the play jury, demonstrates that there was little doubt that *Strange Interlude* would continue its run at the Quincy Theatre.

Strange Interlude may have been a major contributor to the success of the Howard Johnson's restaurant with its scheduled dinner break during the long performance, but within a decade, his restaurants, ice cream stands and franchised restaurants had created and sustained a remarkable business. In a 1938 booklet called *The Story of Howard Johnson's in New England*, Howard Johnson very briefly but proudly recounted the early history of his corner store at 89 Beale Street in Wollaston, Massachusetts:

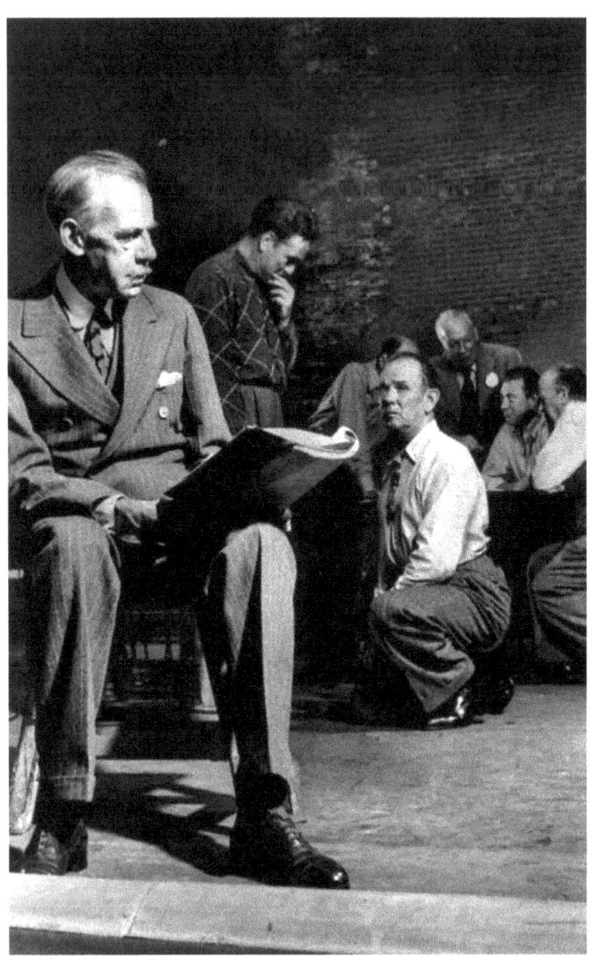

Eugene O'Neill (1888–1953) was a well-respected American playwright whose plays were said to be among the first to include speeches in American vernacular and to include characters on the fringes of society, where they struggle to maintain their hopes and aspirations, but who would ultimately slide into disillusionment and despair. His play *Strange Interlude* catapulted Howard Johnson's new restaurant to a success when it was performed at the Quincy Theatre.

An old-fashioned, hand-cranked ice cream freezer laid the foundation of the Howard Johnson's Ice Cream Shops and Restaurants. Ten years ago I was operating a small news stand in Wollaston, Massachusetts. To add to my "income" I began selling home-made ice cream made in the store's backroom. I was repaid for my efforts by the enthusiasm with which people bought my ice cream—bought it so fast that I and the hand-operated freezer could not keep up.

That was bad, because everyone knew that you couldn't make ice cream in large quantities and still keep that distinctive "home-made" flavor and texture. "Everyone knew!" There's an old Yankee saying: "It ain't the things a man don't know that makes him a fool, it's the awful lot of things he does know that ain't so." I found out the truth of that by studying ice-cream making, experimenting with mixtures, invention new ones, until at last I hit on a formula which could be turned out in quantity and which suited my taste. More important, it seemed to suit many other people, for more and more began to come driving in to Wollaston to ask for "some of that Howard Johnson's home-made ice cream. They coined the phrase that has become my trademark."

Sing a song of Ice Cream, flavors twenty-eight
Simple Simon sampled some, says, "They all are great!"
From A to Z the flavor's fine—this pineapple is prime!
I've only got to Number Ten—but give a fellow time!

CHAPTER 3

Orleans and the Beginnings of the Orange-Roofed Empire

It was fun working for Howard Johnson back in those days. When Mr. Johnson started making his own ice cream, people would actually wait in line to get in.
—Bob Lundy

Orleans is a pleasant town on Cape Cod near the "elbow" of land as it curves north toward Provincetown. The town was settled in 1693 by the descendants of the Pilgrims, who settled Plymouth Colony in 1620 and who were dissatisfied with the poor soil and small tracts of land granted to them as farmland. Originally known as the southern parish of Eastham, Orleans was officially incorporated in 1797 and was named in honor of Louis Philippe, the Duke of Orleans, in recognition of France's magnanimous support for the American colonies against Great Britain during the American Revolution, as well as because the town refused the use of an English name since it had twice been captured by the British during the Revolution. The town's early history, like that of much of Cape Cod, revolved around fishing, whaling and agriculture. As the fishing industry grew, saltworks were established along the town beaches to provide salt for the fish and thereby preserve the catches for shipment.

The town remained fairly small in population until the late nineteenth century, and after the railroad was extended from Boston to Provincetown, it began to attract summer residents who enjoyed the charm of the picturesque village. However, although the population in 1900 was only 1,123 people, the town became increasingly more popular with tourists with the advent of the automobile. Rather than be at the mercy of the railroad timetable, people could tour Cape Cod and stop at restaurants, antique shops, historic sites and points of interest at their leisure.

A prominent family who owned land in Orleans was the Sprague family, who owned a half-acre triangular piece of land at the junction of Routes 6A and 28, near the Eastham town line. Eugene Hale Sprague hailed from Isleboro in Waldo County, Maine, and his family at the turn of the twentieth century lived in Wollaston, Massachusetts, and Orleans on Cape Cod, where he owned the Eagle Wing Inn, a summer hotel that was later operated by his son Rathburn Eaton Sprague. Reginald Heber Sprague (1891–1972), his younger son, was living with his family initially on Park Street at the turn of the century and later on Elmwood Avenue in Quincy and was a friend of Howard Deering Johnson's. A graduate of Quincy High School and Norwich University, class of 1914, and described as "a tall, well-fleshed, ruddy man," he held the distinction of being the first holder of a Howard Johnson's restaurant franchise. As recounted by Blake Clark in his article in *Pageant* in April 1949:

> *Eugene Sprague, a retired packer whom Howard knew, owned a piece of property on Cape Cod that seemed ideal for another ice-cream stand. But Howard could not find the money to lease it or the time to manage it. Driving back from the Cape he conceived his franchise idea. He persuaded Sprague's son, Reggie, to build a combination dairy bar and restaurant. Howard agreed to plan the buildings and furnishings, and provide ice cream, frankfurters and other supplies. There the now famous Howard Johnson color scheme and architecture were introduced...Before Reggie finished his place he was $17,000 in debt. But at the end of the first summer he had cleared $8000, and in two years had repaid all he owed. Soon he was netting twice this amount each summer.*

The restaurant initially opened in the summer for only seven months of the year and provided the famous fried clams, grilled frankforts and twenty-eight flavors of ice cream, all provided by Howard Johnson, who was the franchiser and supplier of foods until World War II, when the popular restaurant was closed during 1943 and 1944; Sprague served in the service and was relocated to Camp Edwards. The restaurant was literally a family business, known as R.H. Sprague Corporation, with Reggie Sprague serving as the cook; his wife, Gladys Lina Bain Sprague, as restaurant hostess; his father cutting and preparing the meat; his daughters, Jean and Barna

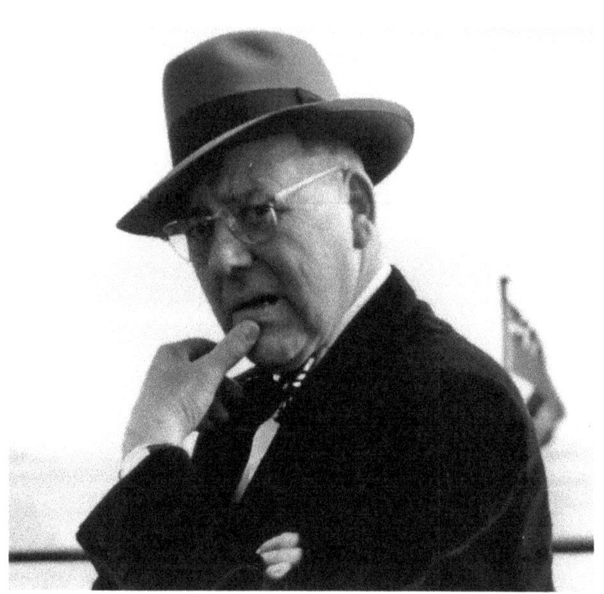

Reginald Heber Sprague (1897–1972) was a lifelong friend of Howard Johnson who was granted the first restaurant franchise in May 1935. Opening a restaurant in Orleans on a corner of his family's property, the new franchise quickly attracted a loyal summer clientele that ensured its success. *Courtesy of Caroline Stewart Macon.*

Sprague, as waitresses; and his sister, Dorothy Sprague, usually preparing salads. As the Orleans Howard Johnson's restaurant was located in a small town, many of the employees worked there for many years, among them Barbara Mayo as head waitress; Marie Knowles, Rowena Taylor, Betty Bremner and Miriam Knowles as waitresses; Louis Fulcher and Clara Fuller as cooks; and Paul Allen, Rodney Dean, Vernon Nickerson and Sidney Pierce as busboys. These people were not just restaurant employees to Reggie Sprague; they were his friends. It was said that he was fond of saying, "It's wonderful what you can do with a few thousand dollars and a couple of friends—especially if one of them is Howard Johnson."

However, although Reggie Sprague's restaurant in Orleans opened in May 1935, it was quickly followed by franchises that Howard Johnson granted to other people, realizing the potential success of these restaurants. It was said that "once the franchise pattern was established, others enjoyed similar success. Don Carlos, a young Bostonian of Greek ancestry, wanted to open a restaurant and use Johnson products. After the agreement was signed, Howard found that his new associate had no money at all, only ideas and a piece of land near Dedham encumbered by a $25,000 mortgage. Yet, once under way, his place cleared more than $15,000 a year…An electrical contractor, a gasoline-station operator, an insurance agent and a bond salesman were among those who found their futures in Howard Johnson franchises."

Beginning in 1935 with franchises in Orleans, Dorchester and Dedham, Massachusetts, there were thirty-nine new franchised restaurants opened in 1936, and by "the fall of 1940, Johnson had more than 130 restaurants (about two-thirds of them franchised) spread through every New England state except Vermont and in seven other states." Although Howard Johnson personally owned some restaurants and roadside ice cream stands, these were establishments that proudly boasted a "Howard Johnson's" sign on the roof. With standardized menus of now familiar foods and identical ice cream dishes, doilies, napkins and chinaware, they gave a sense of uniformity as well as unity throughout the growing chain. This standardization was an important part of the franchise agreement, and Johnson said, "This uniformity, had, I believe, been one of the strongest aids in the rapid growth of the business throughout New England." These franchisees were "furnished with some 450 different items. A fleet of 50 refrigerated trucks transported ice cream and frozen foods, including pies made in the Wollaston kitchen, then quick frozen to be baked and served in the local restaurant" to which it was delivered. These kitchens (or commissaries, as they became known) had a wide array of foods, baked items and, of course, ice cream, as well as the specialty items that were available in the restaurants.

Specialty Items

A few of the specialty items that were mass-produced and individually packaged on a weekly schedule are:

- chicken pies
- beef pies
- charcoal broiled steaks
- curry of shrimp
- halibut au gratin
- clam cakes
- chicken supreme
- fried chickens
- assorted cakes
- cans of assorted soups
- cans of assorted gravies
- cans of assorted sauces
- large cans of clam chowder
- small cans of clam chowder
- assorted pies

The quality of the food, the consistency of its preparation and presentation to the diner was paramount, as Howard Johnson strove to not only protect his name but also to ensure that the franchises operated as a whole. To make certain of this, he would "ensure that his dispersed cadre of restaurant managers upheld a uniform standard, and the company founder issued the 'Johnson Bible'"—a detailed book of instructions on everything from the cooking of vegetables to the maintenance of equipment. Johnson gave his utmost to the restaurant chain and continued to give to his customers what they had come to expect; however, once they arrived, they happily found restaurants that had

> *surroundings that were superior in quality to what they had been accustomed to receiving. Entering a restaurant, customers would find an image of Simple Simon and the Pieman inset in brass in the vestibule floor. To one side was the counter-service area, originally outfitted with stools that could be pulled away when hoards demanding black raspberry, tutti-frutti, or plain old vanilla ice cream crowded up against the fountain on sweltering summer afternoons. The most impressive feature for many years was a mirrored back bar on which ice cream flavors and other specialties were inscribed. To the other side was the main dining room, where the knotty pine walls and booths along the perimeter created a cozy atmosphere.*

In 1938, Howard Johnson, in his booklet *The Story of Howard Johnson's*, noted the following regarding customers liking both the food and the pleasant atmosphere of the restaurants:

> *Because of this increasing patronage, the next year I was able to build two more shops and serve other dishes. But I moved slowly; no food was added to the menus until I was satisfied that people wanted it and that I could prepare and serve it to suit them. I once found, the accepted recipe and method became a strict formula, followed to the letter in every one of my shops, as are my standards of quality, attractiveness and cleanliness. This uniformity has, I believe, been one of the strongest aids in the rapid growth of the business throughout New England, so that still the name of Howard Johnson means "the man who operates our favorite roadside eating-place."*

However, Howard Johnson realized that the colonial-inspired restaurants with their orange tile roofs, which had been provided by Norman W. Pemberton, whose roofing business was in Quincy, as well as the knotty pine

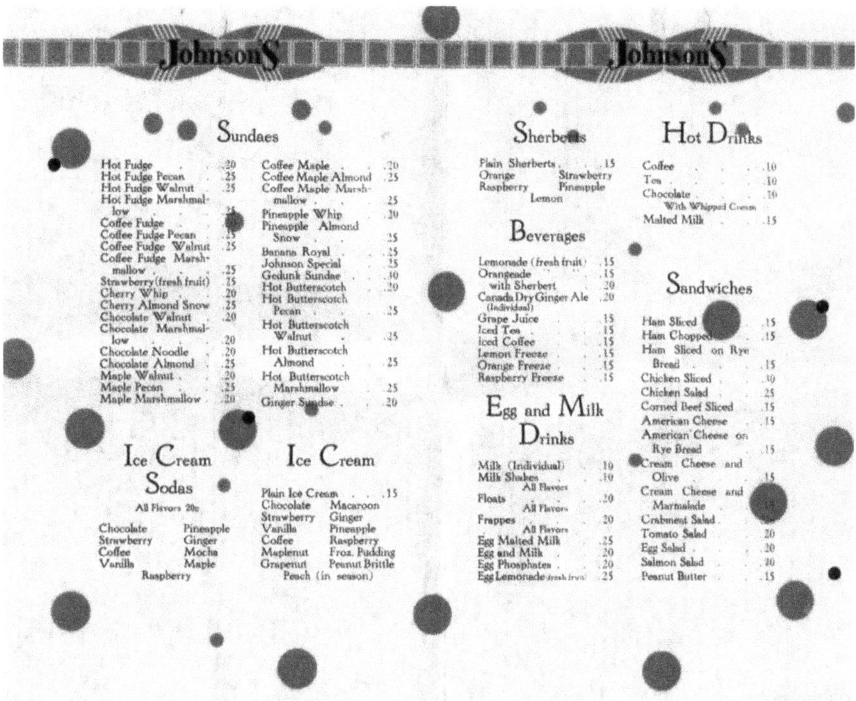

Johnson's

Sundaes

Hot Fudge	.20	Coffee Maple	.20
Hot Fudge Pecan	.25	Coffee Maple Almond	.25
Hot Fudge Walnut	.25	Coffee Maple Marshmallow	.25
Hot Fudge Marshmallow	.25	Pineapple Whip	.20
Coffee Fudge	[illegible]	Pineapple Almond Snow	.25
Coffee Fudge Pecan	[illegible]	Banana Royal	.25
Coffee Fudge Walnut	.25	Johnson Special	.25
Coffee Fudge Marshmallow	.25	Gedunk Sundae	.30
Strawberry (fresh fruit)	.25	Hot Butterscotch	.20
Cherry Whip	.20	Hot Butterscotch Pecan	.25
Cherry Almond Snow	.25	Hot Butterscotch Walnut	.25
Chocolate Walnut	.20	Hot Butterscotch Almond	.25
Chocolate Marshmallow	.20	Hot Butterscotch Marshmallow	.25
Chocolate Noodle	.20	Ginger Sundae	.20
Chocolate Almond	.25		
Maple Walnut	.20		
Maple Pecan	.25		
Maple Marshmallow	.20		

Ice Cream Sodas

All Flavors 20c

Chocolate, Pineapple, Strawberry, Ginger, Coffee, Mocha, Vanilla, Maple, Raspberry

Ice Cream

Plain Ice Cream .15

Chocolate, Macaroon, Strawberry, Ginger, Vanilla, Pineapple, Coffee, Raspberry, Maplenut, Froz. Pudding, Grapenut, Peanut Brittle, Peach (in season)

Johnson's

Sherbets

Plain Sherberts .15

Orange, Strawberry, Raspberry, Pineapple, Lemon

Beverages

Lemonade (fresh fruit)	.15
Orangeade	.15
with Sherbert	.20
Canada Dry Ginger Ale (Individual)	.20
Grape Juice	.15
Iced Tea	.15
Iced Coffee	.15
Lemon Freeze	.15
Orange Freeze	.15
Raspberry Freeze	.15

Egg and Milk Drinks

Milk (Individual)	.10
Milk Shakes (All Flavors)	.10
Floats (All Flavors)	.20
Frappes (All Flavors)	.20
Egg Malted Milk	.25
Egg and Milk	.20
Egg Phosphates	.20
Egg Lemonade (fresh fruit)	.25

Hot Drinks

Coffee	.10
Tea	.10
Chocolate (With Whipped Cream)	.10
Malted Milk	.15

Sandwiches

Ham Sliced	.15
Ham Chopped	.15
Ham Sliced on Rye Bread	.15
Chicken Sliced	.30
Chicken Salad	.25
Corned Beef Sliced	.15
American Cheese	.15
American Cheese on Rye Bread	.15
Cream Cheese and Olive	.15
Cream Cheese and Marmalade	[illegible]
Crabmeat Salad	[illegible]
Tomato Salad	.20
Egg Salad	.20
Salmon Salad	.20
Peanut Butter	.15

A Howard Johnson's menu from the 1930s offered sundaes, sodas, egg and milk drinks and sandwiches, as well as ice cream and sherbets. Howard Johnson said in an advertisement from the 1940s, "When you get the same kind of sundae in New York that you get in Florida, you are more likely to buy one in Maine." Standardization of quality, preparation and portion control ensured uniformity throughout the orange-roofed restaurant chain.

paneled wall interiors, which were provided by Frank B. Curry Company of Boston, were charming in their traditionally inspired New England style. But as he expanded, he sought a more sophisticated style for some of his restaurants, including one that he opened in Somerville, New Jersey. He hired socialite Sister Parish—a nickname given to Dorothy May Kinnicutt Parish by her brother, as she was known then as an aspiring interior decorator—to decorate his new restaurant.

In his review of the book *Sister Parish: The Life of the Legendary American Interior Designer*, William Norwich in the *New York Times* wrote:

> *After coming out in 1927 and then spending a season at the family's apartment on the Quai d'Orsay in Paris, Sister met Harry Parish at a dinner given by her parents at "Mayfields," their house (with gardens*

designed by Ellen Shipman) in Far Hills, N.J. On Valentine's Day, 1930, at St. George's Church in Gramercy Park, Sister and Harry Parish were married by Dr. Drury, the celebrated headmaster of St. Paul's School.

The Parishes had two daughters and one son. After a spell in Manhattan, the family moved to a house in Far Hills, New Jersey. Inspired by "Mayfields" and her parents' beloved place in Dark Harbor, Maine, Mrs. Parish decorated her first country house. It was a smash. Soon she was helping her neighbors with their places. One neighbor, Senator Joseph S. Frelinghuysen, asked her if she would help decorate a new restaurant in nearby Somerville, New Jersey. "The place was called Howard Johnson's," Mrs. Parish remembered. "I did what I could. I dressed the waitresses in aqua, did the walls in aqua, I made the place mats in aqua. I guess I must have thought it was quite chic, but I haven't done a thing in aqua since."

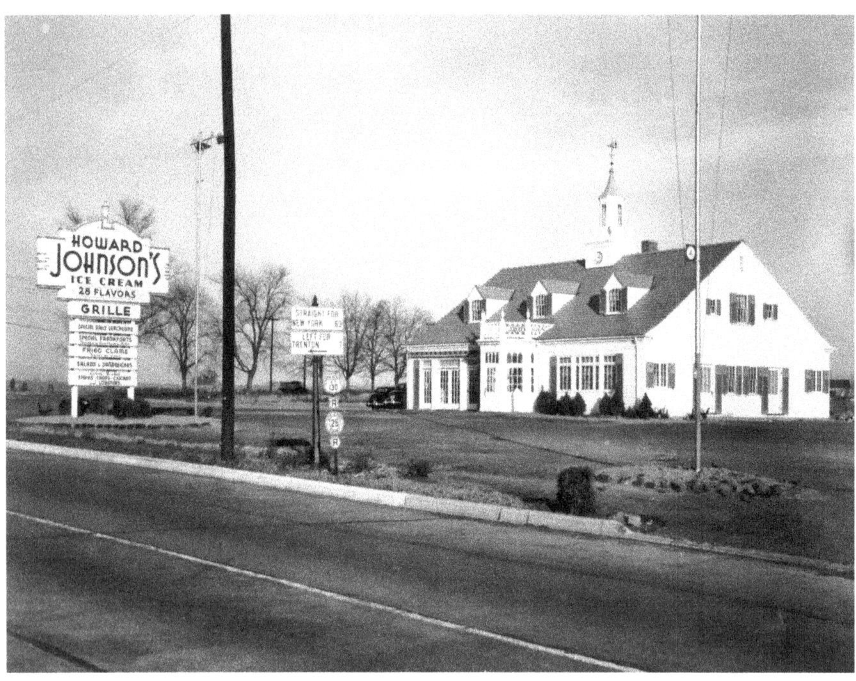

This Howard Johnson's restaurant was located on Route 130 in New Jersey, only seven miles from Trenton, New Jersey, and sixty-three miles from New York City. A Colonial Revival restaurant with the typical orange tiled roof with dormers, octagonal cupola with Simple Simon and the Pieman weathervane, it served a traveling public with fine foods.

In 1933, during the Depression, when her husband's salary at Loeb, Rhodes was cut, Mrs. Parish decided to go into the decorating business officially. "She was a young woman who had, in her own words, 'never opened a window or poured a glass of water myself,' and she decided to take her fate into her own hands," wrote Susan Crater. "She had been accustomed to living a certain way, and she was going to do everything in her power to maintain it for herself and her children."

Her aqua-themed restaurant, albeit with an orange tile roof and turquoise blue shutters, created a dramatic effect as customers walked into the dining room. Sister Parish said that "I had decorated the Hunt Club for pleasure, and the Howard Johnson's for little more than free ice cream," but her taste and her obvious style helped to propel her as a legendary interior decorator of the twentieth century. Howard Johnson "attributes his success to two sound but very simple principles—quality food at sensible prices and assuring the public what to expect before entering a restaurant." But color also proved to be part of the equation, on one hand attracting the passing motorist on the exterior and on the other soothing and creating a sense of pleasantness for the customer on the interior.

CHAPTER 4

The Father of the Franchise Industry and the "Tendersweet" Clam

This is what I like to do best—help a good man to make a go of it himself.
—Howard Deering Johnson, 1949

Franchising is the practice of using another firm's successful business model. The word "franchise" is said to be of Anglo-French derivation—from *franc*, meaning free—and is used both as a noun and as a transitive verb. For the franchisor, the franchise is an alternative to building "chain stores" to distribute goods that avoids the investments and liability of a chain. The franchisor's success depends on the success of the franchisees. The franchisee is said to have a greater incentive than a direct employee because he or she has a direct stake in the business. Essentially, and in terms of distribution, the franchisor is a supplier who allows an operator (the franchisee) to use the supplier's trademark and distribute the supplier's goods. In return, the operator pays the supplier a fee.

Each party to a franchise has several interests to protect. The franchisor is involved in securing protection for the trademark, controlling the business concept and securing know-how. The franchisee is obligated to carry out the services for which the trademark has been made prominent or famous. There is a great deal of standardization required. The place of service has to bear the franchisor's signs, logos and trademark in a prominent place. The uniforms worn by the staff of the franchisee have to be of a particular design and color. The service has to be in accordance with the pattern followed by the franchisor in the successful franchise

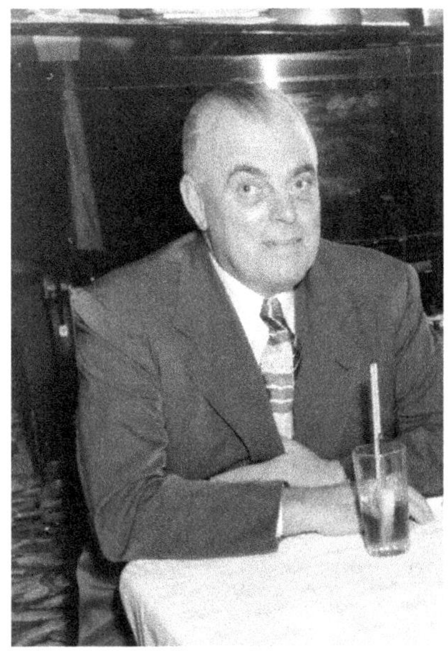

A beaming Howard Deering Johnson had by 1949, the date of this photograph at the Stork Club in New York, successfully franchised his restaurants into one of the largest franchise industries in the United States. From his first restaurant in Quincy Square in 1929, he had parlayed the immensely successful business into a chain of 230 roadside restaurants just two decades later.

operations. Thus, franchisees are not in full control of the business as they would be in retailing.

Howard Johnson's phenomenal growth was based on the application of two relatively new and untried concepts. Its founder, unable to obtain loans from bankers, was a pioneer in the franchising field. Franchisees, rather than the chain, bore the startup costs. These included an initiation fee paid to the company, which then made more money by selling food and other supplies to the franchisees. In addition, Howard Johnson foresaw that the growing popularity of the automobile would send millions of hungry Americans out on the road. By selecting who he wanted to franchise, Johnson was able to get people he trusted to follow his methods. However, to ensure that these franchises followed his directives to the letter, he developed what became known as the "Howard Johnson Bible," which was "an exhaustive set of rules under which franchises had to operate. Johnson laid out menus, recipes, service standards—even a section titled 'Howard Johnson's waitresses—your appearance head to toe.' It was a blueprint for a consistent experience across the chain."

These franchises served the delicious foods provided by the Howard Johnson's commissaries, but the ice cream was a big feature. According to *Fortune* magazine article in 1940, "There's no mystery about good ice cream…All one has to do is to use fresh or frosted fruits, the best cream with whole milk, and the best sirups. The content of butterfat in the mixture of milk and cream must be kept high; Johnson aims to keep it between 21 and 22 per cent. The finished ice cream will have a butterfat content of 18 or 19 per cent because of the addition of other ingredients. In most states the law requires at least 10 per cent. Such simple ingredients always make a success in New England, where any number of establishments have followed this rule and made themselves comfortable."

It was said that the twenty-eight flavors of ice cream—made from milk and cream from the H.P. Hood Company in Charlestown, Massachusetts that Howard Johnson finally settled on became the backbone of his business; "28" was an important number and was even on his license plate (HJ-28). In 1949, it was said that

> *he manufactured and sold more than 3 million gallons, 85% of which were vanilla, chocolate or strawberry. List remains constant at twenty-eight because each promising concoction developed by Johnson's cooks replaces a failing flavor. Thus last May 1949 apple ice cream was slipped into 28th spot in favor of burnt almond, a bizarre item favored chiefly by the very young, daring or desperate customers. Johnson takes great pride in the fact that his ice cream, still made according to his mother's old formula, contains 18% butterfat instead of the 10% to 14% legal minimum.*

Needless to say, his ice cream was not only delicious but also attracted a loyal following of ice cream patrons.

The twenty-eight flavors, with their status of popularity by a voracious ice cream–eating public, ranked from one to twenty-eight like so:

1. vanilla
2. chocolate
3. chocolate chip
4. strawberry
5. coffee
6. maple walnut
7. pistachio
8. butter crunch
9. banana
10. peach
11. peppermint
12. Burgundy cherry
13. butter pecan
14. caramel fudge
15. frozen pudding
16. macaroon
17. orange-pineapple
18. pecan brittle
19. butterscotch
20. black raspberry
21. pineapple
22. coconut
23. fruit salad
24. lemon
25. grape nut
26. peanut brittle
27. ginger
28. apple

There were also four flavors of fruit-flavored sherbet offered: orange, raspberry, lime and lemon. Howard Johnson's *Ice Cream Gazette* once noted,

"Generally speaking, fruit flavors are more popular in the summer, with customers leaning toward nut flavors in the fall. There are also some regional preferences as Frozen Pudding ice cream is most popular in New England, while Coconut is said to be more popular in the Southeast. Pistachio is a big favorite in the New York City area." Wherever the ice cream was served, it was greatly enjoyed.

However, Howard Johnson's delicious ice cream was not the only premium ice cream being enjoyed in New England. The Dutchland Farms was a major rival to his chain of ice cream stands and later restaurants and was said to have strongly influenced the design and development of Johnson's chain. The Dutchland Farms actually had a real dairy farm behind it that had been established in 1897 by Fred F. Field, a wealthy shoe manufacturer in Brockton, Massachusetts. The ice cream and dairy products were produced from the prized Holstein cow herds' milk for the

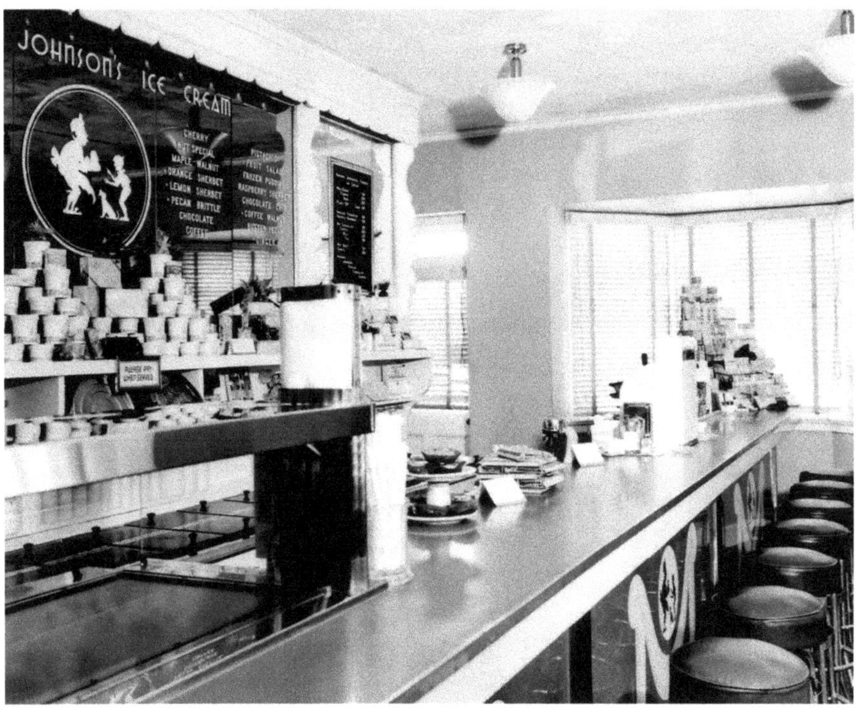

The counter with stools was usually to the right as one entered a Howard Johnson's restaurant. A customer could have a grilled frankfort or dish of ice cream here rather than a full meal in the dining room. The mirrored back board has not only the "Simple Simon and the Pieman" logo but also the twenty-eight flavors of ice cream and a "daily specials board" on the right.

ice cream stands from Grade A milk. Most interestingly, they were offered in twenty-eight flavors and were said to be delicious, premium ice cream. Within five years of opening in 1928, there were almost fifty roadside stores that, in addition to ice cream, sold milk, butter and eggs and served toasted sandwiches, frankfurters, fountain treats and, later, dinners. Menus displayed the Dutchland Farms "registered" colors of orange, blue and white, which also formed the color scheme for buildings. The canvas awnings on the front of the white painted buildings were in eye-catching orange and blue stripes, visible to those passing in automobiles.

In addition to eastern Massachusetts, where most of the Dutchland Farms stands were located, the company offered its dairy fare in New Hampshire, Rhode Island, Connecticut and New Jersey. Some restaurants were operated by the company, but most were franchised, as was true of Howard Johnson's. Dutchland Farms buildings had two outstanding visual characteristics: the orange roofs and the decorative yet functioning windmills that were perched atop the roof or that formed part of the building façade, creating a charming and inviting part of the restaurant. The roadside restaurants, like those of Howard Johnson's, were well situated on busy thoroughfares, and both features were intended to attract motorists' attention. The Depression years were difficult for the Dutchland Farms operators, and quite a few of the restaurants went out of business, with some of the proprietors shifting their allegiance to Howard Johnson's. Irving Carter, a Fairfield, Connecticut operator who opened a Dutchland Farms in 1935, switched to Howard Johnson's after only a few months, and other Dutchland Farms restaurants became independently operated.

Although the ice cream was delicious and the dairy farm productive, times were hard, and Dutchland Farms tried to reorganize its debts. It was eventually sold to rival Howard Johnson in 1940 and merged into his company. Johnson kept the orange, blue and white colors but was barred from using the Dutchland Farms windmills on restaurants operating as Howard Johnson's.

However, it was not just twenty-eight flavors of ice cream that brought customers back to Howard Johnson's. It was also the delicious fried clams, touted as being "sweet as a nut" and native to New England. It was said that the salt, the mud beds of the tidal estuaries and the ocean's numerous nutrients all contributed to the clams' abundance and particular taste, said Ipswich shellfish constable Scott La Preste, a former clam digger. In his opinion, the Ipswich clams "taste real sweet, which is a function of the cold water. It keeps them fresh and firm." However, fried clams have long been enjoyed by New Englanders, for it is known that they have been served since at least 1865 and most likely earlier, and they appeared on an 1865 menu from the Parker House Hotel Restaurant, operated by Peter Drury Parker at the corner of Tremont and School Streets in Boston, Massachusetts. It is not known if the clams were simply deep-fried or if they were dipped in batter and then fried. The same 1865 menu also offers "oysters fried" and "oysters fried in batter." However, it was Howard Johnson, with the four Soffron brothers of Ipswich, Massachusetts, who together in 1951 introduced the now acclaimed clam strip to the American public—henceforth known as the "Tendersweet" clam.

The Soffron Brothers Clam Company was established in 1932 by four brothers—Peter, George, Stephen and Thomas Soffron—sons of Nicholas and Stella Soffron. The family name was originally Soffranas, and they had emigrated from Kalamata, described by Steve Soffron as "olive growing country," a city in the Peloponnese region of southern Greece. The family settled on a farm in Ipswich, Massachusetts, a town forty miles north of Boston. Their parents worked in the textile mills that were the basis of the town's early twentieth-century economy, but after a few years as millworkers, their sons decided to strike out on their own.

According to a brief history of the company by Peter Soffron, the four brothers grew to dislike working in the same mills as their parents and instead found work digging and selling the local soft-shell Ipswich clams. Before the 1930s, soft-shell clams were generally dug up and purchased for use as fishing bait, but clams became an attractive food source for consumption during the Depression years, along with the advent of the fried clam and the growing popularity of clam chowder. In 1932, the Soffron brothers purchased a building on Locust Street in Ipswich and converted it into a soft-shell clam shucking company. They signed a sixteen-year contract with the recently established Howard Johnson's franchise. The contract established Soffron Brothers Clam Company as the sole supplier of shucked soft-shell clams to the restaurants being opened in Massachusetts for use as fried clams. The success of the fried clams at Howard Johnson's restaurants generated an ever-growing demand for larger volumes of the clams available in Ipswich.

With this steadily increased demand for Ipswich clams, the Soffron brothers were compelled to expand their shucking house and develop other shucking houses on other areas of the East Coast rich with soft-shell clams. Their fleet of clam boats included the *Virginia S*, the *Sylvia S*, the *Merle C. Soffron*, the *Theodora S*, the *Stella S* and the *G.N. Soffron*. Soffron Brothers Inc. proudly noted that its selected clams were the "Best for Frying," and it expanded and developed shucking houses in Seabrook, New Hampshire, and Moultonborough, Maine. In 1948, a new sixteen-year contract with Howard Johnson's was negotiated, renewing the exclusivity between the two companies. The Soffrons expanded their business and moved their original shucking house from Locust Street to Brown Square in Ipswich.

With the success and popularity of the Howard Johnson's franchise and the growing success and popularity of their fried clams, the Soffron brothers were forever challenged to meet the ever-expanding demand for clams. The Soffrons were forced to open another shucking house, this time in Digby, Nova Scotia, Canada. Even with their expanded supply of soft-shell clams, the demand became too great for the available supply. During some years, the supply is better than others, and some of the clamming areas are richer in supply than others, but in the early 1950s, a glut in the supply of available soft-shell clams along the entire East Coast of the United States created an extreme challenge for the brothers, and a solution was discovered with the use of an entirely different species of clam, the Atlantic surf clam (*Spisula solidissima*), also known as the sea clam or the hen clam.

The Soffron brothers realized that if the Atlantic surf clam is shucked open and the extremely large digging muscle of the clam removed, it can be cut into thin strips and fried, which was an attractive alternative to the soft-shell clam. The Soffron brothers introduced the new product to Howard Johnson's under the name "Tendersweet" clams, and they became an instant success for the franchise, which shortly afterward purchased the trademark name "Tendersweet" clams from the Soffron brothers. Since the surf clams were fried without the bellies, the sweet flavor was more appealing to a larger customer base and could also be frozen and still retain good quality.

Once again, the demand grew tremendously, and in order to supply the restaurants, the brothers joined forces and worked with the owners of Snow's Clam Company to develop a device to harvest the surf clams. The two companies jointly developed a hydraulic clam dredge that consisted of a large steel cage with foot-long metal spikes on the open end of the cage that could sift through the wet sand to gather the clams. A one-foot-diameter rubber hose also fed air to the opening of the cage in order to loosen the sand. Dragging such a devise from a ship became the new method of harvesting clams and is still used today. With the newly developed technology and the new clam species, the supply was once again abundant. Clams could now be dragged from the ocean floor from Cape Hatteras, North Carolina, up to the southern Gulf of the Saint Lawrence River in Canada and outward to a distance of two hundred miles. The Soffrons converted their shucking houses in Maryland

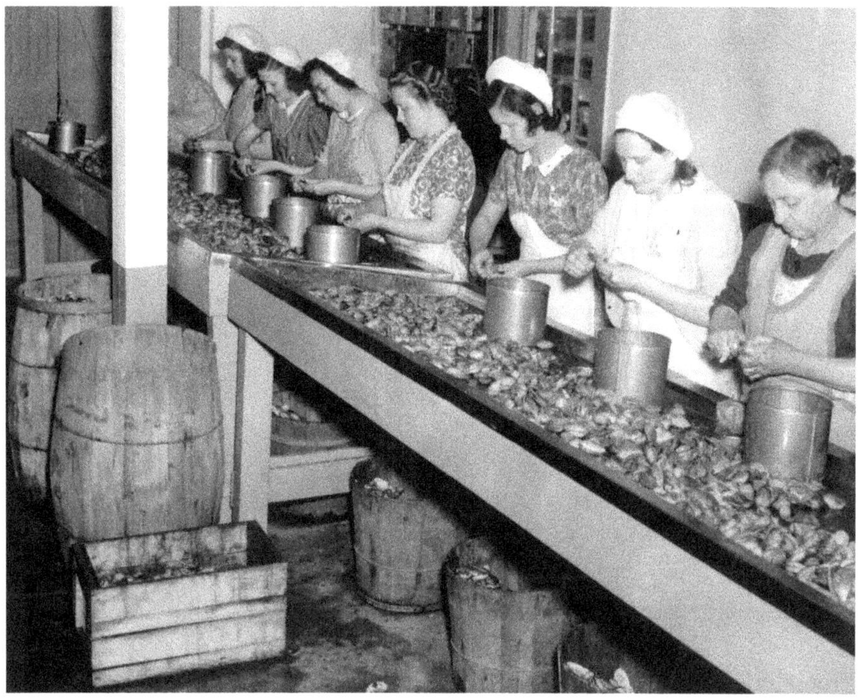

A line of clam shuckers at long troughs filled with fresh Ipswich clams at the Soffron Brothers Clam Company shucking house in 1938. Howard Johnson's exclusive contract with the Soffron brothers extended for thirty-two years, from 1932 to 1964, and the Soffrons provided both soft-shell clams and "Tendersweet" clam strips to the restaurant chain. *Courtesy of Peter Soffron.*

and New Jersey, where the supply of Atlantic surf clams was the greatest. The Soffrons also had built state-of-the-art dredging boats to harvest the clams. Success continued throughout the duration of the remainder of the contract with Howard Johnson's until its expiration in 1966.

In 1966, Howard Brennan Johnson decided not to renew the contract with the Soffron brothers, though the relationship had been mutually rewarding for thirty-two years. As Howard Johnson's was the sole customer of the company, which was a legal point in the contract, the consequences of the cancelled contract were devastating to the business. The Soffron Brothers Clam Company worked diligently to regroup its once thriving business over the next year. In 1968, the company successfully regrouped, and the brothers reopened their shucking house in Ipswich, processing fresh, frozen and canned surf clam products for the wholesale market from the Ipswich-based processing plant until the late 1990s.

Ice cream and fried clams were a delicious and an integral part of the menu served at Howard Johnson's, but they were only a part of the delicious foods, desserts and beverages of all kinds available from a large menu that also had daily specials. In a 1939 booklet entitled *From Maine to Florida with Howard Johnson's*, there was a listing of Howard Johnson's "Stars," the favorite foods that were enjoyed by loyal patrons. These were perennially popular favorites of the public and were enjoyed in every state from Maine to Florida:

> *Delicious Ice Cream*
>
> *Ten years ago* [in 1929] *Howard Johnson devised his original ice cream formula and laid the cornerstone of his present success. This original formula is still in use today and to the single flavor—vanilla—27 additional flavors have been added. Now millions of gallons of this famous ice cream is sold every year because it has retained its rich, delicious goodness and because it is made only of pure, heavy cream and fresh dairy products and flavored with fresh fruits and natural flavorings.*
>
> *Fried Clams*
>
> *Tender, fried clams depend on two important items—the clams and the way they are prepared. Howard Johnson's selects only the freshest clams, certified for purity, and fries them in the finest vegetable oils to a crisp and tempting golden-brown. And because of Howard Johnson's uniform standards you'll find your fried clams equally good in every Howard Johnson's restaurant.*
>
> *Frankforts*
>
> *Howard Johnson's Frankforts are another specialty, exclusive with Howard Johnson's Ice Cream Shops and Restaurants. From beginning to end they're completely different: a frankfort made up according to Howard Johnson's own recipe, grilled in pure creamery butter and served piping hot on a flaky, toasted roll with mustard and relish—truly a feast for a king.*
>
> *Salads*
>
> *Whether it is made from fruits and vegetables fresh from the garden, sea foods with the salty tang of the blue ocean, choice poultry or tender, tasty*

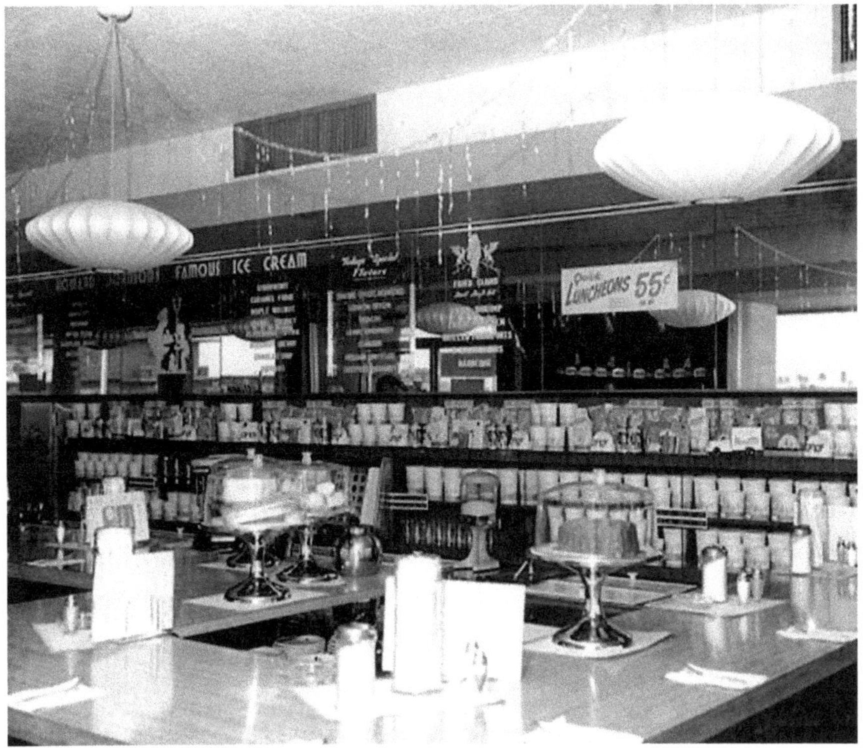

A Howard Johnson's restaurant in 1952 had Formica counters where customers could sit on stools to enjoy a quick snack, a cup of coffee or a dish of ice cream. Various cakes, kept under glass tops, included carrot cake, coconut cake and sour cream cake, supplied from the commissaries and available at all restaurants.

meats—a Howard Johnson's salad is not complete without these. Still to be added are the crisp lettuce and creamy mayonnaise—and that touch of genius which makes a Howard Johnson's salad a work of art.

Three-Decker Sandwiches

Like the old three-decker merchantman, this Howard Johnson's specialty carries a splendid cargo between its three golden slices of perfect toast. Your choice of mouth-watering meats, delightful cool salads or tangy cheeses in a host of tempting combinations, the Howard Johnson's Three-Decker on its mountainous sea of potato chips provides in itself a hearty and well-balanced meal.

BAKERY PRODUCTS

From Howard Johnson's own spotless bakeries come the rolls, cake, pie and pastries to make the perfect complement to the perfect meal. Baked by long-tested home recipes these products are always fresh and delicious.

SIZZLING STEAKS

Some day when you hanker for a real meal order a Howard Johnson's Sizzling Steak, ceramic-broiled and served in a glow of sizzling, crackling, sputtering splendor—that's steak at its very best. Again you can be sure of quality for all Howard Johnson's meat is of the highest quality.

COFFEE

Howard Johnson's Coffee is blended for these restaurants and is always freshly brewed—the perfect accompaniment to a delicious Howard Johnson's meal.

CANDIES

Howard Johnson's candies are made in his own spotless candy kitchen according to original recipe using only the purest of ingredients. A great variety of tempting, delicious candy in a wide choice of attractive packages.

Johnson had wanted to expand his company, but the stock market crash in October 1929, and the resulting lack of credit, prevented him from doing so. After waiting a few years and maintaining his business with the restaurant in Quincy Square, the Uptown Theatre in Boston and the store in Wollaston, Johnson was able to persuade his friend Reggie Sprague in 1935 to open a second Howard Johnson's restaurant in Orleans, Massachusetts, on Cape Cod. The second restaurant was franchised and not company-owned, and this restaurant was one of the first franchising agreements in the United States. By the end of 1936, there were over 36 more franchised restaurants, creating a total of 41 Howard Johnson's restaurants. By 1939, there were 107 Howard Johnson's restaurants along the highways and busily traveled roads of the eastern United States, generating annual revenues of $10.5 million. In less than fourteen years, Howard Johnson was now directing a franchise network of over ten thousand employees with 170 restaurants, said to be serving more than 1 million people per year.

The unique icons of orange tile roofs, cupolas and weathervanes on Howard Johnson's properties helped patrons identify the chain's restaurants and motels. The restaurant's very recognizable trademark "Simple Simon and the Pieman" logo was created by artist John Alcott in the 1930s and has long been one of the most recognized brands in the United States food industry.

When the Pennsylvania Turnpike, the Ohio Turnpike and the New Jersey Turnpike were built, Johnson bid on and won exclusive rights to serve food to drivers at service station turnoffs through the turnpike systems. There were two hundred Howard Johnson's restaurants when America entered World War II. By 1944, only a dozen Howard Johnson's restaurants remained open for business. The effects of war rationing and fuel rationing had crippled the

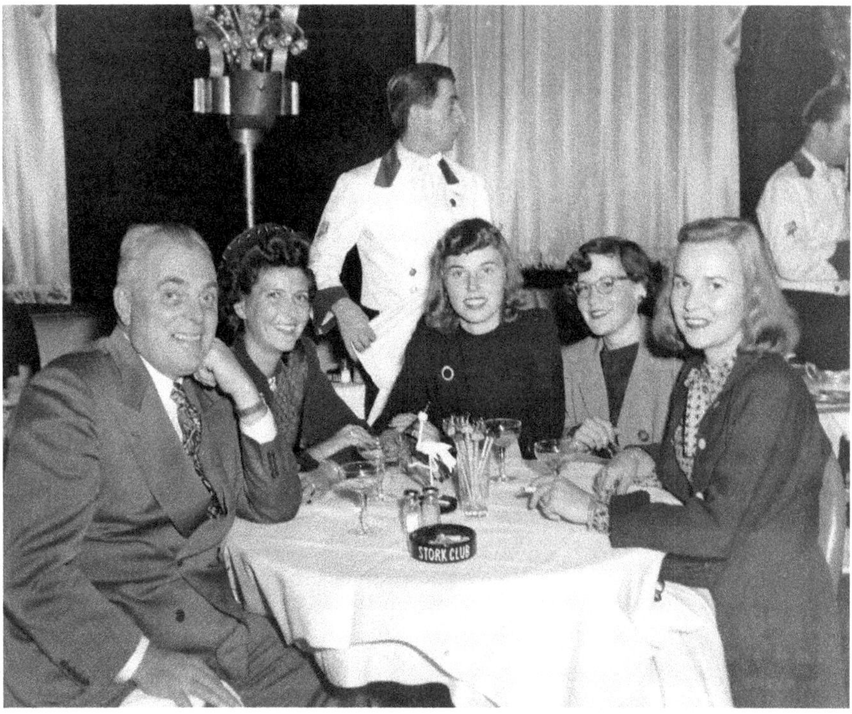

Seen here in November 1948 at Sherman Billingsley's Stork Club in Manhattan are (left to right) Howard Deering Johnson, Marjorie Smith Burgin Johnson, Dorothy V. Johnson, Wiff Waterman and Polly Weeden. The Johnsons were entertaining Dorothy and two of her college friends from Briarcliff Junior College, in Briarcliff Manor in Westchester County, New York, at dinner.

company, as it had been built on the ascendancy of the automobile. Johnson managed to maintain his business by serving commissary food to war workers and United States Army and Navy recruits. In the process of recovering from these losses, the Howard Johnson's company began construction in 1947 of two hundred new restaurants throughout the American South and the Midwest. By 1951, the sales of the Howard Johnson's company totaled $115 million.

As Howard Johnson expanded his business, so too did he expand the geographic area in which he opened restaurants, moving from New England and down the East Coast of the United States. Franklin Delano Roosevelt started the Works Progress Administration (WPA), which put people to work building and repairing roads, among them the Pennsylvania Turnpike. "Howard Johnson's was a precedent-setting organization. It was the first to capitalize on the huge business potential that lay along the nation's highways. Not until the development of Howard Johnson's could families travelling by car be guaranteed of finding palatable food in agreeable surroundings almost wherever they drove."

The Pennsylvania Turnpike had been planned in the 1930s to improve automobile transportation across the mountains of Pennsylvania. It utilized seven tunnels that were built for the abandoned South Pennsylvania Railroad in the late nineteenth century, and construction began in November 1938. The road opened on October 1, 1940, between Irwin and Carlisle, Pennsylvania, as the first long-distance limited-access highway in the United States and led to the construction of other limited-access toll roads and the Interstate Highway System.

The Pennsylvania Turnpike is a toll highway operated by the Pennsylvania Turnpike Commission and is a limited-access highway, running for 360 miles across the state. The turnpike begins at the Ohio state line, where the road continues west into Ohio as the Ohio Turnpike. The toll way ends at the New Jersey border at the Delaware River and extends over the river, where it continues into that state as the Pearl Harbor Memorial Extension of the New Jersey Turnpike.

The roadway runs east–west through the state, connecting the Pittsburgh, Harrisburg and Philadelphia areas. As it passes through the Appalachian Mountains in the central part of the state, the turnpike has seven tunnels and uses four former railroad tunnels.

In the late 1940s, the turnpike was extended east to Valley Forge, opening in 1950, and west to the Ohio border, opening in 1951. In 1954, the road was extended east to the Delaware River, and the mainline turnpike was completed in 1956 when the Delaware River Bridge was finished. In the

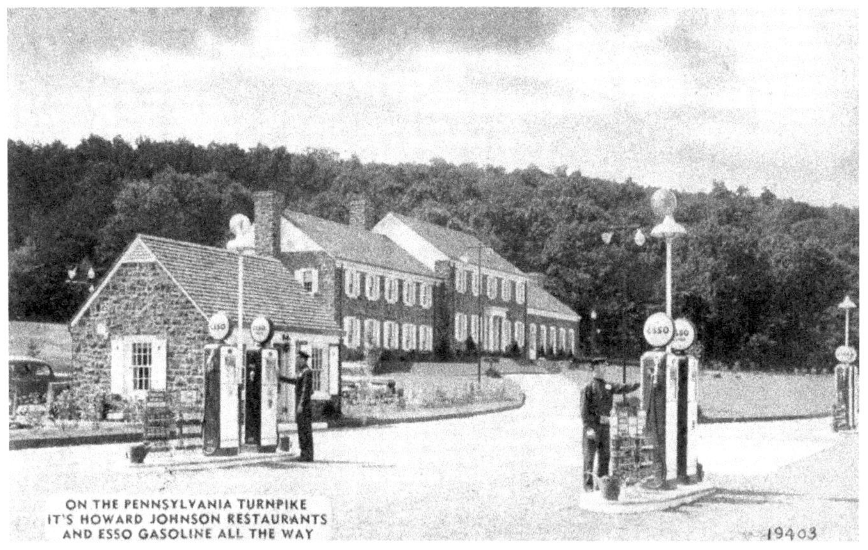

The Pennsylvania Turnpike was opened in 1940 from Harrisburg to Pittsburgh, and Howard Johnson's was granted the concession to open eight restaurants along the turnpike, serving its famous foods and twenty-eight flavors of ice cream in distinctive fieldstone buildings. Esso Gasoline of the Standard Oil Company received the concession to provide gasoline at these turnpike service areas.

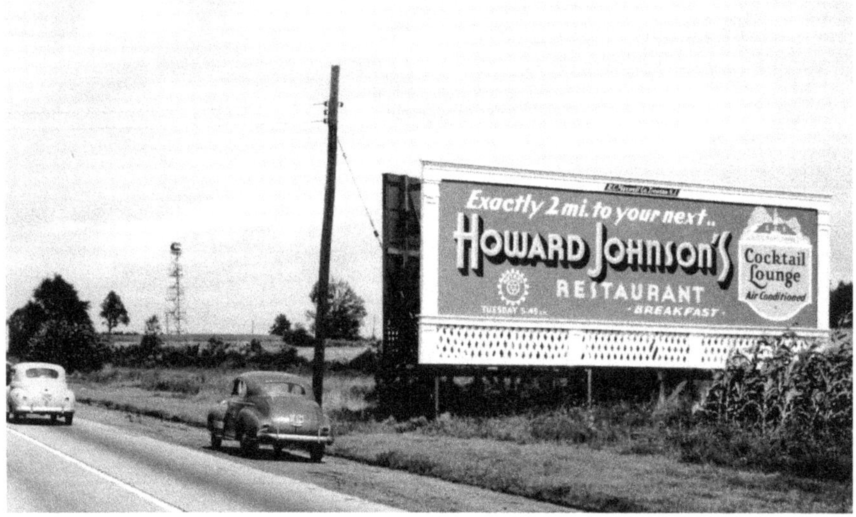

Roadside billboards were erected near Howard Johnson's restaurants, alerting travelers that the restaurant was exactly two miles up the road. The R.C. Maxwell Company in Trenton, New Jersey, prepared well-designed billboards, which were often erected on the edge of farmland. The John Donnelley and Sons Advertising Company had since 1929 produced the billboard advertising in the Boston area.

1960s, an additional tube was bored at four of the two-lane tunnels, while the other three tunnels were bypassed. These improvements made the entire length of the highway four lanes wide.

As the first section of the highway was built through a rural part of the state, food or gas was not easily available to motorists, so the commission decided to construct service plazas at thirty-mile intervals. The service plazas would have buildings constructed of native fieldstone resembling colonial-era buildings of the Pennsylvania region rather than the white painted buildings in New England. In 1940, Standard Oil of Pennsylvania was awarded a contract to operate ten Esso service stations along the turnpike. Eight of the service plazas would consist of service stations along with a restaurant, while the service plazas at the halfway point in Bedford would be larger. The South Midway service plaza, which was the largest on the turnpike, contained a dining room, a lunch counter, a lounge and lodging facilities for truckers, and a tunnel connected it to the smaller North Midway service plaza. The remaining service plazas were smaller and contained only lunch counters. Food service at the service plazas was provided by Howard Johnson's restaurants, and it was said in *A Colorful Souvenir Book of Pennsylvania Turnpike System* that "each service station provides restaurants and dairy bar service and many of them have table service where hungry motorists can have a variety of delicious meals. All of the dairy and lunch counters, as well as the restaurants and dining room service, are under the direct supervision and management of the celebrated caterer—Howard Johnson."

After World War II, the food facilities were greatly enlarged. Service stations sold gasoline, repaired cars and had towing services available. On the extensions of the turnpike, the service plazas were built larger and farther back from the road. Gulf Oil would operate the service stations on the extensions; Howard Johnson's still provided food service at sit-down restaurants. With the creation of the Interstate Highway System, restaurants and gas stations were prohibited along interstate highways, and the turnpike, which became a part of the system, was grandfathered in and allowed to continue operating its service plazas.

In 1978, as Howard Johnson's exclusive contract to provide food service was nearing an end, the turnpike commission considered bids for competitors to provide food service. That year, ARA Services was awarded a contract to provide food service at two service plazas, ending Howard Johnson's monopoly. The toll way became the first toll road in the country to offer more than one fast-food chain at its service plazas. At this time, gas stations along the turnpike were operated by Gulf Oil, Exxon and ARCO.

CHAPTER 5

The New York World's Fair and the "Queen of Rego Park"

Expositions are the timekeepers of progress. They record the world's advancements. They stimulate the energy, enterprise, and intellect of the people, and quicken human genius. They go into the home. They broaden and brighten the daily life of the people. They open mighty storehouses of information to the students.

These evocative words were spoken by United States president William McKinley at a public address in 1901 at the opening of the Pan-American Exposition in Buffalo, New York. His words were poignant and thought provoking but clearly stated that expositions and fairs were not simply places for entertainment, but rather they should strive to "[s]timulate the energy, enterprise and intellect of the people." Held annually, these fairs brought nationwide countries together in the twentieth century to showcase modern technology and development and foster a sense of shared camaraderie.

The 1939–40 New York World's Fair was said to have covered 1,200 acres of the Flushing Meadows in Queens, New York, and was the second-largest American world's fair of all time. Many countries around the world participated in the fair, and more than 45 million people were said to have attended its exhibits in the two seasons that it was open. This was the first exposition to be based on the future of the world, using as its catchy slogan "Dawn of a New Day" and allowing awestruck visitors to see and experience through exhibits "the world of tomorrow." According to a pamphlet of the New York World's Fair:

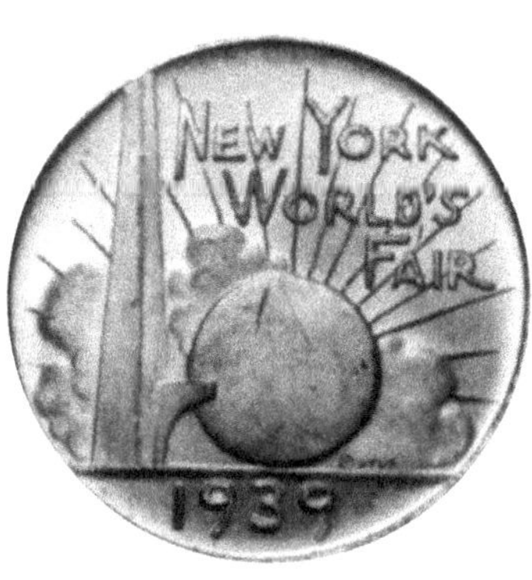

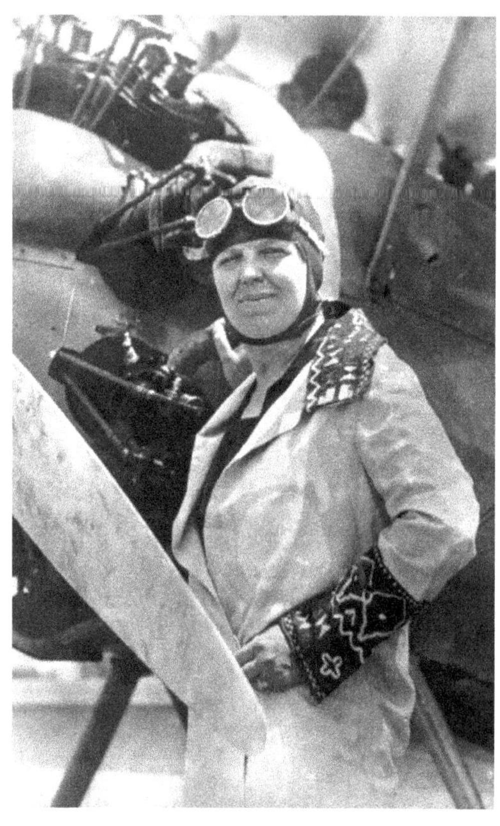

Above, left: Howard Johnson's minted a gold-colored token for use in its restaurant for those traveling to the 1939 New York World's Fair. Showing the Trylon and the Perisphere, symbols of the world's fair, this token had no monetary value but was redeemable for a discount on food and ice cream for those stopping at the restaurant on Queens Boulevard in Rego Park in Queens, New York.

Above, right: Lydia Pinkham Gove (1885–1948) was an investor in the Howard Johnson's restaurant that opened in Rego Park in Queens, New York, on the road to the New York World's Fair. She invested a huge sum in the Queens Boulevard restaurant, which was the largest Howard Johnson's restaurant ever built. *Courtesy of Schlesinger Library, Radcliffe Institute, Harvard University.*

> *The eyes of the Fair are on the future—not in the sense of peering toward the unknown nor attempting to foretell the events of tomorrow and the shape of things to come, but in the sense of presenting a new and clearer view of today in preparation for tomorrow; a view of the forces and ideas that prevail as well as the machines. To its visitors the Fair will say: "Here are the materials, ideas, and forces at work in our world. These are the tools with which the World of Tomorrow must be made. They are all interesting and much effort has been expended to lay them before you in an interesting way. Familiarity with today is the best preparation for the future."*

In 1935, at the height of the Great Depression, it was widely discussed how the lingering effects of the Depression could be dispelled, and it was decided to create an international exposition. The New York World's Fair Corporation, whose office was in the Empire State Building, was a way of not only fostering interest in a nationwide exposition but also to bring much-needed tourist revenue to New York. The New York World's Fair would hopefully foster a new age of global communication, nationwide superhighways and suburban living, and surprisingly, it delivered on this hope.

Over the next four years, the committee planned and organized the fair and its exhibits, with countries around the world taking part in creating the biggest international event since World War I. Working with the committee was Robert Moses, a well-known developer and the New York City parks commissioner, who saw great value to the city in having the World's Fair Corporation remove a vast ash dump in the borough of Queens on Long Island that was selected to be the site for the exposition. This event turned the area into a city park after the exposition closed.

Edward Bernays directed public relations of the fair in 1939, and Grover Whalen, a public relations innovator, saw the fair as an opportunity for corporations to present consumer products rather than just as an exercise in presenting science. The promotion and advertising of this great event took many forms, all of them effective. In 1938, even the Brooklyn Dodgers, New York Giants and the New York Yankees baseball teams did their part to promote the upcoming fair by wearing patches on their jerseys featuring the Trylon, Perisphere and "1939" on their left sleeve. Howard Hughes flew a special world's fair flight around the world to promote the fair the year before it was opened. It seemed that this advance publicity fueled the excitement and, in a way, brought people still suffering from the lingering Depression hope with a streamlined world of new consumer goods, such as teardrop cars and smoking robots, electric dishwashers and nylon stockings, all manufactured by companies such as Westinghouse, General Motors and AT&T.

While the main purpose of the fair was to lift the spirits of the United States and drive much-needed business and tourism to New York City to fuel the economy, it was also felt that there should be a cultural or historical association. It was planned that the fair would be officially opened on the 150th anniversary of George Washington's first inauguration as president of the United States, which took place in New York City.

Opened with great media fanfare on April 30, 1939, the fair welcomed an incredible 206,000 people on the first day. Although many of the

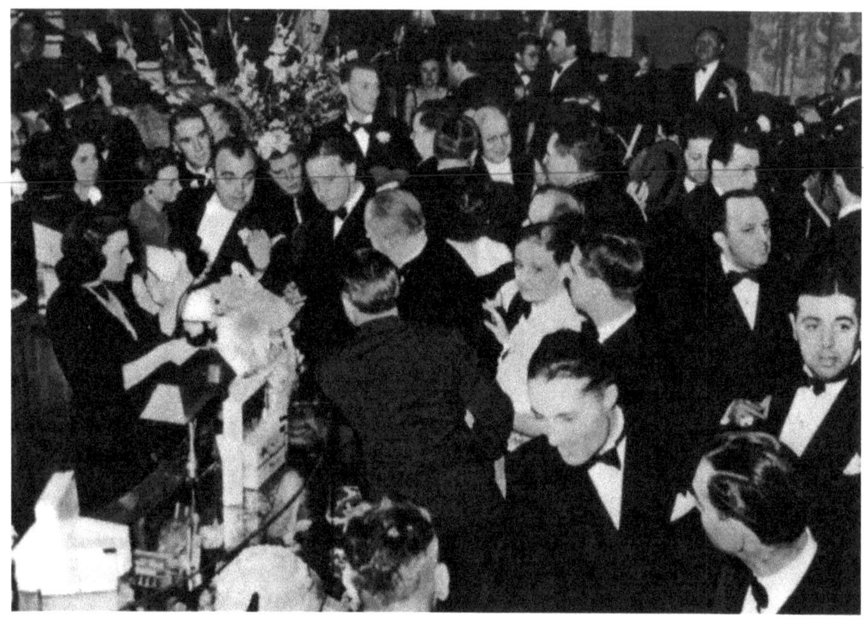

Opening night brought hundreds of Howard Deering Johnson's and Lydia Pinkham Gove's family and nearest and dearest friends to marvel at the new restaurant in Rego Park in Queens, New York. Seen just below the floral arrangement is Howard Deering Johnson, debonair in white tie and tails, gesturing to a friend as he holds a conversation with honored guests.

pavilions and other facilities were not quite ready for the opening day, the ceremonies were put on with great éclat, and President Franklin Delano Roosevelt gave the opening-day address. His speech discussed the wide range of technological innovation showcased at the fair, not only broadcast over the various radio networks but also televised. NBC used the event to inaugurate regularly scheduled television broadcasts in New York City over its station W2XBS, now known as WNBC. An estimated 1,000 people viewed the Roosevelt telecast from about two hundred television sets scattered throughout the New York area, many of them in store windows, where they gathered to watch as a group. The world's fair was themed and divided into different sections, and the buildings and pavilions erected on the fairgrounds were extraordinary, with many of them experimental in design. Architects were encouraged by their corporate or government sponsors to be as creative, energetic and innovative as possible.

The "Theme Center" consisted of two all-white landmark monumental buildings named the Trylon, which was more than seven hundred feet tall, and the Perisphere, which could be entered by a moving stairway and exited via a grand curved walkway named the Helicline. Inside the vast Perisphere was a model city of the future that visitors viewed from a moving walkway placed high above the floor level. The Theme Center was designed by the architect Wallace Harrison and his associate Max Abramovitz. Ironically, the colors blue and orange had been chosen as the official colors of the fair, not only the colors of New York City but also Howard Johnson's; they were featured prominently, and only the Trylon and Perisphere were built in brilliant white and could be seen from great distances. Avenues stretching out into the various areas from the Theme Center were designed with rich colors that actually changed the farther one walked from the center of the grounds. It was said that at night, with the latest in lighting technology switched on, the effect was felt by many of those attending to be a "magical" experience.

Another theme of the world's fair was the emerging new middle class, leading an ardently hoped-for recovery from the Great Depression. The fair also promoted the prototype "Middleton Family"—Bud, Babs and their two children, all of whom appeared in ads showing them taking in the sights of the fair and the new products being manufactured to make life easier and affordable, such as the new automatic dishwasher and Elecktro, a seven-foot-tall walking, talking robot. This advertising encouraged families to visit the fair and hopefully not just enjoy the exhibitions but also spend their money.

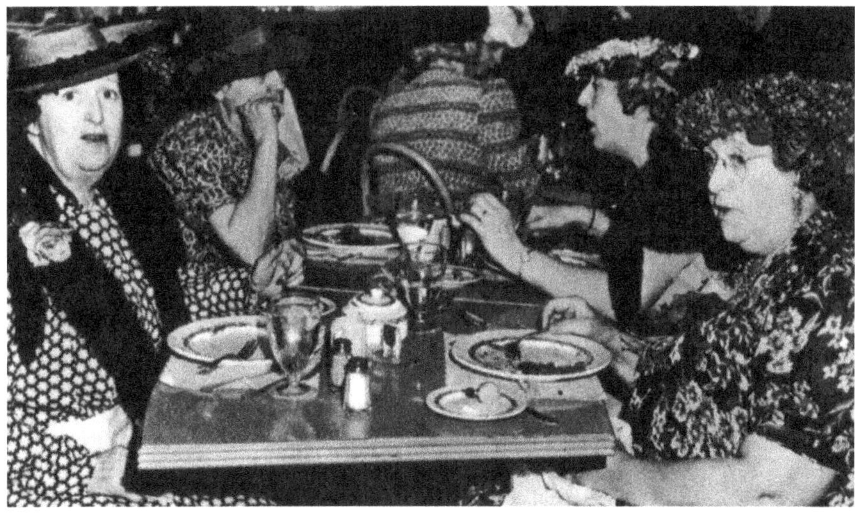

Diners at Rego Park at the Queens, New York restaurant stopped before or after visiting the New York World's Fair, often enjoying a dinner from a long menu that had daily specials. These two women, replete with stone martens furs, seem to have enjoyed the dinner as their plates were empty. However, there was always room for a dish of ice cream.

In 1940, the theme of the fair was changed to "For Peace and Freedom," as the war in Europe was escalating. The fair was to be open for two seasons, from April to October each year, and was eventually closed on October 27, 1940. The world's fair was said to have attracted more than 45 million visitors and generated roughly $40 million in revenue, but it was unfortunately a financial failure, and the corporation declared bankruptcy. Although the United States would not enter the Second World War until the end of 1941, the fairgrounds poignantly served as a window into the troubles overseas. The pavilions of Poland and Czechoslovakia did not reopen for the 1940 season, and countries under the thumb of the Axis powers in Europe in 1940, such as Poland, Czechoslovakia and France, ran their pavilions with a special nationalistic pride. The only major world power that did not participate for the 1939 season was Germany, citing budget pressures. The USSR's pavilion was dismantled after the first season, leaving an empty lot called "The American Commons."

World War II presented additional problems with what to do with the exhibits on display in the pavilions of those countries under Axis occupation. In the case of the Polish pavilion, most of the items were sold by the Polish government in exile in London to the Polish Museum of America and shipped to Chicago. A notable exception was made for a monument of King Jagiello to which city of New York mayor Fiorello La Guardia took such a liking that he helped spearhead a campaign to have it installed in Central Park.

Some of the buildings from the 1939 fair were used for the first temporary headquarters of the United Nations from 1946 until it moved in 1951 to its permanent headquarters in New York City. The former New York City building was used for the United Nations General Assembly during that time. This building was later refurbished for the 1964 fair as the New York City pavilion, featuring a panorama of the city of New York, an enormous scale model of the entire city. It is the only building that survives from the 1939–40 fair that remains in its original location. It is now the home of the Queens Museum of Art, which still houses the panorama.

The 45 million visitors to the New York World's Fair were impressed, astonished and given new hope for a brilliant and prosperous future, but as they traveled to the fair by bus, train or automobile, they had to pass the new Howard Johnson's restaurant that was built at 95-25 Queens Boulevard in Rego Park, an area developed in 1920 by the Real Good Construction Company. Here Howard Deering Johnson, and his major investor Lydia Pinkham Gove, who had already invested in a Howard

Johnson's restaurant franchise in 1938 on the Jericho Turnpike on Long Island outside Garden City, were building the biggest and most elaborate orange-roofed restaurant in the chain, said to have cost $600,000 of which half was invested by Miss Gove.

The restaurant was designed by Howard Johnson's chief architect, Joseph G. Morgan, and was erected by W.F. Babor & Company Inc. The restaurant was said to have had wood tables and booths, burgundy rugs and maroon leather seating. A grand opening cocktail reception and dinner was held on January 17, 1940, and ushered in Howard Johnson's short-lived foray into the realm of near luxury dining:

> *The Largest Roadside Restaurant in the World. Masterpiece of restaurants opened in 1940 on Queens Boulevard in the Forest Hills section of New York City, just outside the World's Fair park. Three stories in height and built at a cost of $600,000, this building boasts its own bakery and two complete kitchens. Seating capacity in winter is about 700. In summer two awninged terraces on the second floor, furnished in cool wicker and pastel cushions, invite 300 more guests to linger over a frosty drink. The three dining rooms are so restful and so attractive that at first we miss some of the details which go to make their perfection…the thick soft carpets…the glittering chandeliers…the blue green Venetian blinds, the maroon leather upholstery…the restrained use of color in walls and draperies…the charm of a light-fountain playing in the Empire Room. Across the hall from the Empire Room upstairs is the Colonial Room. Both are available for private parties, weddings, Communion breakfasts, bridge parties, and other social gatherings. The kitchens are marvels of efficiency. Everything moves like clockwork. Four thousand dinners are served on Sunday with less fuss then you or I would entertain our in-laws. When you're in New York, don't fail to eat at "Queens." Tell your friends about it. It isn't just another restaurant. It's a Waldorf Astoria of a place! It's a dream come gloriously true!*

No expense had been spared, even in the midst of the Great Depression, and the restaurant was to be awarded a bronze plaque for excellence in design and construction of buildings erected in the Queens Borough during the year ending October 31, 1940, by the Queens Chamber of Commerce. The restaurant proved an immediate success, with a steady flow of people stopping for breakfast, lunch, dinner and late-night suppers or even just for an ice cream cone as they waited in front of the restaurant for the bus to take them back to the city.

Howard D. Johnson was fortunate in his friendship with Lydia Gove, as her wealth and income were incredible even at the height of the Great Depression. She had attended the Salem Classical High School and graduated from Smith College in 1907 and Radcliffe College as a graduate student in 1916. She was one of five daughters of William and Aroline Chase Pinkham Gove, her father being a graduate of the Harvard Law School and who served as president of the Lydia E. Pinkam Medicine Company. Lydia Gove served as the treasurer of that company, which was started in the 1870s by her Quaker grandmother, Lydia Estes Pinkham (1818–1883). It was described in a company brochure as "a positive cure for all those complaints and weaknesses so common to our best female population." Following Lydia Pinkham's death in 1883, the company and its medicine would survive the scrutiny of the Pure Food and Drug Act of 1906, subsequent regulations and a protracted family feud. Lydia Gove was a strong and enterprising woman who, in addition to her role as treasurer of the family company and as investor in two of Howard Johnson's restaurants, was an aviator of sorts. In a history-making five-day flight in August 1926, Lydia Pinkham Gove was the first woman to fly in an airplane across North America from Boston to California as a paying passenger.

An unnamed and undated newspaper clipping noted:

> *Miss Lydia Pinkham Gove, oldest daughter of Mrs. Aroline Pinkham Gove and granddaughter of Lydia E. Pinkham, is a twentieth century pioneer. Miss Gove is a tall, healthy looking young woman who has not bobbed her hair. She is Assistant Treasurer and Advertising Manager of the Lydia E. Pinkham Medicine Company and is very active on the Board of Directors. Last July, Miss Gove made a trip to the Pacific Coast with a party of relatives. For six weeks, they climbed mountains, descended canyons, rode on horseback and in speed boats, arriving at last in Southern California. Here they found a new and fascinating sport—riding in aero planes. Miss Gove and one other member of the party were thrilled by the experience of skimming like birds through the bright California sunshine. Upon learning of a passenger aero plane service to Salt Lake City they decided to fly as far as Utah on the homeward trip, picking up the rest of the party there.*

So popular had she become, especially as a role model for women of all ages, that she would sponsor a prize contest among college women in New England to write essays on why they would want to travel by "aero plane" from Boston to California:

> *Women have gone in for cross-country flying. Miss Lydia P. Gove of Salem, Mass., is the first woman to make a coast-to-coast airplane trip. She arrived in Boston as a member of the first Los Angeles to Boston passenger trip. When Miss Lydia P. Gove embarked on her transcontinental flight, little did she dream of the publicity that would result. From coast to coast newspapers blazed the story of these pioneers of the sky trial. Miss Gove was interviewed, photographed, questioned and congratulated. Reporters and photographers lay in wait for her. Letters and telegrams piled up on her desk. Enthusiastic over this interest in flying, Miss Gove promptly announced a prize contest, offering free trips by aero plane from Boston to California to the two students of any New England College who should write the best 250 word letters telling why they wanted to go. Within 48 hours after Miss Gove's contest was announced, over 1000 letters were received at her residence in Salem. By every mail they came, until practically every college in New England was represented. From early morning until late at night the judges read letter after letter in their efforts to keep ahead of the rising tide of mail. Sunday morning the papers proclaimed in great black headlines the fact that Miss Gove had increased the prizes to four. Two girls were to fly from East to West and two boys from California back to Boston.*

Lydia Pinkham must have been pleased with the profits of her large investments in two of Howard Johnson's restaurants, but the one on Queens Boulevard in Rego Park had the added cachet that it was not just near the entrance to the New York World's Fair but also the most elegant restaurant ever to be built in the chain. In *Fortune* magazine in 1940, it was noted that Howard Johnson and Lydia Gove "didn't spare the horses this time but hired Andre Durenceau to paint exotic beasts with erotic ladies upon the walls of the curving stairway, which leads to rooms for banquets and wedding breakfasts." The monumental entrance was flanked by four Corinthian fluted columns supporting a life-sized cartouche of "Simple Simon and the Pieman," and the interior had plush carpeting, crystal bronze dore chandeliers and elegantly appointed dining rooms. It was said that "Johnson's glorification of the roadside stand culminates in this $600,000 palace."

Lydia Pinkham Gove was a shrewd investor and lived in splendor at Sky High, her fabled waterfront mansion on Ocean Avenue in Marblehead Neck, Massachusetts. Built in 1935 as a replica of the famed Castle Carcassonne in the south of France, the mansion had fourteen rooms, an outdoor pool and tennis courts. Built at the height of the Great Depression for the reputed sum of $500,000, Lydia Gove was said to have received a letter of thanks from

President Franklin Delano Roosevelt for providing so many construction jobs in the midst of such difficult economic times. She also founded the Lydia Pinkham Memorial Clinic in Salem, Massachusetts, in memory of her grandmother. After her death in 1948 from ovarian cancer, the castle was sold for a pittance to Guido L. Rugo, who was part owner of the Boston Braves professional baseball team. Howard Johnson, her business partner, must have greatly respected her and valued her friendship, for he donated $5,000 in her memory to the Damon Runyon Cancer Memorial Fund.

CHAPTER 6

From Maine to Florida, Plus a Few Favorite Recipes

Howard Johnson would often show up at a Howard Johnson's eatery to test meals and listen to customers' conversations.
—Time *magazine*

Since the day he opened his first restaurant in 1929 in the Granite Trust Bank Building in Quincy Square, Howard Johnson's orange-roofed restaurants evolved in style and design, but always with an orange tile-roofed restaurant, with white siding and turquoise shutters. The revolving "Simple Simon and the Pieman" weathervane didn't just swerve with the prevailing wind, but it also boldly claiming that travelers could stop here at a "Landmark for Hungry Americans."

In just two decades, Howard Johnson's architectural and engineering department grew from one "mechanical and architectural draftsman-designer" who was located in a three-decker on Beale Street opposite the store to a large staff that oversaw the individual design of new restaurants and, later, the motor lodges, making them "superior in quality, efficiency and décor" to any other being built at the time.

The five architectural variations of Howard Johnson's restaurants, beginning in the mid-1930s, were as follows.

COLONIAL HOUSE. This was the first design for the restaurants. Used from the 1930s through the mid-1950s, the design was modeled after the prevailing colonial architecture of New England. Howard Johnson's "Colonial House"

1934	Charles Smith was the mechanical and architectural draftsman-designer and later became the chief engineer. Joseph G. Morgan served as the first chief architect and designed all the buildings.
1937	John Ferrante had started in the syrup and ice cream department and later became a draftsman.
1938	Head Architect Joseph Cicco started as chief draftsman. Charles Goodale started as an architectural designer, later becoming head architect of the Red Coach Grills.
1939	Julius Baldi and Ernest Sveden were architectural draftsmen, later becoming chief draftsman and construction supervisor, respectively.
1950	Herbert Olsen started as junior draftsman, later becoming design assistant for Red Coach Grills.
1952	Kenneth Benson started as an office boy and studied architecture nights, later becoming senior draftsman.
1953	Charles Newell started as an architectural draftsman, later becoming commissary designer. Joseph Kennedy started as a junior draftsman, later becoming senior draftsman.
1955	Edmund Zapasnik started as the kitchen equipment draftsman, later becoming equipment expediter and kitchen equipment design draftsman.

design was made famous by the orange tile roof, which stood out against the other architecture of the surrounding New England area.

Nims. This was the second design for restaurants. This mid- to late 1950s design would become the most famous and recognizable design due to the majority of the restaurants being built with this design. This design would continue for years to come. The name is credited to Rufus Nims, an architect who was chosen to design new Howard Johnson's restaurants that would reflect not only the changing times in America but also the modernization of the Howard Johnson's company.

Concept 65. This was the third design for the restaurants. This mid-1960s design would only be used in three new restaurants built circa 1965. The design was once again created to reflect the changing times in America, including the modernization of the Howard Johnson's company. The design was chosen for three busy locations for Howard Johnson's restaurants. It played heavily off of the A-frame designed structure of the gate lodge, which was the structure that housed the offices for the Howard Johnson's motor lodges. The design used wide-open spaces to accommodate more guests than the "Colonial House" and "Nims" designs could.

T-Shape. This was the fourth design for the restaurants. This late 1960s design was created for the remodeling and expansion of the already built "Nims" restaurants at various busy locations; however, only two of the "Nims" restaurants would actually be remodeled and expanded for this design. It was more or less a scaled-down version of the "Concept 65" design—most notable was the shorter-pitched A-frame roof.

Mansard. This was the fifth and final design for the restaurants. This early 1970s design was created once again to reflect the changing times in America, as well as the modernization of the Howard Johnson's company. The design was used only at a handful of the final Howard Johnson's restaurants to be built. It was created with a various rectangular or square design but always topped with a Mansard roof. The design was primarily used to make the cost of constructing new restaurants as cheap and energy-efficient as possible. It was the least popular and least recognizable of the Howard Johnson's restaurant designs, for it lacked the charm and familiar feeling of the previous designs that guests had come to know over the years.

The design of the restaurant from the 1930s to the 1950s was a traditional "Colonial" design and fit into the New England landscape quite well, but according to Brian Miller:

> *As time went on, new restaurants were added to the chain that were far from New England. The more traditional elements were removed and modernized. In 1948, in preparation for a new restaurant construction in Miami, Florida, Johnson called upon Rufus Nims. Rufus eschewed the traditional Howard Johnson design in favor of a sleek single story structure that featured long strands of plate glass that put the interior of the restaurant on display. The traditional Cupola was refashioned into a contemporary styled spire that houses the exhaust system. In a few short years this new Nims design became the brand's prototype. Over the next 30 years the design of new restaurants and refurbishments*

1925	Howard Johnson starts his empire in the former Walker-Barlow drugstore in Wollaston, Massachusetts.
1926	He starts his first ice cream stand on Quincy Shore Drive at Wollaston Beach.
1927	He expands his ice cream stands to include Nantasket Beach in Hull, Massachusetts, and Revere Beach in Revere, Massachusetts.
1929	He opens his first restaurant in the Quincy Trust Building in Quincy Square; the restaurant was designed by J. Williams Beal Sons and offered traditional New England fare and twenty-eight flavors of ice cream.
1935	He opens his first restaurant franchise in Orleans, Massachusetts, on Cape Cod, quickly followed by restaurants in Dorchester and Dedham, Massachusetts.
1939	There are 150 Howard Johnson's restaurants, from Maine to Florida, west to Pennsylvania.
1940	Pennsylvania Turnpike opens from Harrisburg to Pittsburgh, with eight Howard Johnson's restaurants being opened.
1943	World War II government contracts are supplied for marmalade, candy and syrups; Howard Johnson's feeds workers in factories and universities training officers in the service.
1950	Agents and the company start a fund for cooperative advertising.
1953	Pioneering efforts in freezing continue; Brockton commissary demonstrates a complete meal with clam chowder, chicken pot pie, rolls and apple pie, all frozen two months previously.
1953	First combined restaurant and motor lodge was opened on December 3 on Route 17 in Savannah, Georgia.
1954	The first store on Beale Street in Wollaston is closed and later used as a company office.
1955	The Howard Johnson's brand is now available in supermarkets.
1956	There are five hundred restaurants in thirty states.
1959	Howard D. Johnson becomes chairman of the board and treasurer, and his son, Howard Brennan Johnson, assumes the position as president.
1961	Howard Johnson's becomes publicly owned.
1962	Howard Johnson's stock is listed on the New York Stock Exchange; the first multi-story lodge is opened in New York City.
1963	The commissary plants manufacture and distribute to restaurants more than seven hundred items, among them clam chowder, claret sauce, cream sauce, French dressing, chocolate fudge cake and date nut bread.

1964 There is a reservation system implemented in all lodges, allowing advance reservations to be made by the traveling public.

1965 With the opening of a restaurant in Mesa, California, Howard Johnson's is now truly a coast-to-coast chain; the iconic fashion designer Dior designs the new waitress uniform; Howard Johnson Cola goes nationwide.

1966 The total income of Howard Johnson's exceeds $200 million; corporate reorganization with first executive Vice Presidents is appointed; the automatic merchandising division is created.

1967 Howard Johnson fundraising effort for the United States Olympic Team takes place; Howard Johnson's opens a restaurant in San Juan, Puerto Rico.

1969 A new Howard Johnson's restaurant is said to open every nine days, and a lodge every two weeks; a fire destroys the building in Wollaston, Massachusetts, that housed the first Howard Johnson's store.

1972 Howard Deering Johnson died at his home at 861 Fifth Avenue in New York City and is buried at the Milton Cemetery in Milton, Massachusetts.

1979 The company is sold to Imperial Group Limited of the United Kingdom.

1985 Marriott Corporation buys Howard Johnson's for $314 million; Marriott keeps the 418 company-owned restaurants but immediately sells the franchise system and the company-owned lodging units to Prime Motor Inns Inc. for $97 million.

1990 Prime Motor Inns sells Howard Johnson's to Blackstone Capital Partners L.P.

1992 Hospitality Franchise Systems Inc. goes public; Blackstone Capital Partners retains 65 percent ownership.

1995 Hospitality Franchise Systems changes its name to HFS Inc.

1996 Howard Johnson's adopts the Howard Johnson International Inc. moniker.

1997 HFS merges with CUC International to form Cedent Corporation.

2005 The first restaurant was opened by the company in Alaska.

2013 Only two restaurant franchises survive from the hundreds at one time; today, the only Howard Johnson's restaurants still open are in Lake Placid, New York, and Bangor, Maine.

of existing units would tweak these brand image features to reflect contemporary appeal but they never deviated from a feeling of quality, comfort and boldness.

As Howard Johnson's restaurants continued to expand, the name became synonymous with good food and sensible prices. Brian Miller said:

From the beginning, Johnson had a knack for marketing and merchandizing his products and services. Examples of this ability were successfully demonstrated over the 25 years he led the company. Initially the ice cream shops were developed to maximize the amount of space for advertising that would be seen by people passing by. Johnson had the aptitude to position his units on well-traveled roadways to maximize exposure and he worked diligently to find the right location each unit. After the perfect location was acquired he developed a building that provided the appropriate décor for the location and time. Once the restaurant was in operation Johnson negotiated with landowners to provide billboards that were positioned around or near the location that advertised his ice cream and food products.

His obvious success in opening restaurants, which were either own outright or as franchises, over almost two decades ensured that when he opened on December 3, 1953 the first combined Howard Johnson's restaurant and motor lodge on Route 17 in Savannah, Georgia, the company took on a new aspect with not just delicious foods and ice cream but a comfortable place to stay. W.W. Saunders was the first Howard Johnson's Motor Lodge operator, and W.D. McLendon was the first manager, and they ensured that the traveling public, whether it was a businessman on the road, or a family taking an automobile vacation, that clean, comfortable and affordable lodging was available.

As the highway system continued to expand and improve, scores of sales persons were deployed to develop sales territories and many of these new sales opportunities were located along Interstate Highway System that provided easy access to customers. These soon to be coined "road warriors" spend many nights away from home making sales contacts. This new brand of business travelers were a perfect market to help support existing restaurants and develop a network of motels that help to foster continued growth for the company.

There was one restaurant that did not boast an orange roof and turquoise blue shutters: the Howard Johnson's in Williamsburg, Virginia. The ice cream shop was located on the Duke of Gloucester Street, in what was known as Merchants Square, and the Howard Johnson's was in a period-looking building adjacent the historic section of Colonial Williamsburg. The site was a Howard Johnson's from about 1951 until 1963 and was a licensed unit owned by William Biggs.

However, with America's entry into World War II, gasoline rationing took such a toll on the Howard Johnson's chain that the number of restaurants fell in little more than a year from about two hundred (seventy-five of them company-operated) to fewer than seventy. By the summer of 1944, only twelve remained in business. The company took up part of the slack by turning some of the restaurants into jam factories and by operating cafeterias for workers in war plants. It was said that "Johnson's ingenuity surfaced and he sought and won institutional feeding contracts for defense plants, shipyards, military posts and colleges. He concentrated on maintaining the basic strength and quality in his food manufacturing plants during the war years." Once the war ended, Howard Johnson adopted a policy of smaller units in place of big, showy "roadside cathedrals." By the summer of 1947, construction was underway on the first of two hundred new branches to stretch across the Southeast and Midwest of the United States. Still owned exclusively by its founder, the Howard D. Johnson Company was providing its restaurants with several hundred items, including the saltwater taffy always found on the counters.

By 1954, there were close to four hundred Howard Johnson's restaurants in thirty-two states, of which about 10 percent were highly profitable company-owned units on turnpike locations. That year, Howard Johnson entered the motel business, which was a great success. A number of factors contributed to the popularity of these motor lodges, but "the most important is the public's appreciation of the policy of offering comfortable accommodations conveniently located and geared to the needs of the entire family—at sensible prices." In 1959, the company founder, who had accumulated three homes, a sixty-foot-long yacht and an art collection, as well as had gone through four marriages, turned the reins over to his son, twenty-six-year-old Howard Brennan Johnson, who succeeded him as president of the company. The junior Howard Johnson, called "Bud" by family and friends, was a graduate of Phillips Andover, Yale and the Harvard Business School and quipped, "My father felt that I should start at the top and work my way down."

When the Howard D. Johnson Company went public in 1961, it consisted of 605 Howard Johnson's restaurants (265 operated by the company and 340 by licensees), 10 Red Coach Grill company-owned restaurants and eighty-eight Howard Johnson's Motor Lodges, all of them franchised, in thirty-three states and the Bahamas. There were seventeen manufacturing and processing plants in eleven states. There were said to be fourteen thousand people who invested in the company, and as the annual report noted in 1961, "To you our stockholders we express the sincere hope that your association with us will be long and mutually beneficial." Both annual sales and earnings per share increased every year between 1959 and 1966; however, between 1961 and 1967, the company's founder, his son and his daughter sold nearly 2 million shares of stock for a sum estimated in the neighborhood of $1 billion.

In 1963, when the firm's profit margin rose to an all-time high for the fourth straight year, the number of company-owned Howard Johnson's exceeded the franchised units for the first time. "It's simple," Howard B. Johnson explained to a *Forbes* reporter in 1962. "Last year our own 279 stores and restaurants had sales of nearly $79 million, on which we got both the wholesale and the retail profit. Naturally, we'd like more of these double-barreled profits." The number of motels reached 130 in 1964, each with a Howard Johnson's restaurant on the site or adjacent to it. Popular Howard Johnson's staples were now being frozen and distributed through supermarkets in the Northeast. In the mid-1960s, Howard Johnson's became a coast-to-coast chain for the first time by opening California outlets. The Ground Round—a limited menu, pub-style suburban chain with banjo strumming entertainment—was initiated in 1969.

Marked by occasional gasoline shortages and frequent gas price hikes, the 1970s were a difficult decade for companies catering to motor traffic, but especially for Howard Johnson's, which depended on highway operations for 85 percent of its business. Yet except for 1974, the first full year of the energy crisis, Howard Johnson's continued every year to post record sales and earnings per share. It reacted to the challenge by instituting around-the-clock service in more than 80 percent of the company-owned restaurants, installed cocktail lounges in place of soda fountains in about 100 of these locations, increased seating capacity and stepped up special menu promotions. New HoJos, the company's leader pronounced, would be concentrated in population centers rather than along highways. By the end of 1975, the Howard Johnson's chain had grown to 929 Howard Johnson's restaurants (649 company-operated), 32 Red Coach Grill restaurants, 63 Ground Round restaurants and 536 motor lodges (125 company-operated) in forty-two states, the District of Columbia, Puerto Rico, the Bahamas, the British West Indies and Canada.

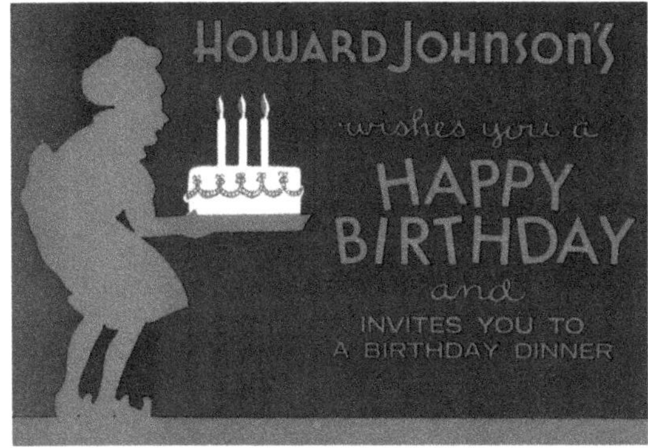

All children twelve years of age or under were invited to be the guest of Howard Johnson's restaurants on their birthday. These colorful orange and blue cards were sent to children, who could select a birthday dinner from the children's menu, with a special "Birthday Cake baked by the Pieman" served with candles for dessert. There were also balloons and lollipops offered as Johnson Girls serenaded the birthday child with "Happy Birthday."

Nevertheless, in the competitive struggle for the traveler's dollar, Howard Johnson's restaurants were lagging behind competitive fast-food franchisers such as McDonald's and Burger King and growing lodging chains such as Holiday Inns, Ramada Inns and Marriott. The classic orange-roofed Howard Johnson's were often thought of as past their prime, and customers complained of slow service and overpriced, bland, predominantly frozen food that gave rise to the gag, "Howard Johnson's ice cream comes in twenty-eight flavors and its food in one." Howard Johnson's outlets accounted for two-thirds of the restaurant group's sales volume in 1977. By contrast, the company's motels, although also cited as increasingly behind the times, accounted for only 16 percent of the company sales in 1978 but more than 43 percent of its earnings.

Criticized for choosing to stand pat and not spend or reinvest company profits, Howard Brennan Johnson tried to explain his dilemma to a *Forbes* reporter in 1978: "My expansion plans got stalled in the 1974 oil embargo. I overreacted. I stopped all expansion, and once you stop, you know how hard it is to get the monster going again." Others, however, blamed management's tight-fisted focus on the balance sheet for the company's lack of dynamism and its results. One of its former executives said, "HoJo always seemed to have ideas to upgrade the restaurants and hotels. But they never wanted to spend the money." By the late 1970s, the future of the Howard D. Johnson Company was beginning to look better on the balance sheet than its actual operations indicated.

The following recipes are drawn from familiar foods served by Howard Johnson's restaurants. The menus since 1929, when the first restaurant in the Granite Trust Bank in Quincy Square, offered foods prepared by Helen Church that became favorites of the customers, from chowders and soups to steaks, chops, chicken, the special fried clam plate and such special dinners

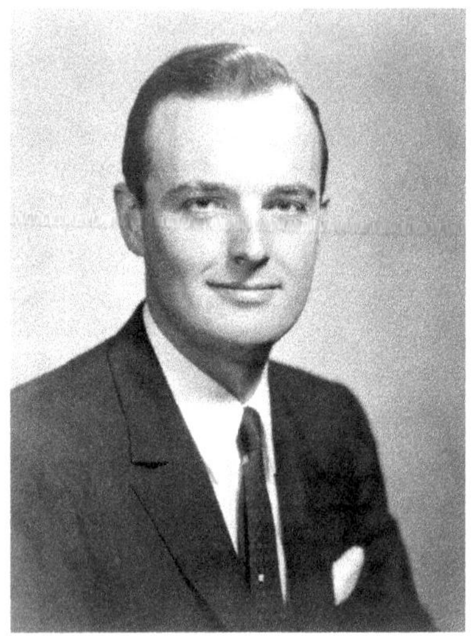

Left: Howard Brennan Johnson became president of Howard Johnson's in 1959. A graduate of Phillips Andover, Yale University and the Harvard Business School, he had been primed to take over his father's company since he was a child.

Below: A group of dignitaries poses for a photograph in front of a tractor trailer that had merchandise "transferred directly from storage refrigerators and freezers into…stainless steel trailers, filled to capacity, then start their long journeys to outlying commissaries who in turn supply the restaurants in their areas."

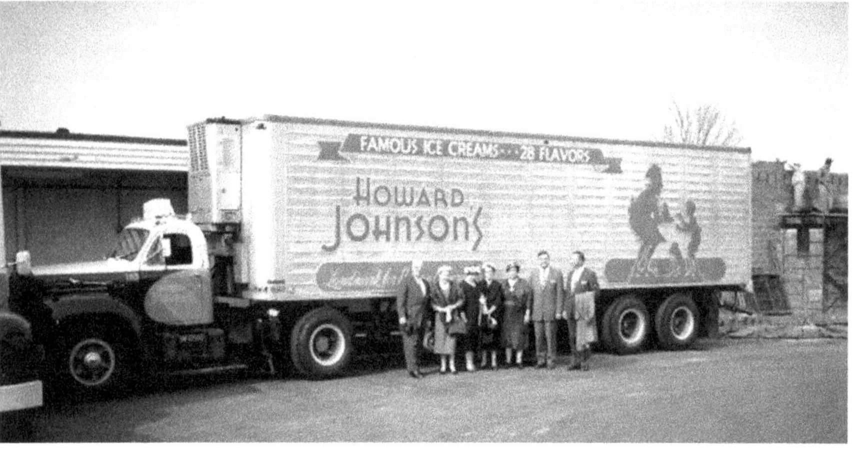

as broiled lobster tail with drawn butter, deviled crab with tartar sauce and chicken chasseur. The food was always delicious, attractively served and reasonable priced. As it was noted in his *New York Times* obituary, "During his active years, Johnson sensed that the food tastes of Americans were becoming more sophisticated, but he was careful not to get ahead of his customers. If you say Halibut Dante, the average American will never buy it, but if you say halibut with cream and tomato sauce, he'll not only buy it but say it's great."

These recipes give a glimpse into what the steady customers had come to expect: tried-and-true meals served to appreciative guests.

Clam Chowder

Clam chowder has been a mainstay of New England fare since the time of the seventeenth-century settlement by English settlers. It combines the plentiful clams found along the ocean with milk and butter, and it became a popular mainstay of the menu at Howard Johnson's restaurants. Jacques Pépin, a young Frenchman, was hired by Howard Johnson to work in the New York's Queens Commissary, testing and perfecting recipes that would be served throughout the country in restaurants and franchises. Among Pépin's tried and tested recipes was clam chowder. The following recipe, though, is not the exact one served at the orange-roofed restaurants, as the recipes were never shared with the public.

1 medium onion, diced
½ pound salt pork, cubed
4 cups cubed, cooked potatoes
1 pint steamed clams (or canned clams)
2 cups milk
2 cups light cream
2 tablespoons butter

Sautee the diced onion and cubed salt pork in a frying pan until golden brown. Add the potatoes, clams, milk, cream and butter and gently simmer until chowder has thickened and the flavors are mixed. Serve with oyster crackers or Bent's Water Crackers.

"A bowl of Howard Johnson's clam chowder was my absolute favorite," said Kathleen Lawlor.

Grilled Frankforts

Using all-beef frankforts, Howard Johnson's would clip both ends of the frankfort and then notch them lengthwise, grilling them in creamery butter that would infuse the meat. Then they were placed in a butter-toasted roll, served in a paper sleeve. These were not just simple hot dogs; they were a delicious way of serving something at the beach or in one of the restaurants. Howard Johnson's served the grilled frankforts in toasted buns with potato salad.

***

Welsh Rarebit

2 tablespoons butter
1 tablespoon flour
¼ teaspoon dry mustard
½ teaspoon salt
1 cup milk
1 cup grated cheddar cheese
1 egg, slightly beaten

In a double boiler, add the butter, flour, mustard and salt and mix until smooth. Stirring constantly, add the milk until thick. Sir in the grated cheese and stir until melted. Take off the double boiler and add the egg, returning the boiler and cooking a few minutes longer until the rarebit is thick and creamy.

Spoon the Welsh rarebit over toasted English muffins or toast points. One can also serve it with thinly sliced tomatoes and grilled bacon strips.

The author's grandaunt often served Welsh rarebit on a Sunday evening for supper, but to this basic recipe, she often added a bottle of beer to the double boiler, and this added another dimension to the delicious concoction.

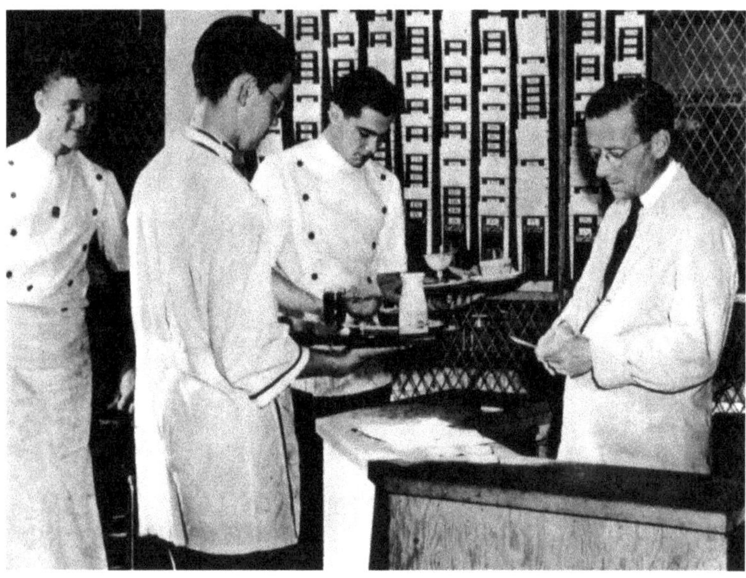

Two men hold trays of food as they are checked by a statistician in 1940. There were rigid rules on the sizes of portions, from the amount of clam chowder served to the size of the scoop of ice cream. The checker on the right, standing in front of a wall of time cards, made sure that servings were neither too small nor too large.

Boston Brown Bread

1 cup unsifted whole wheat flour
1 cup unsifted rye flour
1 cup cornmeal
1½ teaspoons baking soda
1½ teaspoons salt
¾ cup dark molasses
2 cups buttermilk

Grease and flour a two-quart mold. Combine flours, cornmeal, soda and salt and stir in molasses and buttermilk. Pour the mixture into the mold and cover tightly. Place the mold on trivet in deep kettle and add enough boiling water to kettle to come halfway up the sides of mold and then cover. Steam for three and a half hours or until just done. Remove from mold to cool on a cake rack. Serve hot with baked beans.

Jon Robert Hogan remembered that Boston brown bread, with lots of butter, was served with baked beans in the little brown pots. "We'd drive to my mother's family in Indiana every year and probably stopped at every Howard Johnson's between there and New Jersey!"

***

Chicken Pot Pie

¼ teaspoon dried thyme
salt and pepper, to taste
1½ pounds chicken breasts, skinned and boned and cut into 1-inch chunks
olive oil cooking spray
1 large onion, finely chopped
1¾ cups chicken broth
2 cloves garlic, chopped
5 medium parsnips, peeled and thinly sliced
3 medium carrots, thinly sliced
3 stalks celery, thinly sliced
2 tablespoons cornstarch
½ cup water
2 cups frozen peas, thawed
¼ cup finely chopped fresh flat-leaf parsley, plus more for garnish

Preheat oven to 425°F.

Sprinkle thyme and ¼ teaspoon each of salt and freshly ground black pepper evenly over chicken. Lightly coat a skillet with olive oil spray and heat on medium-high. Add chicken in single layer and cook 3 minutes or until lightly browned, turning pieces over once halfway through cooking; transfer to plate.

To same skillet, add onion and ¼ cup of chicken broth. Cook 5 minutes or until browned, stirring and scraping up browned bits. Add garlic and cook 1 minute, stirring. Stir in parsnips, carrots and celery and then add remaining 1½ cups of chicken broth. Heat to boiling on high and then cover, reducing the heat to maintain a slow simmer. Cook 10 minutes or until vegetables are tender-crisp.

In a small saucepan, stir cornstarch into water to dissolve and then stir into the vegetable mixture. Simmer 2 minutes or until thickened, stirring occasionally. Stir in peas, chopped parsley, reserved chicken, ½ teaspoon salt and ¼ teaspoon freshly ground black pepper. Heat to simmering and then transfer to 13x9-inch baking dish. Cover the chicken mixture with a pie crust and bake 15 minutes or until golden brown. Garnish with parsley to serve.

***

Chicken Curry Served Over Rice

1 onion, chopped
1 stalk celery, sliced
2 carrots, julienned
⅓ cup flour
3 cups chicken broth
1 teaspoon curry powder
½ cup evaporated milk
2 tablespoons mayonnaise
3 cups cooked chopped chicken (shrimp could be substituted)
⅓ cup butter

Place the butter in large frying pan over medium-high heat. Add the onion, celery and carrots. Cook for 5 minutes. Sprinkle the flour over the mixture, mixing well, and sauté for another 2 minutes. Pour in the broth and cook, stirring constantly until the mixture thickens, about 4 minutes.

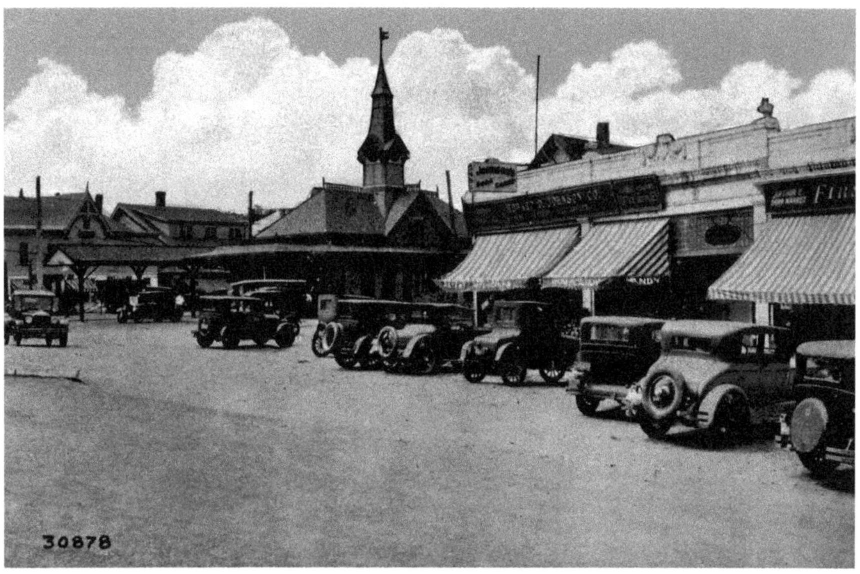

Quincy's Depot Square was where the Wollaston Station was located on the Granite Branch of the Old Colony Railroad, which connected downtown Boston to the South Shore communities. Howard Johnson's store was on the corner, and here he sold candy, cigarettes, cigars, newspapers and magazines to those traveling to Boston.

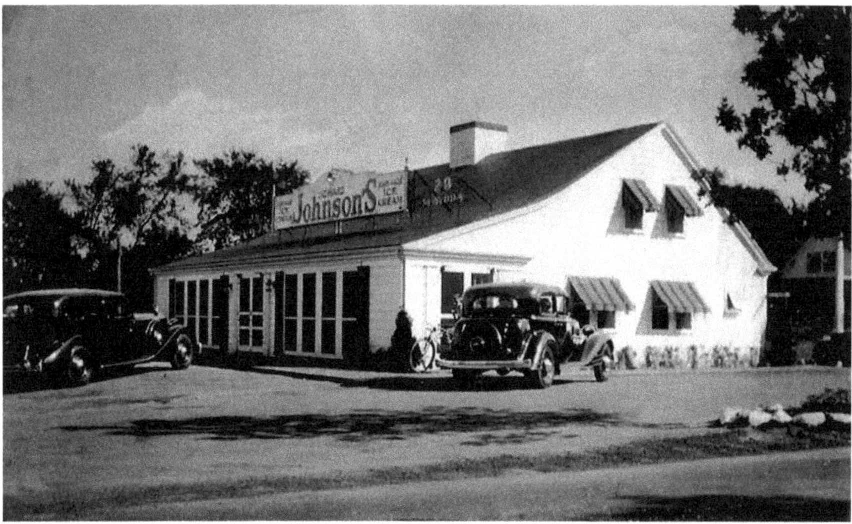

The Howard Johnson's restaurant in Orleans, Massachusetts, was opened by Reginald H. Sprague in May 1935 and was the first restaurant franchise in the restaurant chain that had a prominent sign surmounting the roof and served the traditional fried clams, grilled frankforts and twenty-eight flavors of ice cream, all provided by the franchiser, Howard Deering Johnson.

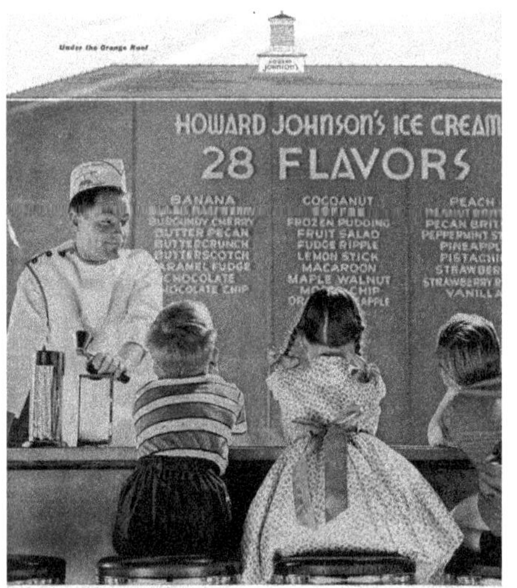

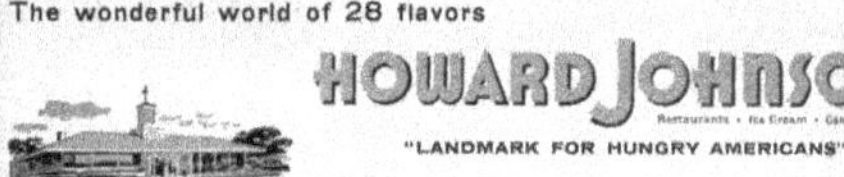

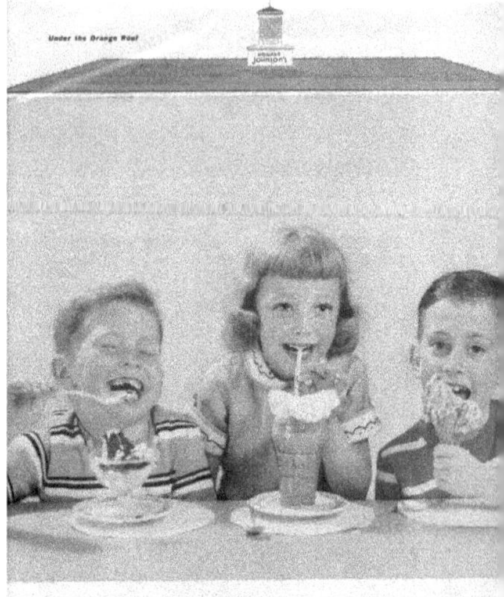

Above, left: "The wonderful world of 28 flavors," an advertisement for Howard Johnson's twenty-eight flavors of ice cream, shows a white-uniformed ice cream server with his scoop at the ready as three children intently study the sign of ice cream flavors from which they could choose.

Above, right: The full text for this advertisement reads, "Everything's better than make-believe at Howard Johnson's…We've got 28 ice cream flavors in this wonderland. That shows how much Howard Johnson's loves the kids. And we have special menus, special chairs, a special smile for big eyes and little stomachs. Sure we love Mom and Pop, too—see our delicious foods and easy prices! Come to a friendly, courteous Howard Johnson's tonight."

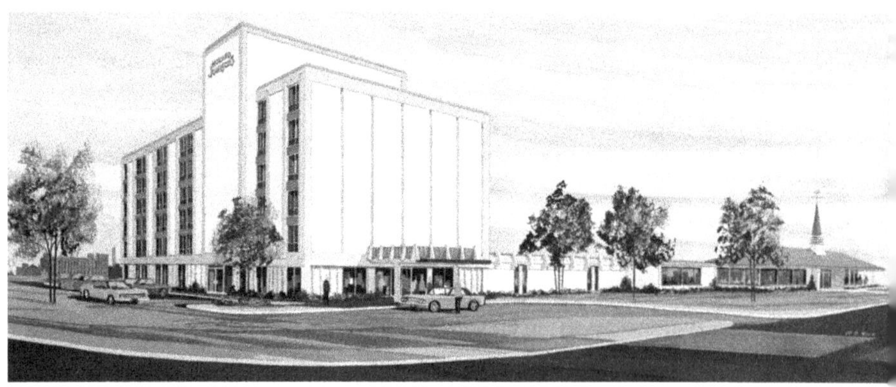

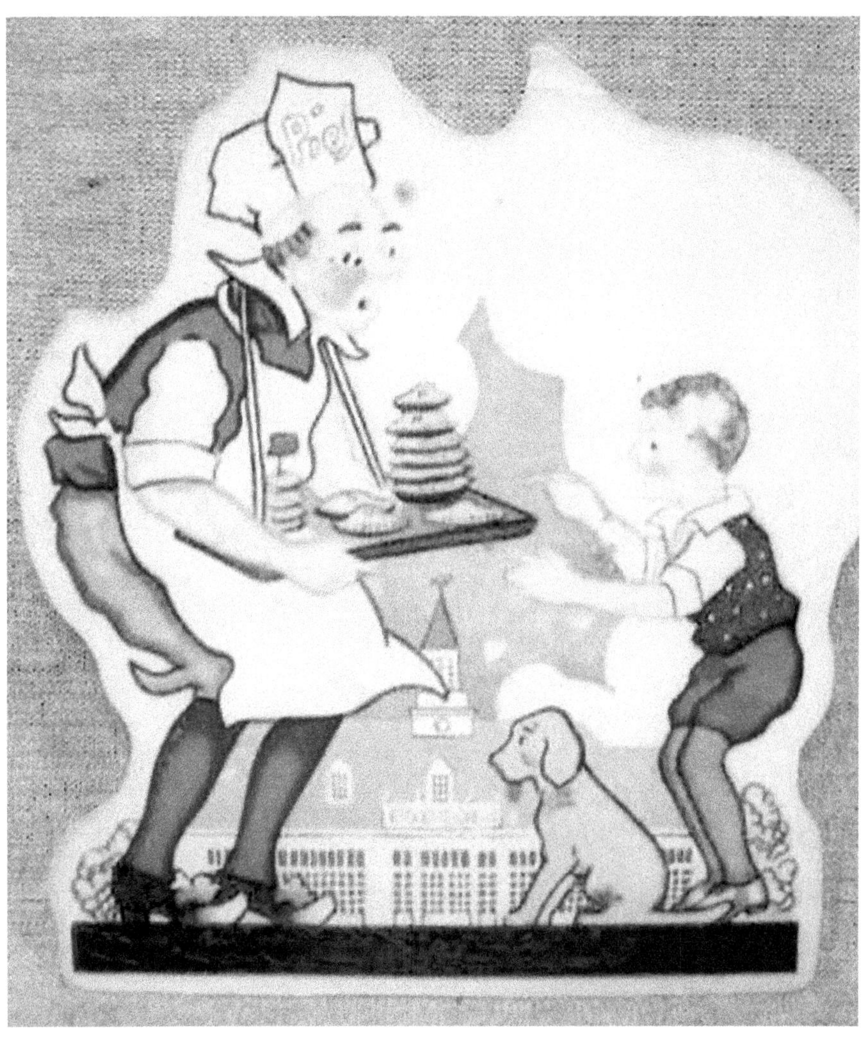

Above: The "Simple Simon and the Pieman" logo, designed by John E. Alcott, was often printed in full color on cardboard stock and used as displays in the restaurants. The logo had become one of the most readily recognizable brands in the United States food industry.

Opposite, bottom: This Howard Johnson's Motor Lodge and Restaurant was opened in 1967 on Boston Street in Dorchester, Massachusetts, facing the Southeast Expressway, and known as the HoJo Plaza. The six-story motor lodge had one hundred air-conditioned rooms—each with a television, a radio and a direct-dial telephone—an Olympic-size swimming pool and a "Coach'n Four" cocktail lounge.

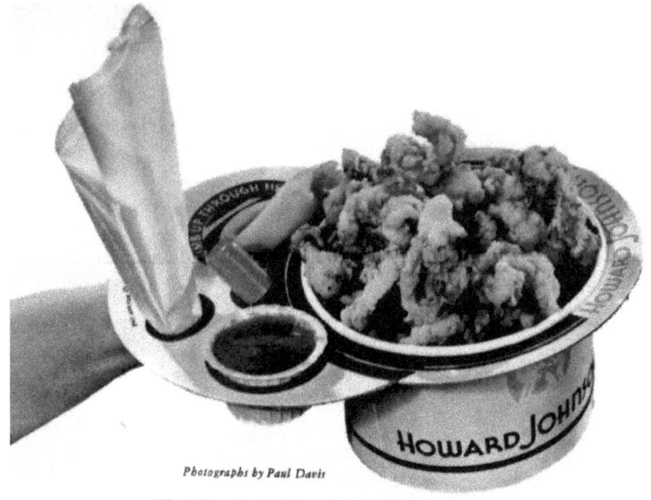

Photographs by Paul Davis

CLAMS: "SWEET AS A NUT"

The Ipswich clams served by Howard Johnson's restaurants were supplied by the Soffron Brothers Clam Company in Ipswich, Massachusetts. Their clams were so fresh and delicious that they were called as "sweet as a nut." The Soffron brothers introduced the "Tendersweet" clams, which were strips of the Atlantic surf clam (*Spisula solidissima*) without bellies, and they were the first clam strips to ever be served to the public.

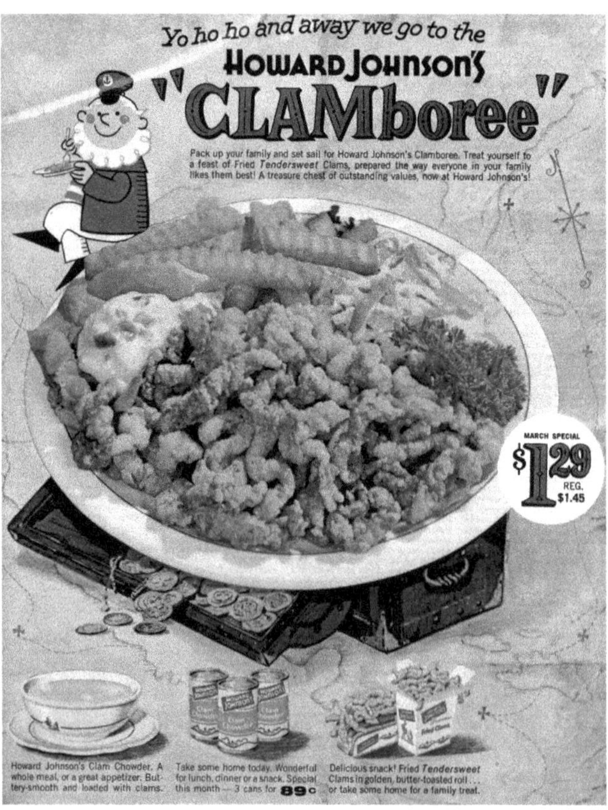

Yo ho ho and away we go to the Howard Johnson's "CLAMboree." This advertisement offered a special price on clams and instructed the public to "Pack up your family and set sail for Howard Johnson's Clamboree. Treat yourself to a feast of Fried *Tendersweet* Clams, prepared the way everyone in your family likes them best! A treasure chest of outstanding values, now at Howard Johnson's."

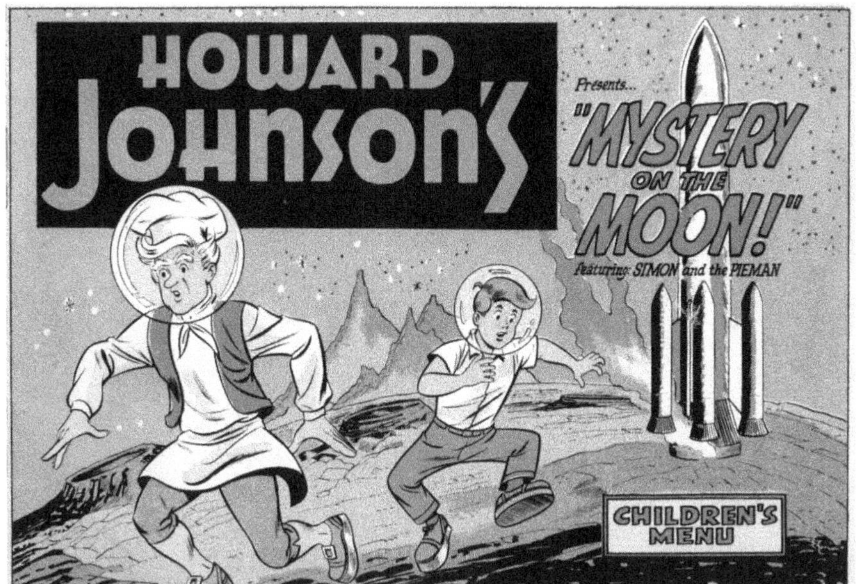

A children's menu from Howard Johnson's in the 1960s presented "Mystery on the Moon!" which featured "Simon and the Pieman" in an "epic space-saga, of near galactic proportions!" The menu had meals such as the Little Boy Blue (grilled hamburger patty), the Jack and Jill (golden brown fish fillet), the Humpty Dumpty (tuna fish salad) and the Miss Muffet Lunch (a petite garden vegetable plate).

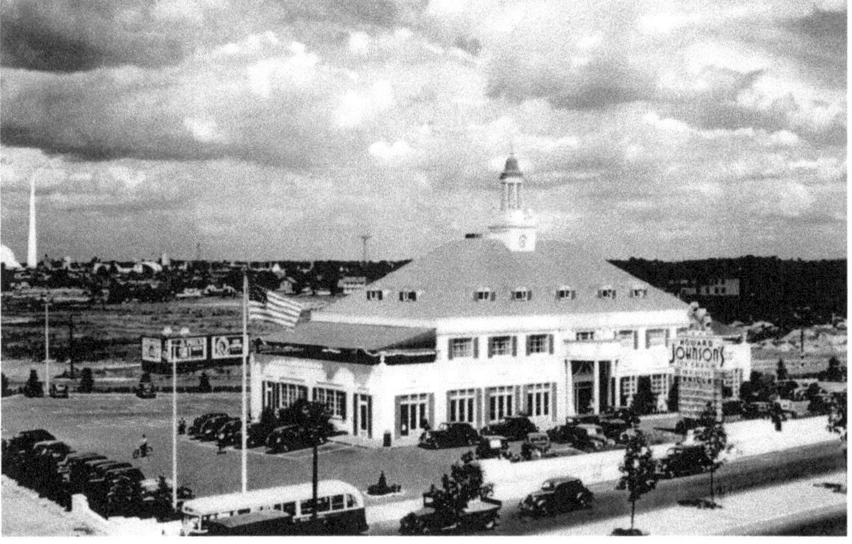

The Howard Johnson's restaurant in Rego Park in Queens, New York, was the largest restaurant ever built with an orange tile roof! On the far left can be seen the Trylon and the Perisphere, the symbols of the 1939–40 New York World's Fair, so those attending the fair had to pass the restaurant. The restaurant had elegantly appointed dining rooms and wall murals painted by Andre Durenceau.

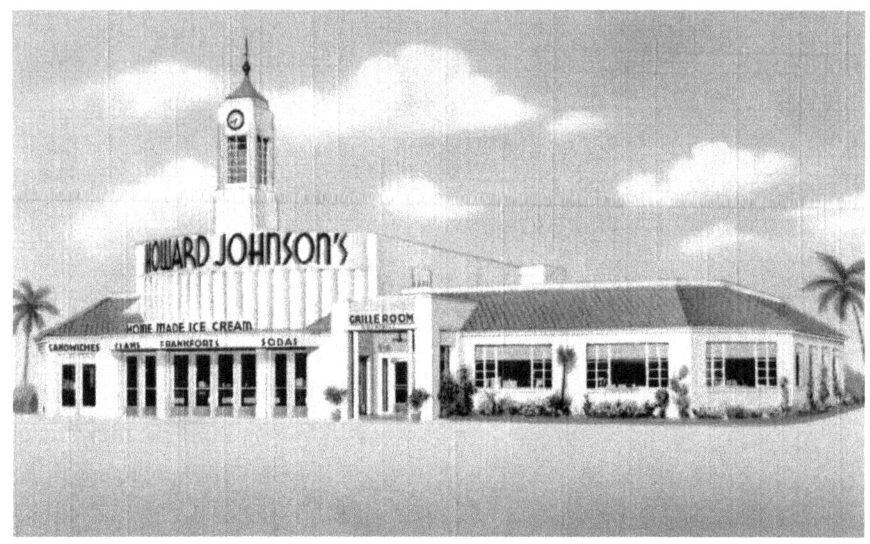

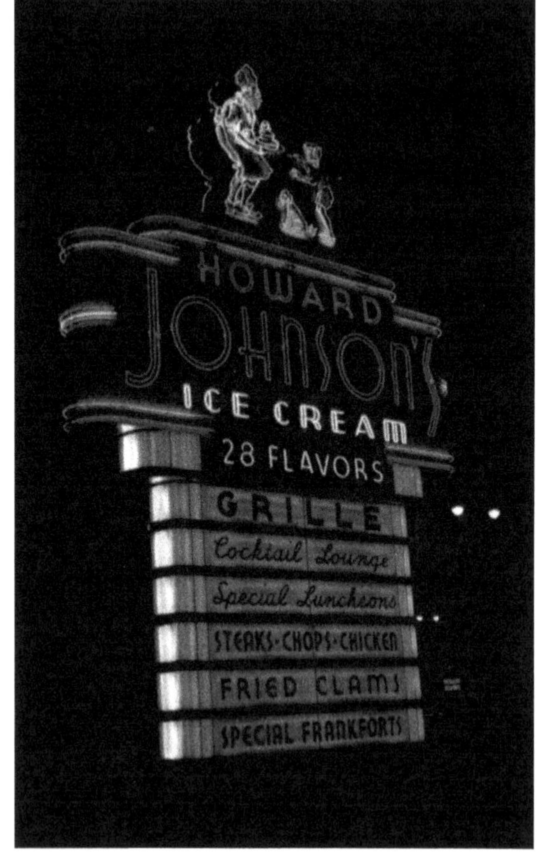

Above: The Howard Johnson's ice cream shop and restaurant in Miami, Florida, was at 1100 Biscayne Boulevard and was similar to the other restaurants in the chain, but it had a decidedly eclectic Art Deco façade, a marquee that resembled a theater and a tall, square cupola. With a weathervane of "Simple Simon and the Pieman," it was said to be "like a lighthouse beacon calling the hungry and curious to its doors."

Right: The neon-illuminated marquee stood in front of the Queens Boulevard restaurant at Rego Park in Queens, New York, and beckoned to passing motorists, noting that the Cocktail Lounge was open and that there were steaks, chops and chicken on the grill, fried clams, special frankforts and, of course, the famous twenty-eight flavors of ice cream.

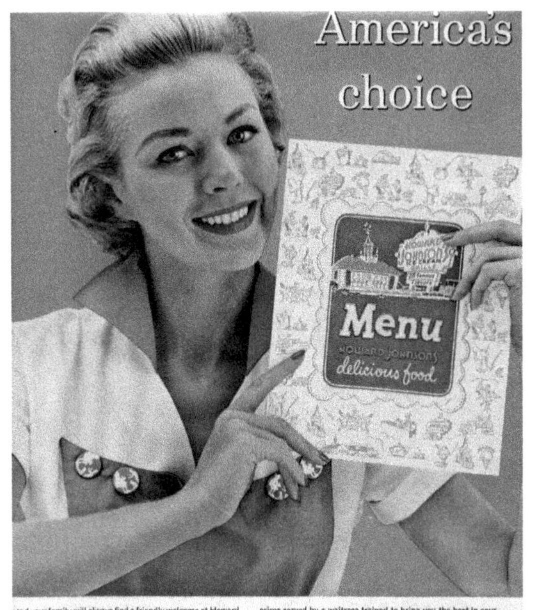

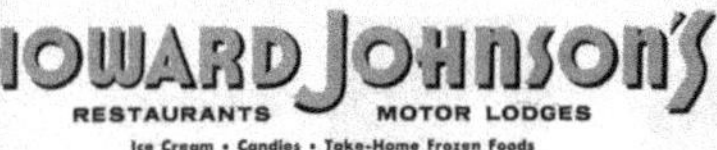

A smiling Johnson Girl waitress in her aqua and white uniform holds a Howard Johnson's menu. "You and your family will always find a friendly welcome at Howard Johnson's…a pleasant atmosphere…good food at sensible prices served by a waitress trained to bring you the best in courteous, efficient, friendly service…no matter where you travel!"

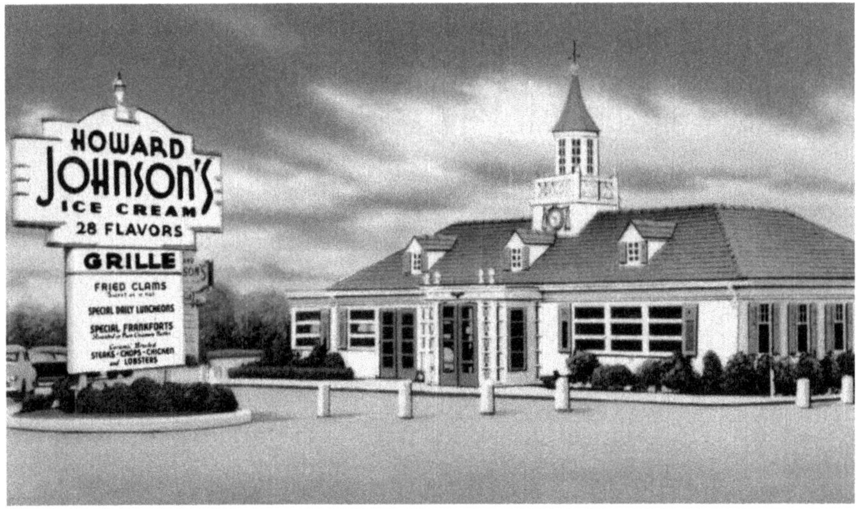

The prototype of the Howard Johnson's restaurant in the late 1930s was a one-story white restaurant with a dormered orange tile roof, turquoise blue shutters and a cupola with a "Simple Simon" weathervane. The interiors were knotty pine walls and banquet tables, crafted by Frank B. Curry of Boston.

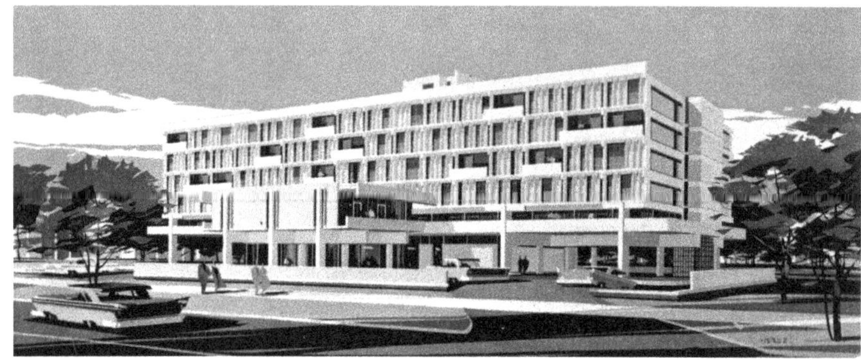

The Howard Johnson's Motor Lodge on Boylston Street in Boston was known as the "Kenmore" and was said to be "Boston's most talked about, most luxurious new hotel in decades." The modern six-story motor lodge had one 178 air-conditioned rooms with Italian Provincial furnishings, televisions and radios; a rooftop swimming pool; and a health club.

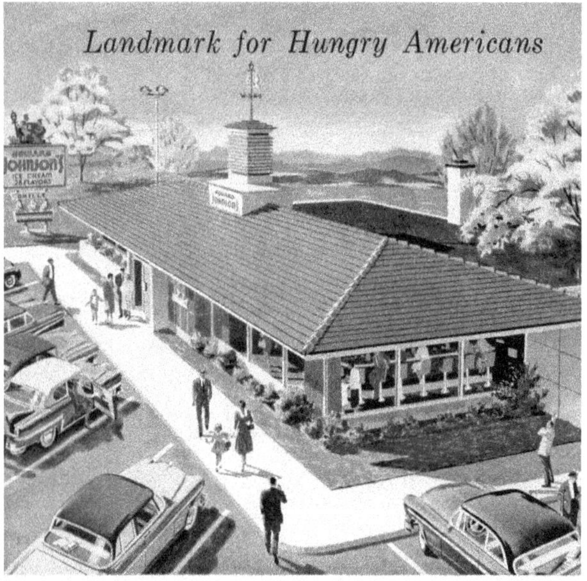

From happy experience millions of Americans know they will find a wide range of prices and courteous, friendly service under the familiar orange roofs. Howard Johnson's restaurants—featuring full-course meals, salads, sandwiches and tempting desserts—can be found on important highways. Today there are over 500 and we're still growing.

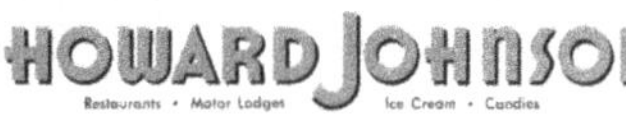

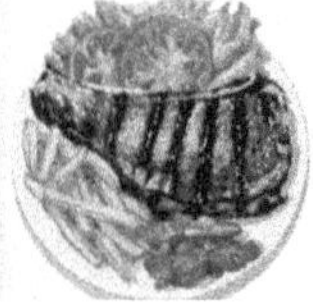

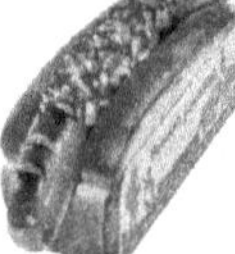

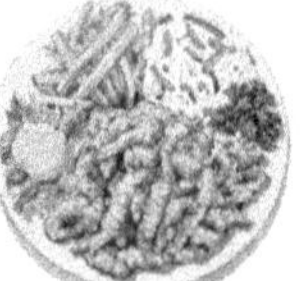

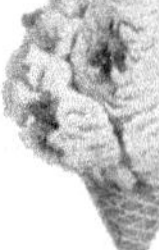

"From happy experience millions of Americans know they will find a wide range of prices and courteous, friendly service under the familiar orange roofs. Howard Johnson's restaurants—featuring full-course meals, salads, sandwiches and tempting desserts—can be found on important highways."

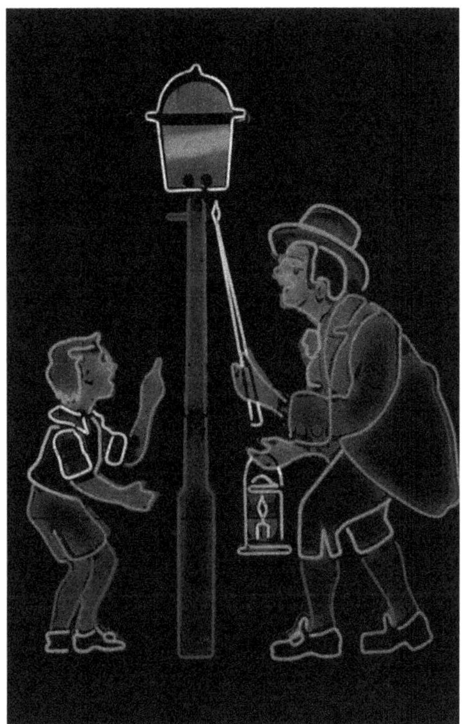

"The Lamplighter" was the colorful neon-illuminated logo sign for the Howard Johnson's "Lamplighter Room" in the motor lodges. These large exterior signs showed an old-fashioned streetlamp being lit as Simple Simon points to the spot, and they were a popular part of the motor lodge décor. The Lamplighter Rooms offered "guests leisurely dining in a relaxed atmosphere created with carpeted floors, wood paneled walls, distinctive paintings, and comfortable furnishings."

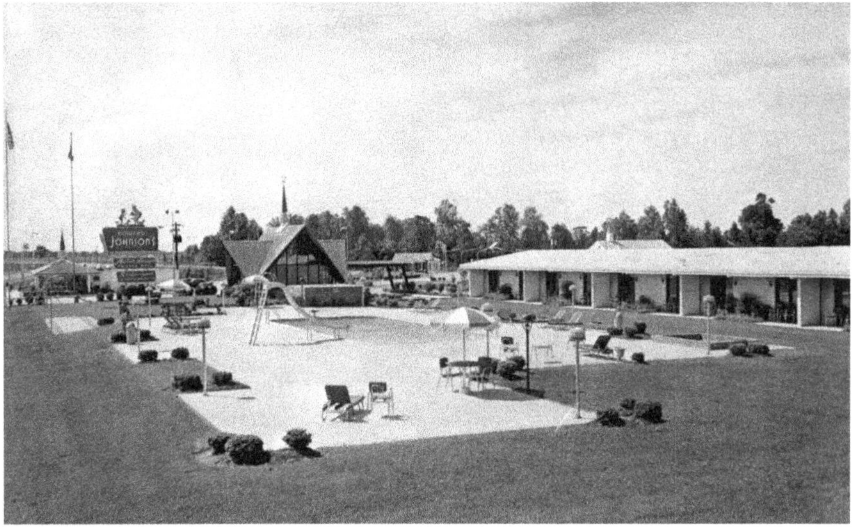

The Dunn, North Carolina motor lodge and restaurant was located on Interstate 95 and was advertised as being 545 miles south of New York City and 465 miles north of Jacksonville, Florida, making it almost the halfway point between the two cities. The restaurant can be seen on the far left, with the four-sided orange-roofed office to the motor lodge just beyond the in-ground pool in the center.

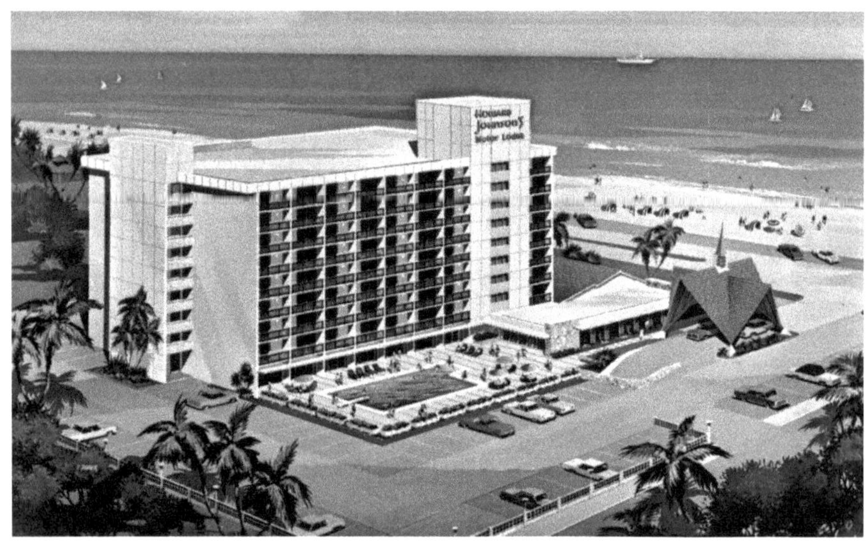

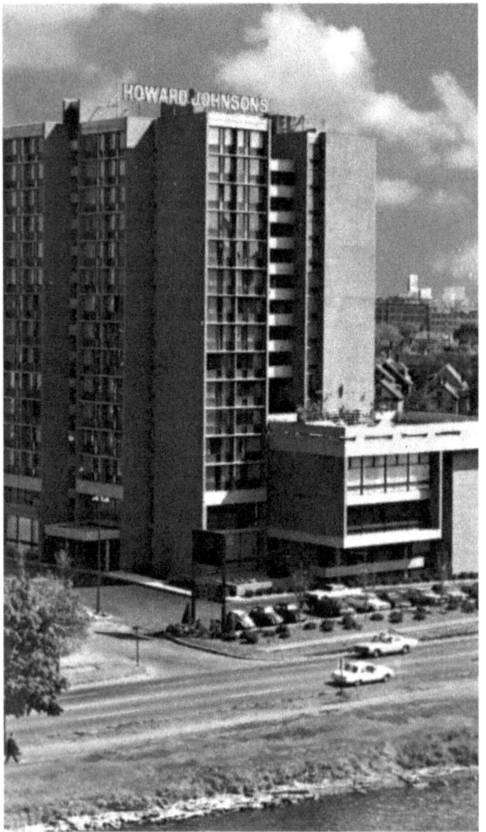

Above: The Howard Johnson's Motor Lodge and Restaurant in Fort Lauderdale, Florida, was located at 700 North Atlantic Boulevard and was advertised as being "Planned Entirely for your Pleasure." The nine-story motor lodge had 144 luxurious air-conditioned rooms, a cocktail lounge and a private in-ground pool that was adjacent to the famous beaches of Fort Lauderdale.

Left: The Howard Johnson's Motor Lodge in Cambridge, Massachusetts, was located at 777 Memorial Drive, facing the Charles River. The sixteen-story motor lodge had two hundred guest rooms, a swimming pool, a cocktail lounge and a Red Coach Grill restaurant. Today, the lodge is a Courtyard Marriott.

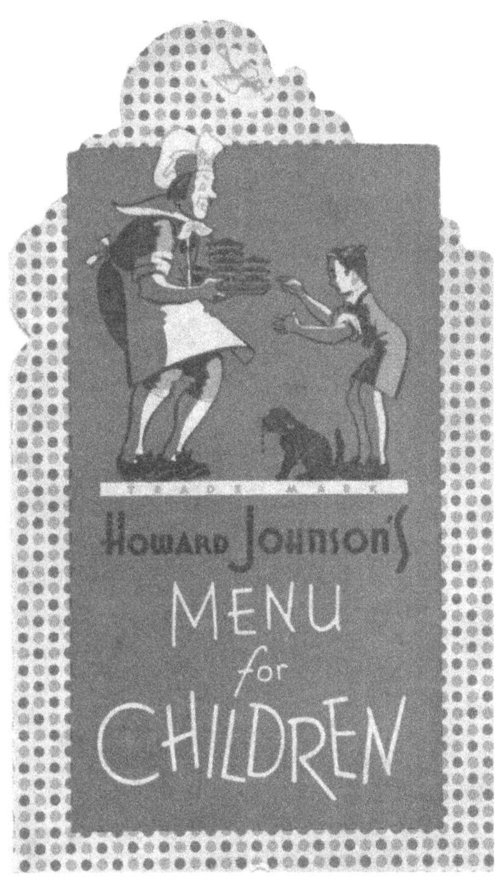

Left: A Howard Johnson's children's menu from the early 1940s had "Simple Simon and the Pieman" on the front and such popular children's meals as the Simple Simon Special (a broiled lamb chop), the Tommy Tucker Plate (sliced chicken), the Davey Jones (broiled fillet of haddock) or the Jack Horner Lunch (peanut butter and jelly sandwich). Of course, each meal came with a dessert of Howard Johnson's ice cream and a cookie.

Below: The only Howard Johnson's not to have an orange tile roof was the one in Colonial Williamsburg, a two-story brick building conforming to the architectural prototype of Perry, Shaw & Hepburn, the firm that restored Williamsburg. "Rather than an effort to preserve antiquity, the combination of restoration and re-creation of the entire colonial town attempts to re-create the atmosphere and the ideals of 18th-century American people and revolutionary leaders."

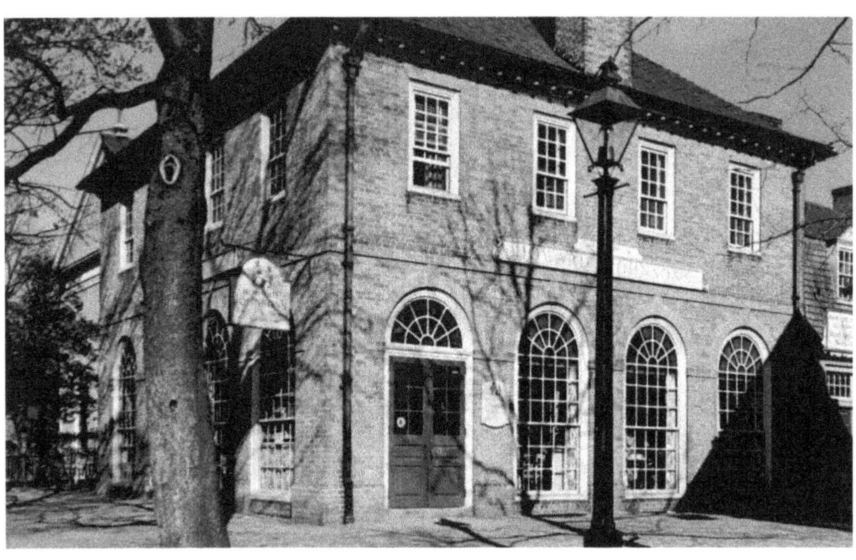

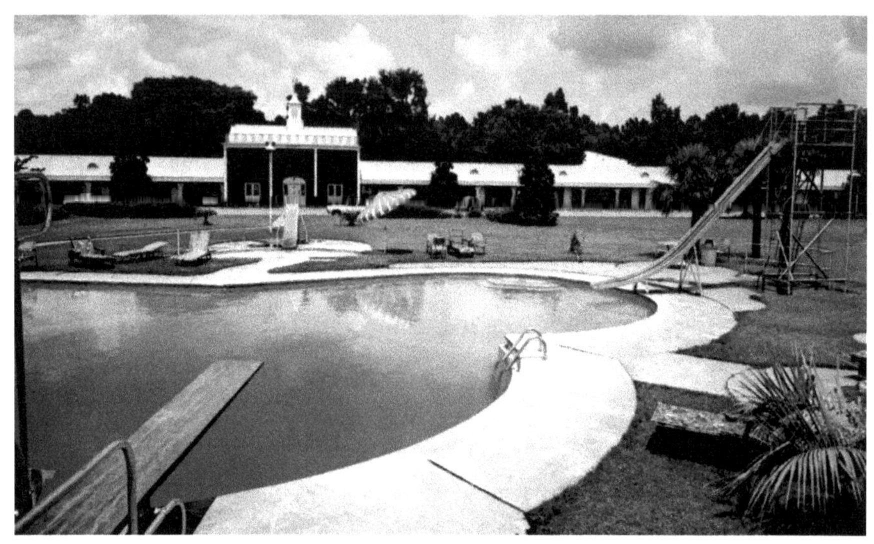

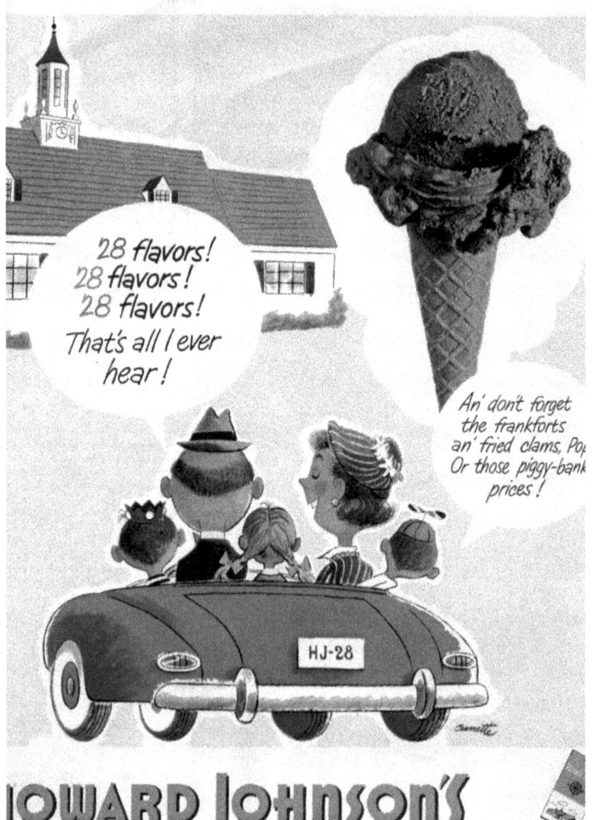

Above: The first motor lodge in the Howard Johnson's empire opened in 1954 in Savannah, Georgia, on Route 17A and 17. A popular and convenient stop for those traveling south, "its fine reputation has made it a favorite of tourists and travelling businessmen alike." Built facing a large manicured lawn, it had a swimming pool with both diving board and slide that brought much enjoyment to families stopping at the lodge.

Left: A family drives toward a Howard Johnson's restaurant, with the father saying, "28 flavors! 28 flavors! 28 flavors! That's all I ever hear!" as his son in the rear seat pipes in and says, "An' don't forget the frankforts an' fried clams, Pop. Or those piggy-bank prices!"

In an advertisement on "How to succeed in carving a turkey without really trying," a red-vested Rudy Vallee is seen carving a roast turkey and offering a tip to put the family in the car, head for the orange roof and order Howard Johnson's turkey special. Vallee was at the time performing at the Forty-sixth Street theater in New York in the immensely popular musical *How to Succeed in Business without Really Trying*. In the 1960s, the Harold Cabot & Company was the advertising agency for the company.

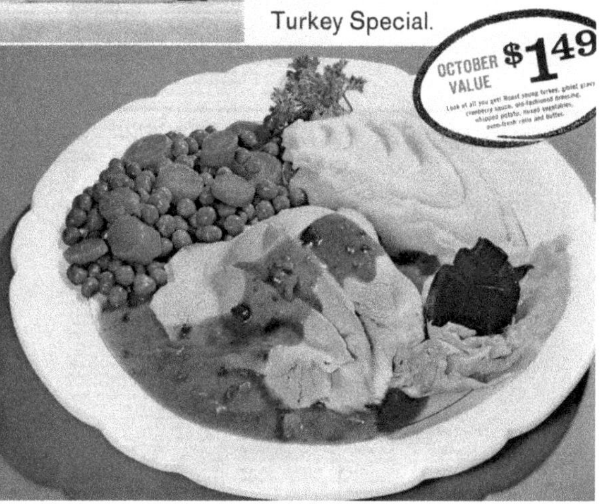

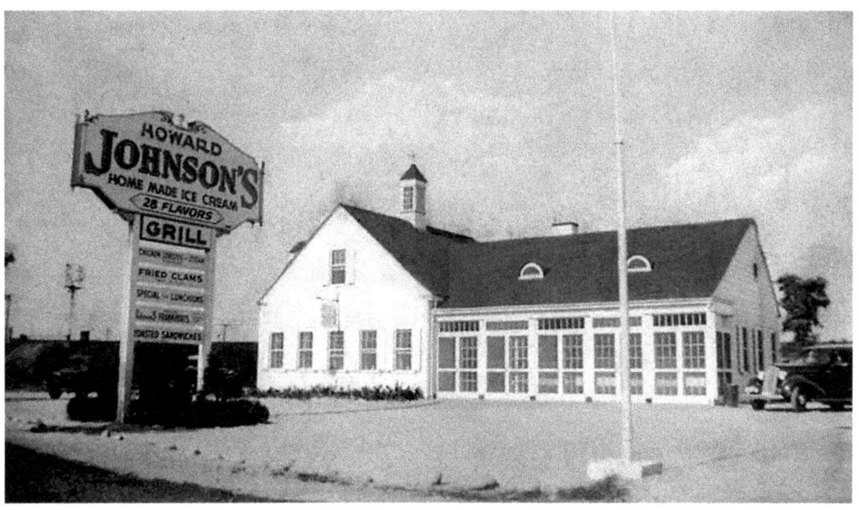

The Howard Johnson's restaurant in Dorchester, Massachusetts, opened in June 1935 on Old Colony Parkway (now William T. Morrissey Boulevard). The restaurant was on the main road leading to the South Shore from Boston prior to the construction of the Southeast Expressway, so it was strategically well located. With its orange tile roof by Norman W. Pemberton Company, it could be seen from either direction.

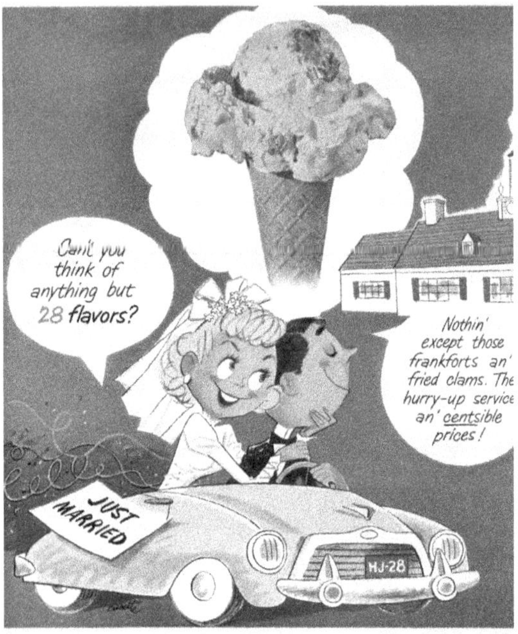

HOWARD JOHNSON'S

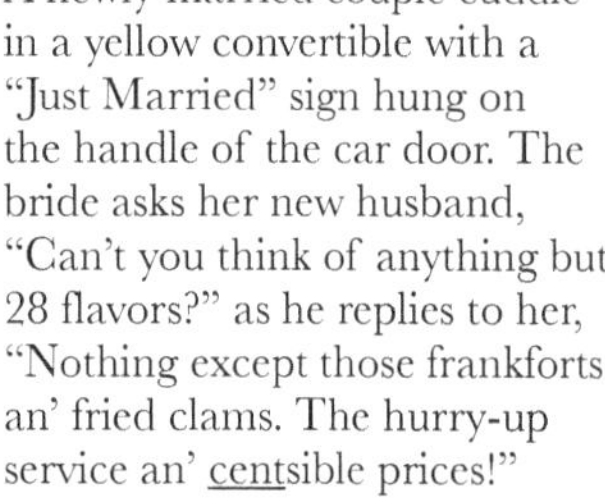

A newly married couple cuddle in a yellow convertible with a "Just Married" sign hung on the handle of the car door. The bride asks her new husband, "Can't you think of anything but 28 flavors?" as he replies to her, "Nothing except those frankforts an' fried clams. The hurry-up service an' centsible prices!"

HOWARD JOHNSON'S Smart idea!

He built an ice cream cone into a chain of 230 roadside restaurants that gross $150,000,000!

"I STARTED in 1925 with a hand-cranked ice cream freezer and a recipe I borrowed from my mother," says Ford Truck user Howard Johnson. Last year, the nation-wide chain of 230 orange-tiled restaurants that Johnson owns or supervises grossed over $150,000,000.

Food is prepared and served according to uniform standards. "When you get the same kind of sundae in New York that you got in Florida, you are more likely to buy one in Maine," says Johnson. His formula has succeeded so well he now owns 6 ice cream factories, 4 candy and jam plants, and 40 Ford Trucks to service 230 restaurants.

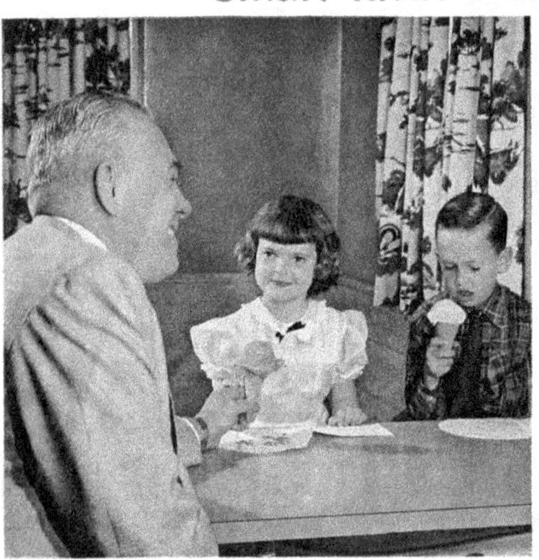

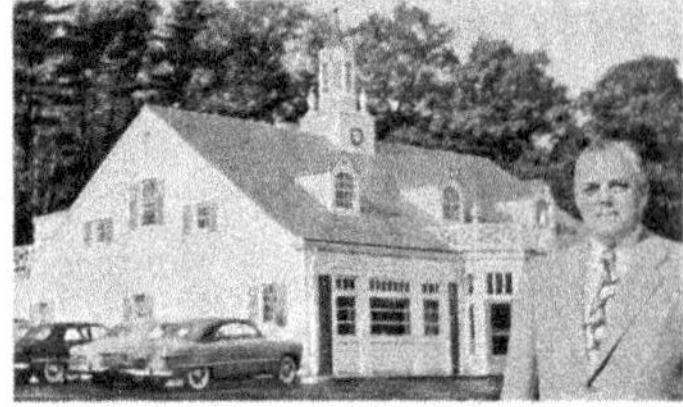

◀ **OVER 5 BILLION** ice cream cones have passed over Ford Truck user Howard Johnson's counters. Although he promotes "28 famous flavors," old favorites like vanilla, chocolate, strawberry account for 85% of his ice cream sales.

▲ **LARGEST** operator of roadside restaurants in the United States is Howard Johnson of Wollaston, Mass. Familiar to travelers from Maine to Florida, his restaurant chain is now invading the Midwest and Pacific Coast.

Howard Johnson beams with pride as he hands a chocolate ice cream cone to his daughter, Dorothy, as his son, Howard, enjoys a vanilla ice cream cone. It was said, "Although he promotes '28 famous flavors' old time favorites like vanilla, chocolate, strawberry account for 85% of his ice cream sales." The Johnson children were often featured in advertisements as young children saying, "We love our Daddy's ice cream!"

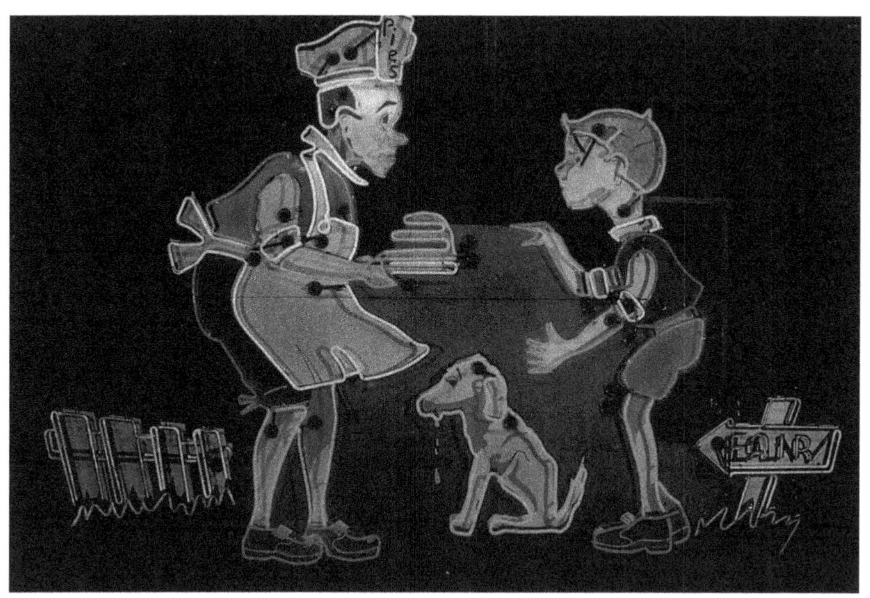

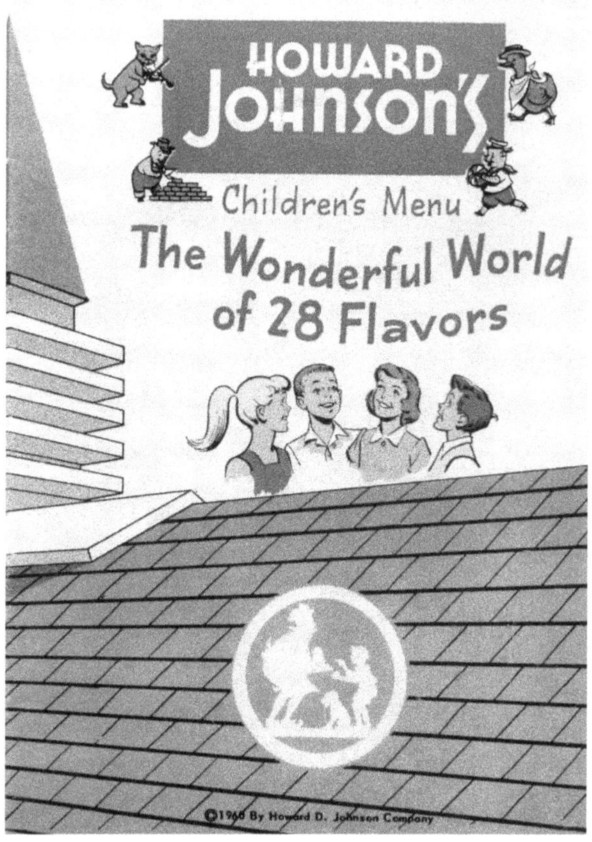

Above: A porcelain and neon light sign of "Simple Simon and the Pieman" was often distributed to franchise restaurants in the 1950s. With John Alcott's logo, it could be seen in the evening, attracting passing motorists to stop for dinner or a dish of ice cream.

Left: The Howard Johnson Ice Cream Game was greatly enjoyed by children who visited Howard Johnson's restaurants and tried the various flavors of ice cream. Once they had tried all twenty-eight flavors of ice cream, they were qualified for a free ice cream cone. What child wouldn't persistently ask Mom and Dad to stop at a Howard Johnson's so they could play the game to the finish?

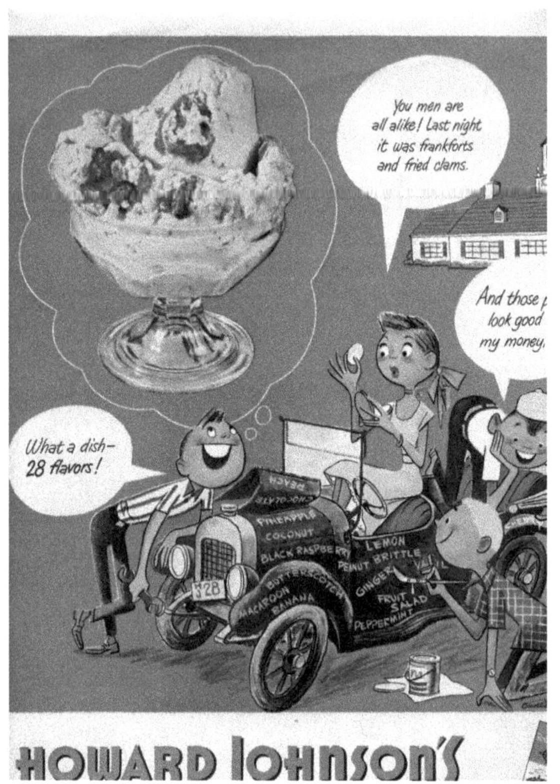

A teenage boy is seen leaning on the hood of a Model T Ford dreaming of a dish of Howard Johnson's ice cream, while his friend paints the twenty-eight flavors on the sides of the automobile. A young lady who is applying makeup says, "You men are all alike! Last night it was frankforts and fried clams," and now it's twenty-eight flavors…yet is it the dish of ice cream in his mind or the "dish" in the automobile he is really dreaming about?

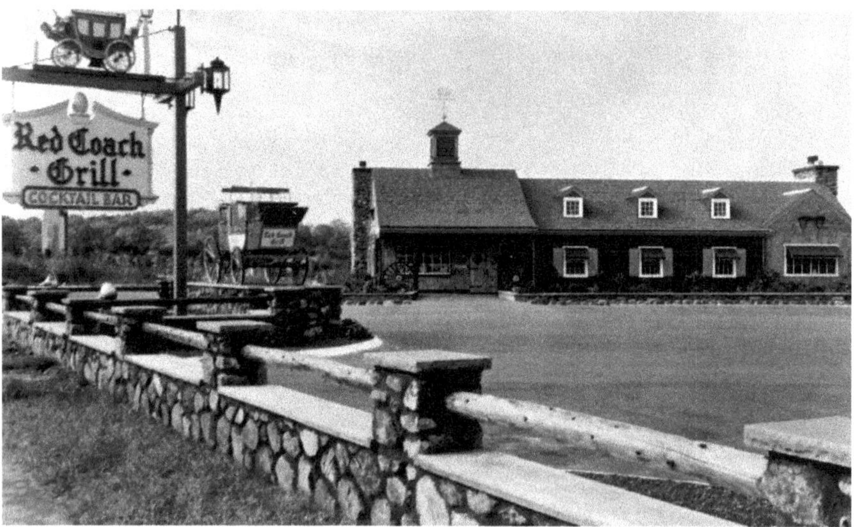

The Red Coach Grill was founded in 1937. In the early 1960s, it was acquired by Howard Johnson's as an upscale restaurant chain. These restaurants were distinctive in character, with a red coach as its motif and with a rustic, red-roofed restaurant of fieldstone and California redwood.

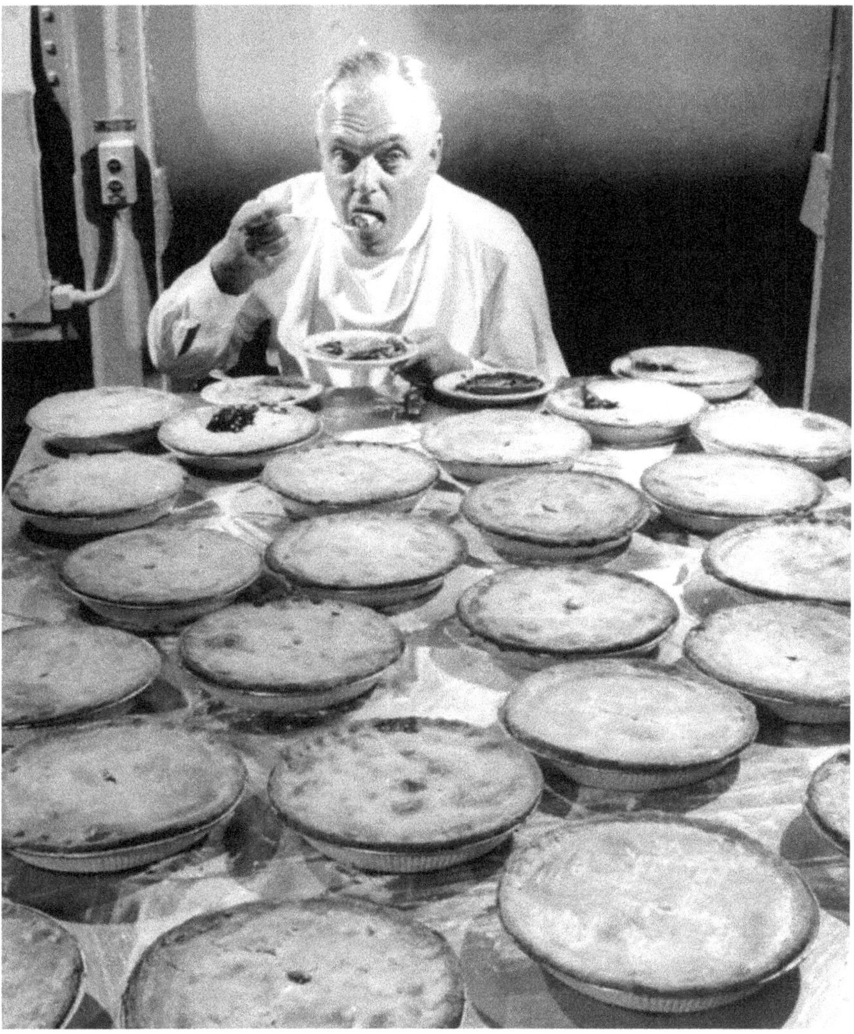

Howard Deering Johnson was a perfectionist and a very hands-on manager who ensured quality control by taste-testing foods prepared at his commissaries. Here, with a large napkin bib, he tastes a slice of cherry pie that had been baked at his Quincy, Massachusetts commissary to judge the consistency of flavor, filling and the flakiness of the pie crust. Unless he was satisfied, it would not be served to his guests.

Combine curry powder, evaporated milk and mayonnaise in a separate bowl. After mixing, pour into the vegetable mixture and then add the chicken (or shrimp). Stir occasionally and heat until hot. Serve over hot rice.

Chicken and shrimp curry was a favorite standby at Howard Johnson's and was served as early as the 1930s as an entrée on the menus.

Chicken Liver en Brochette

1½ pounds chicken livers
¾ teaspoon dried marjoram
¾ teaspoon dried thyme leaves
¾ teaspoon salt
⅓ teaspoon fresh ground black pepper
12 large button mushrooms
9 slices bacon, halved crosswise
6 tablespoons butter
¼ cup dry white wine

Rinse chicken livers and pat dry with paper towels. In medium bowl, combine the marjoram, thyme, salt and pepper. Add livers and toss to cover with seasonings. Remove stems from mushrooms and wipe the mushroom caps with a damp towel. Wrap each liver in bacon. On each of six wooden skewers, alternate three livers and two mushrooms. Arrange skewers (if using wood, soak in water overnight) on rack in broiling pan. Brush with half of the butter. Broil for 5 minutes. Turn skewers and brush with remaining butter and the wine. Broil 5 to 7 minutes longer or until bacon is crisp.

Howard Johnson's served chicken livers en brochette with French-fried potatoes, lettuce and tomato.

***

Chicken Croquettes

For the Chicken:

1 onion, quartered
2 carrots, scraped and cut into slices
2 stalks celery, cut into slices
2 bay leaves
2 chicken breasts, bone in and skin on
salt and pepper

For the Croquettes:

4 tablespoons butter
1 small onion, very finely chopped
2 large cloves garlic, minced
salt and pepper to taste
½ teaspoon ground thyme
pinch of cayenne pepper
freshly grated nutmeg, to taste
6 tablespoons flour
2½ cups chicken stock
⅓ cup heavy cream
4 egg yolks
1 cup fine breadcrumbs, divided
½ cup panko breadcrumbs
small handful of flat-leaf parsley, very finely chopped
⅓ cup grated Parmigiano-Reggiano cheese
1 large egg
¼ cup water
frying oil

For the Gravy:

3 tablespoons butter
4 tablespoons flour
2 tablespoons Worcestershire sauce
salt and black pepper
1 extra-large egg yolk, beaten

To poach chicken, place onion, carrots, celery and bay leaves in a pot. Add chicken, cover with water and bring to a boil. Season with salt and reduce heat to simmer; poach at gentle, low rolling boil for 1 hour. Remove chicken and let cool. Strain stock, simmer 30 minutes more and strain again. Remove chicken from bones and separate from skin. Chop chicken meat and add to food processor; pulse to a fine chop. Should yield about 2½ cups chopped meat. Cool in refrigerator in a large mixing bowl.

For the croquettes, heat butter in a skillet over medium heat. Add onions and garlic and season with salt, pepper, thyme, cayenne pepper and nutmeg. Stir-fry to soften and then add flour and whisk for 1 minute. Whisk in chicken stock and then the cream. Add some to a small bowl with the egg yolks to temper, then add everything back to the sauce and let thicken. Remove from heat and stir in about ½ cup of the regular breadcrumbs—the sauce should be very thick. Let cool and then pour room-temperature sauce over cold chicken. Combine and chill at least 1 hour more. Heat a few inches of oil in a Dutch oven or in a countertop fryer to 360°F. Heat oven to 275°F and place a wire rack in a rimmed baking sheet. Combine remaining breadcrumbs with panko breadcrumbs, parsley and cheese in a shallow dish. Beat egg with water in a second shallow dish.

For the gravy, melt butter in a saucepot or skillet over medium to medium-high heat. Whisk in flour, cook 1 to 2 minutes, add some stock and let thicken. Season the gravy with Worcestershire, salt and pepper. Ladle some gravy into egg yolk to temper and then add back to gravy. Adjust seasoning to taste and reduce heat to low.

Roll balls of the chicken mixture and form a dozen croquettes. Dip the croquettes in egg wash and then gently press breading mixture evenly all over the croquettes. Fry croquettes four at a time until golden brown, turning them gently as they cook to evenly brown, 5 or 6 minutes per croquette. Place on a wire rack in rimmed baking sheet and bake gently for 12 to 15 minutes. Serve with parsley sprigs.

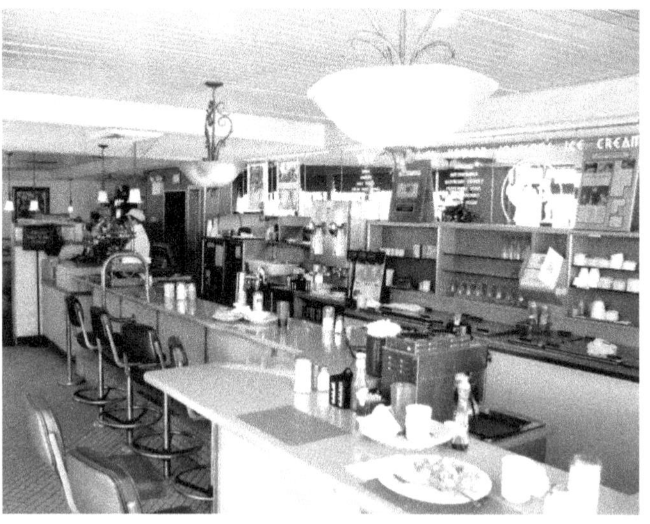

A Howard Johnson's restaurant was always a popular place, with counter service available for those who did not wish to be seated in the dining room. Whether it was a quick sandwich, a slice of cake and coffee or a dish of ice cream, the friendly and welcoming Johnson Girl waitress was there to make your visit pleasant.

Chocolate Cake

For the Cake:

Follow your preferred instructions/recipe to bake a chocolate cake with two 9-inch layers. Cool on a rack and then split each layer so that you have four thin layers.

For the White Filling:

3 tablespoons flour
1 cup milk
½ cup Crisco shortening
½ cup butter
1 cup sugar
1 teaspoon vanilla

Mix flour and milk well and then cook in a double boiler until very thick. Let the mixture cool and then add the remaining ingredients. Beat until fluffy and then spread on inside layers. Make chocolate icing and put on top and sides of cake.

For the Chocolate Icing:

½ cup milk
2 cups sugar
4 tablespoons cocoa
½ cup butter
1 teaspoon vanilla

Cook milk, sugar and cocoa together in a double boiler until it forms a soft ball. Remove from heat and add butter and vanilla. Beat until glossy and frost the cake.

***

Howard Johnson's Carrot Cake

3 cups flour
1 teaspoon baking soda
2 teaspoons cinnamon
1 teaspoon salt
2 cups sugar
3 eggs
1½ cups vegetable oil
1 teaspoon vanilla
8-ounce can crushed pineapple, drained
2 cups grated carrots
½ cup chopped pecans

Combine and sift together flour, soda, cinnamon, salt and sugar. Break eggs into small bowl; add oil and vanilla. Beat together and then add to sifted ingredients with pineapple, grated carrots and pecans. This makes a stiff mixture, and I find it best to fold the flour and sugar in by hand. Pour batter into a greased and floured 10-inch tube pan and bake in preheated 300°F oven for 90 minutes. This cake will keep moist a long time.

***

Howard Johnson's Sour Cream Cake

2 sticks butter
3 cups sugar
6 eggs
3 cups all-purpose flour
1 cup sour cream
1 teaspoon vanilla

Cream butter and sugar and add eggs, two at a time, alternately with the flour and sour cream. Add vanilla flavoring and mix well. Turn into a buttered and floured pan; smooth top. Bake at 300°F for 90 minutes or until it tests done.

***

Coconut Cake

¾ cup unsalted butter, room temperature
1¼ cup sugar
3 eggs, room temperature
2¼ cups flour
1 teaspoon salt
1 teaspoon baking powder
1 cup canned coconut milk
1 teaspoon vanilla extract
½ cup sweetened coconut

For the Coconut Cream Cheese Frosting:

½ cup butter (1 stick), room temperature
8 ounces Philly cream cheese, room temperature
1 cup powdered sugar
¼ cup sweetened desiccated coconut

Preheat the oven to 350°F.

Cream the butter until light and fluffy. Add sugar and cream until light and fluffy again, scraping down the sides halfway through to ensure even mixing. Add the eggs, one at a time, beating for 30 seconds each to ensure mixing. Be sure to scrape down the sides after each egg to ensure even mixing.

Combine the flour, salt and baking powder in one bowl. In another, add 1 cup of a well-shaken can of coconut milk and a teaspoon of vanilla. In a mixing bowl, add half of the dry ingredients and mix; then add half of the wet ingredients. Mix in the reaminder of the wet and dry ingredients, ending with the dry. Stop mixing once the ingredients become incorporated, but do not overbeat.

Fold in the sweetened coconut. Scoop gently into a buttered baking pan or Bundt pan and bake for 30 minutes, rotating the pan after the first 15 minutes to ensure even baking. Be sure to check with a toothpick to see if the cake is done. If the toothpick comes out of the cake clean, then it is ready. Allow the cake to cool for a minute or two in the pan and then transfer to a wire rack to cool completely. After the cake is cool, frost with the coconut cream cheese frosting, made by mixing ingredients together in a bowl.

This cake is often more delicious after having been covered and refrigerated overnight.

***

Clams as "Sweet as a Nut"

1 cup evaporated milk
1 cup milk
1 egg
¼ teaspoon vanilla
dash salt and pepper
4 dozen freshly shucked clams
1 cup cake flour
1 cup yellow cornmeal
oil for frying

Combine evaporated and whole milk, egg, vanilla, salt and pepper. Soak clams in liquid and then dredge in combination of cake flour and cornmeal, fluffing them in the flour mix for light but thorough coverage. Shake off excess flour and fry in oil.

Howard Johnson's served its famous Ipswich clam plate with French-fried potatoes, tartar sauce and homemade rolls and butter.

***

Macaroni and Cheese

1 pound cooked elbow macaroni
1 pound sharp cheddar cheese, grated
⅓ cup all-purpose flour
3 teaspoons sea salt
3 teaspoons dry mustard
¼ teaspoon cayenne pepper
½ teaspoon black pepper
1⅓ cups sour cream
4 eggs
4 cups half-and-half
2 cups heavy cream

Cook the elbow macaroni according to package directions and drain. Butter a 9- by 15-inch casserole and put the macaroni and some grated cheese in the pan. Heat the oven to 350°F. In a large bowl, whisk together the flour, salt, mustard, cayenne and black pepper. Mix the sour cream into the dry ingredients until incorporated. Mix in the eggs, followed by the half-and-half and heavy cream. Pour the custard over the macaroni.

Top the macaroni and custard with the remaining cheese. Bake the macaroni and cheese for 30 minutes or until the cheese is melted and browned around the edges. The custard will be a bit soft in the center, but it firms up as it cools.

***

Filet of Scrod, Fisherman-Style

3 ounces salad oil
4 pieces of scrod, filleted
¾ cup flour
1 egg, beaten
¾ cup milk
8 ounces fresh mushrooms, sliced
8 ounces butter
2 ounces pimento, diced
1 ounce fresh lemon juice

Heat the salad oil in a frying pan. Season the fish fillets with salt and pepper and then dip in flour, egg, milk and flour again in that order. Fry slowly until golden brown. Turn the fish fillets with a spatula and fry the other side.

Place the fish in a buttered baking dish. Sautee the mushrooms in butter and then add pimento and lemon juice. Pour the mushrooms over the fish and bake at 325°F about 10 minutes or until the fish is tender.

***

Cole Slaw

1 large head of green cabbage
2 large green bell peppers
2 medium white onions
1 cup sugar

For the Marinade:

1 teaspoon dry mustard
1 teaspoon celery seed
2 teaspoons sugar
1 tablespoon salt
1 cup vinegar
¾ cup vegetable oil

Coarsely shred cabbage and slice the peppers and onions into thin rings. Layer them in a large bowl and sprinkle a cup of sugar over them. Let stand for one hour or until the sugar is dissolved and the slaw is juicy.

In a saucepan, combine the marinade ingredients, stirring to mix, and bring to a boil. Pour the marinade over the slaw mixture, cover and refrigerate overnight.

Howard Johnson's cole slaw was a delicious accompaniment to fried clams and fish, as well as sandwiches.

***

CHAPTER 7

Ephemera, Advertisements and Children's Menus

Should Simple Simon Seek a Pieman While Going to the Fair,
He'd Now Head for a Johnson Stand—"Tis Best" He Would Declare
—placemat, circa 1940

Howard Johnson was well aware of the benefits of advertising, and his corner store in Wollaston, his ice cream stands at both Wollaston Beach and Nantasket Beach and his first restaurant in Quincy Square all had large signs reading "Howard Johnson's." Yet by 1929, Howard Johnson had posted his first billboard, which was produced by the John Donnelly and Sons Company, near Boston to promote his new restaurant in Quincy Square. Howard Johnson's chain of restaurants and motels became virtually synonymous with travel among American motorists and vacationers, according to cultural historians, in part because of Johnson's ubiquitous outdoor displays.

Ephemera has been described as "any transitory written or printed matter not meant to be retained or preserved." The word "ephemera" is said to be derived from the Greek, meaning things lasting no more than a day. So, Howard Johnson's menus, birthday card notices, posters and printed material were not really thought of as permanent but rather something the public would discard and which could be replaced as the need arose. However, ephemera was an important vehicle by which the company and its delicious foods and ice cream could be advertised to the public. Signs, newspaper advertisements and word-of-mouth publicity all worked in unison to make

Simple Simon met a pieman,
Going to the fair;
Says Simple Simon to the pieman,
Let me taste your ware.
Says the pieman to Simple Simon,
Show me first your penny;
Says Simple Simon to the pieman,
Indeed I have not any.
Simple Simon went a-fishing,
For to catch a whale;
All the water he had got,
Was in his mother's pail.
Simple Simon went to look
If plums grew on a thistle;
He pricked his fingers very much,
Which made poor Simon whistle.
He went to catch a dickey bird,
And though he could not fail,
Because he had a little salt,
To put upon its tail.

the public aware of his orange-roofed restaurant and the delicious foods and ice cream that were served.

Howard Johnson hired John E. Alcott to begin to brand his restaurant. Alcott created the font type for "Howard Johnson's" and began to oversee the graphic design of everything from restaurant placemats to napkins, menus and chinaware, as well as graphics on the ice cream trucks, roadside billboards and advertisements that were seen by thousands of people on a daily basis. The branding of the company with the "Simple Simon and the Pieman" logo became the basis of name recognition, as did the color combination of orange roofs and turquoise blue shutters that the traveling public saw during the day or the neon-illuminated marquees that stood in front of the restaurants and acted as beacons during the evening.

The Howard Johnson's restaurants were among the first and most family-friendly restaurants, and they offered special menus for children that included tasty and visually appetizing meals that had eye-catching names such as the Peter Piper Plate, the Miss Muffet Lunch, the Little Boy Blue, the

Davey Jones, the Tommy Tucker Plate, the Humpty Dumpty Lunch and the Simple Simon Special.

These meals would be advertised on paper menus shaped like a baseball cap, a rabbit face at Easter, a Santa Claus face at Christmas or a face composed of sausages and pancakes. They were fun to order from, but then, with yarn or string, they could also be worn as a mask until lunch or dinner arrived. There was also the "Ice Cream Game" that allowed a child to have a check mark placed in a box beside one of the twenty-eight flavors of ice cream. Once all twenty-eight boxes were checked, the game player was entitled to a free ice cream cone. One can only imagine how children must have wished to play this game at Howard Johnson's on a nightly basis during the summer months.

Often the children's menus were colorful and full of interesting cartoons in addition to a menu, which hopefully kept them occupied until dinner arrived. One of the booklets was not just interesting but also informative. It was "All About the Metric System with the Menu on the Back." A child could not only read but also learn about metrics. Another proudly boasted, "There's loads of fun to be had with a Howard Johnson's Tracie Pad!" The children could draw in the booklet after ordering their meal.

One of the most successful promotional campaigns geared toward children was the "Howard Johnson Birthday Club," which allowed children to be fêted on their birthday with "Free dinner for the child—free cake—lighted candles and all—free balloons and lollipops, free serenade 'happy birthday to you!'" by the Howard Johnson Girls and, of course, the honoree's family and friends. The Birthday Club was promoted by a brilliantly colored blue-and-orange card depicting the "Simple Simon and the Pieman" logo that requested the name, address, birthdate and age of the child. When completed, it would be sent to the Howard Johnson's restaurant. A few weeks before the upcoming birthday, a birthday card and "Celebration Certificate" were sent to the child, and the mother would call for a requested date. Once the party arrived at the restaurant, the table was reserved, often with party hats, and the birthday dinner was celebrated. Said Bob Corker, who was the manager of the Springfield, New Jersey restaurant:

> *We send out over 10,000 cards each year and get better than a 50% return. We average about five guests in each party. Friday's our busiest time, then Sunday and Monday...Johnson Girls* [often] *sing Happy Birthday more than 6000 times a year...These birthday parties were big business for the restaurant chain, and though the birthday child's dinner and birthday*

cake were free, those celebrating were paying guests...Birthday business is extra business—and extra tips for Johnson Girls. You might say it's the frosting on the cake.

As an affirmation that Howard Johnson's was truly a family-friendly restaurant chain, a 1968 press release on the Birthday Club noted, "When you're a child...The world is all yours, and it's such a happy place. Birthdays are big occasions; parties, once-a-year thrills. Happiness is making a wish! Our family restaurants are part of that childhood scene; HJ's is glad to fulfill a child's sense of wonder. And the HOJO Birthday Club helps make it happen."

CHAPTER 8

Employees and Associates

Mr. Johnson included us in his dream of expansion. He relayed a sense of tremendous potential, made us part of something exciting.
—Bill Prendergast

In the mid-1960s, Howard Brennan Johnson began publishing a small booklet series titled *Advertised in Life*, and they were real-life dramas about Howard Johnson's employees. It noted that the "booklet is a tribute to the Howard Johnson's people who have figured prominently in the first year of the Howard Johnson's Spotlight Award Program. The program is designed to honor and reward those who have performed an unusual service to the public above and beyond the demands of their immediate responsibilities. These services have run the gamut from friendly little acts of kindness to major acts of heroism. But, for the people of Howard Johnson's, it's all in a day's work."

In a press release, the Howard D. Johnson Company said that it hoped that

> *these dramatic, real-life stories will give you some insight into the kind of friendly, hopeful people you can always expect to find at Howard Johnson's Restaurant or Motor Lodge. We are enormously pleased with them. Howard Johnson's is a company devoted strongly to the ideal of people helping people. In selecting our employees on every level, we make a determined effort to seek out the obviously helpful, friendly and courteous type of person. Today, we see many people who are interested*

in entering the business on every level—advanced teenagers, management trainees, chefs, cooks, hostesses and others, all eager for an opportunity with Howard Johnson's.

Well, not every employee of Howard Johnson's since its founding in 1925 was awarded the $1,000 savings bond and a gold spotlight emblem pin like those in the Spotlight Award Program received, but they did their various jobs conscientiously and worked as a cohesive group to serve the public in the best way they could.

Some were waitresses, architects, engineers, line chefs or busboys and busgirls; some were hostesses greeting diners, graphic designers or managers of the restaurant. But all employees and associates formed an integral part in furthering the business. Other employees—such as Jacques Chirac, who worked at the Harvard Square restaurant in Cambridge, Massachusetts, in 1953 when he was attending Harvard Business School and went on to become mayor of Paris, prime minister of France and president of France—made their own unique contributions and were a vital part of the business.

Although not all of the following employees and associates—chosen at random to highlight the wide diversity of jobs—were part of the Spotlight Award Program, they combined their individual talents to perpetuate the "orange-roofed empire."

John E. Alcott

John Eagles Alcott (1899–1978) was an industrial designer who designed the Howard Johnson's "Simple Simon and the Pieman" logo with a salivating dog, thus branding the fast-growing company with one of the most recognizable trademarks in the United States food industry.

A designer and teacher, John Alcott was born in Chelsea but raised in Everett, Massachusetts. He served in the U.S. Navy during World War I and then graduated from the State Normal Art School (now known as Massachusetts College of Art and Design). He served as chairman of four departments at the Rhode Island School of Design for many years and was employed at Bird & Son as head designer. Mr. Alcott was the organizer and managing partner in the design firm of Alcott, Thoner & Marsh. Shortly thereafter, he started his own business known as Alcott Associates, which was located in Westwood, Massachusetts, where he resided, and was active

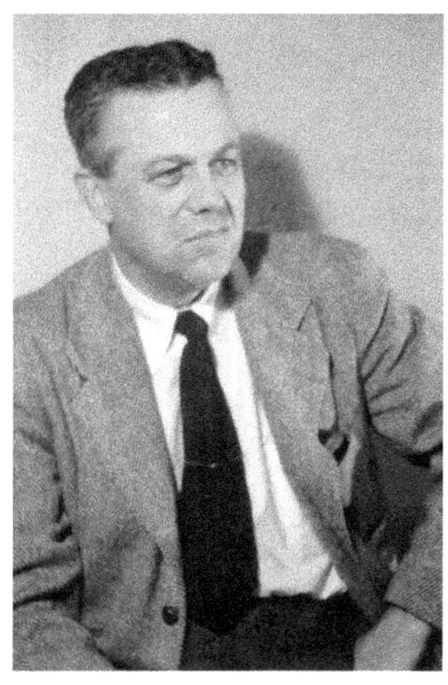

John Eagles Alcott was an industrial designer and educator whose legacy is his design of the logo that branded the Howard Johnson's restaurant chain. His skills as a designer were also used to standardize the lettering font used for Howard Johnson's name, as well as the selection of orange and blue as the company's colors. *Courtesy of Steve and Christine Alcott Baptiste.*

in town affairs. In his obituary, it was said that he "served the town [of Westwood] continuously from 1935 until early this year [1978] as selectman, assessor, finance commission member and sewer commissioner." He founded in 1960 (and was also a charter member of) the Westwood Rotary Club and served as its first president; he was "honored by the Rotary as a Paul Harris Fellow for his outstanding contribution to the community."

His lasting legacy, however, is the logo that branded the Howard Johnson's restaurants and was seen and recognized by the traveling public as the embodiment of quality foods, fast service and a fun tradition. Paper placemats set before diners had the famous logo, with the caption "Should Simple Simon seek a Pieman while going to the fair / He'd now head for a Johnson Stand—'Tis best' he would declare." Mr. Johnson had seen the work that John Alcott had done in designing Mary Hartigan's Restaurant, a former Dutchland Farms, with a consistent theme throughout. "It wasn't long after that Mr. Johnson called me. 'I see what you did for Mary Hartigan's and I like it,' he said. 'I have a truck being built and I'd like you to come up with a design to put on the side of it.'"

The idea for the logo came to Mr. Alcott during a brainstorming session at Johnson's Wollaston office when he noticed a small sketch "on a metal candy container that was in the office. I went back to my studio—a converted stable—and developed the idea. The result was Simple Simon...and the company now had something besides its orange roofs that people could easily recognize." Alcott's business was successful, but the Howard Johnson's account became his biggest account, and he said, "Designing for Howard Johnson's became a continual thing as the company expanded."

During the first years of designing for Howard Johnson's, Alcott's designs were not just artistic but also fun for the restaurant patrons.

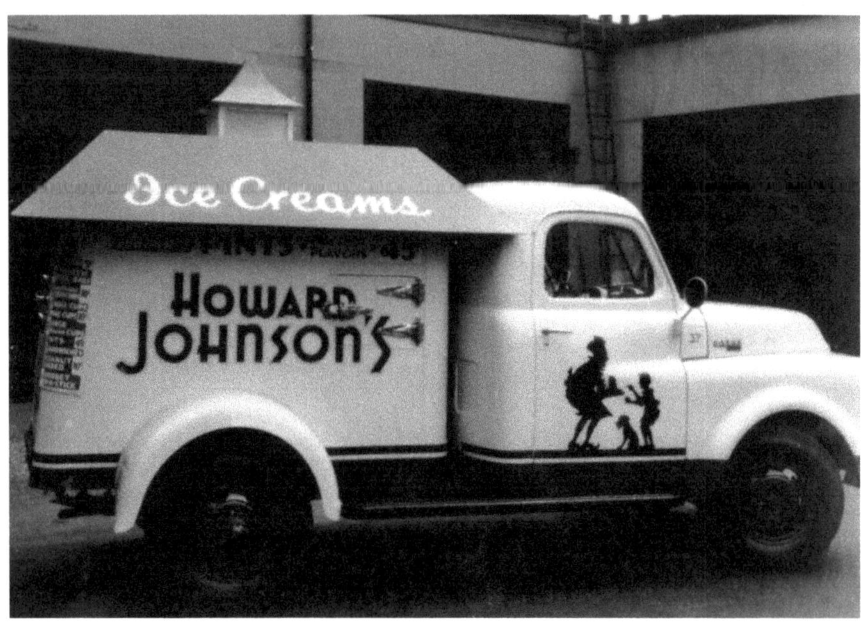

A fleet ice cream freezer truck was purchased from Dodge, and to customize them, John Alcott designed an orange roof with a cupola over the freezer section, with the "Simple Simon and the Pieman" logo on each of the side doors. These trucks would arrive in residential neighborhoods with a distinctive melodic bell to alert all children within hearing distance that a Howard Johnson's ice cream truck had arrived. *Courtesy of Steve and Christine Alcott Baptiste.*

He started "designing placemats for the company. Some of the earliest designs were maps of the eastern U.S. with HJ restaurants marked off in orange." The placemats were an immediate success, but by 1936, the full-color logo had been "simplified to a single color poster silhouette. This was then used on placemats, menus, candy and food packages." His skills as an industrial designer were also employed to standardize the lettering font used for Howard Johnson's name and select the orange and turquoise as the corporate colors that became as recognizable from coast to coast as the vivid colors of the nationwide restaurant chain. He said that he and Howard Johnson "experimented with different shades of orange at one of the restaurants. I suggested that we use the white background to set off the orange and turquoise. I eventually developed a chart of color shades that were the only ones that could be used. This ensured that everything printed for the company was standardized—and that was always a goal."

Although Howard Johnson's was a major account, Alcott had many other successful ventures. The Rhode Island and Massachusetts buildings at the 1939–40 World's Fair in New York were essentially his creations; he "designed the interior of the buildings, planned the exhibits and assembled the parts into a successful whole…[and when] the Massachusetts exhibit was in jeopardy in the second year of the Fair because of lack of Funds, he helped arrange for the opening of a restaurant which subsequently paid the building's way."

As a man said to have "a friendly, congenial personality [which has] given him a good measure of success," he was also a noted designer of kitchen ranges, telephones, lawn mowers, lamps and numerous plastic products. He generously donated eight of his paintings shown at the World's Fair to the Westwood High School, where they hung in the cafeteria.

Margaret Anderson

There she stood—not much bigger than the heavy bag she struggled with, fighting back tears—the weight of the world on her little shoulders. She asked the price of a room, pushing a crumpled dollar bill across the counter. Astonished, Margaret Anderson, desk clerk at Howard Johnson's Motor Lodge, Kingsport, Tennessee, sized up the situation immediately. Filled with pity, she assumed the unhappy little girl was determined to run away from home.

With tender sympathy, she talked to the child who revealed a misunderstanding at home. She was convinced her parents no longer loved her. Finally, wracked with sobs, convinced that Miss Anderson was, indeed, her friend, she told her name. Her parents, near hysteria, came as fast as they could.

For her sympathy and understanding and for safely reuniting the youngster with her parents, Margaret Anderson received Howard Johnson's Spotlight Award.

Note: This section was taken directly from the Advertising in Life *booklet. Margaret Anderson was one of the employees who was recognized by the 1964 Howard Johnson's Spotlight Award Program, which appeared in* Life *magazine.*

Ronald J. Brodeur

Fresh off a destroyer—weeks since he'd seen his girl—the sailor left his Boston base and was enroute to Attleboro, Massachusetts, to see her when trouble developed in a front wheel. Pulling into a Howard Johnson's Restaurant, he removed the wheel and found a broken bearing. What now?

Inside the restaurant Ron Brodeur, 17, Quincy, Massachusetts, high school senior and part time trainee, saw the sailor struggling unsuccessfully to remount the wheel. He asked permission to take an early break so he could help the sailor. Taking his entire break period, the young trainee succeeded in remounting the wheel. Ron's efforts made it possible for the grateful sailor to reach a garage. Repairs made, he was able to continue his sentimental journey.

What is Ron Brodeur planning to do with the $1,000 Savings Bond he received for his Spotlight Award? He'll be able to go on to further schooling. His ambition? To be a master chef.

Note: This section was taken directly from the Advertising in Life *booklet. Ronald Brodeur was one of the employees who was recognized by the 1964 Howard Johnson's Spotlight Award Program, which appeared in* Life *magazine.*

Robert Burrows

Robert Burrows worked at the Howard Johnson's restaurant in Andover, Massachusetts, which was on Route 28, about halfway between Boston and the Rockingham Racetrack in New Hampshire. Because of its location, the restaurant was often busy with both businessmen during the day and racetrack aficionados at night and on weekends.

Raised on Martins Pond in North Reading, he attended the L.D. Batchelder School in North Reading and later the Reading High School. He would work after school and during the summer, when he worked sixty hours per week for twelve dollars, with fourteen cents being deducted for social security. He remembered that the restaurant was fairly new in 1938 and that it was considered by his peers as being prestigious to work there. "It was a friendly place to work."

During his employment, he did kitchen work and operated the dishwashers, but one job he was assigned was to prepare the famous whipped potatoes served at the restaurant. After peeling and boiling ten gallons of potatoes, he would strain them and pour the potatoes and some milk into a large machine that would whip them for five minutes. When they were light and fluffy, he began to add melted butter to the mixture as it was being steadily whipped by large paddles. The result by the end of the week was an increase in side orders for the whipped potatoes, as they were so delicious! The waitresses told the chef that businessmen, who often ordered the seventy-five-cent businessman's lunch, ordered extra potatoes, and it translated into a larger tip, thanks to Bob Burrows's extra melted butter. While he was at Howard Johnson's, he was allowed seventy-five cents per day for food, which could be enjoyed any way he wished. He could help himself to one of the twenty-eight flavors of ice cream, which were kept in large freezers, or enjoy a meal.

In March 1942, just a few months after the bombing of Pearl Harbor, he enlisted in the United States Marine Corps but waited a week for his father's permission as he had only just graduated from high school. He was sent to Parris Island, where he began training, and would be there for almost a year until the spring of 1943, when he and his fellow marines were transported by Pullman cars across the United States to Camp Pendleton, California, at Oceanside. There they trained until shipped overseas into the Pacific conflicts.

Because the Marine Corps refused to take draftees (until ordered to do so), as they traveled from the East Coast, every time the train was scheduled to stop at noon in major cities en route, they were paraded down the main street behind the regimental band in dress blues and playing the blood-stirring Sousa marches, with Marine Corps recruiters following along the march and busily enlisting volunteers. Although it was done to ensure that civilians knew that the war effort took on many aspects, these men were proud of their accomplishment after a year's training and knew that they had the support of the people. Once, as they marched as a unit in Salt Lake City, Utah, the 1,200 marines were marched into the Mormon Tabernacle and were entertained by an organ recital from the organist.

When the battalion arrived in California, it was soon sent into the Pacific Campaign. A few days before it sailed, Burrows was one of two men in the battalion selected, along with fifty others from all over the Pacific operation, for Officers Candidate School at Quantico, Virginia. They were told that they were being sent to college, as they were too young to receive officer training. From a long list of colleges, his second choice was Colorado College in Colorado Springs, which a friend had suggested they choose. Following World War II, he returned to Colorado College and finished his degree. He later did graduate studies at the University of Edinburgh and was later awarded his PhD at the University of Pennsylvania. Throughout his career, he was a professor of American literature and American studies at the University of Wisconsin at Whitewater.

Often returning to New England with his wife and their three young sons along the Pennsylvania Turnpike, they would always stop at the Howard Johnson's restaurants along the highway, as they were welcoming, had clean facilities, were distinctive in architecture and had the famous twenty-eight flavors of ice cream. As he had said, "It was a friendly place to work," but it also was a place the traveling public could rely on for good food and sensible prices.

Helen Church

Helen Nichols Church (1902–1997) was a pioneer nutritionist who, according to her obituary, "began her career telling Howard Johnson what to serve at his very first restaurant."

Born in Le Roy, Illinois, on the Nichols family farm, she attended the University of Illinois, where she received her degree in home economics. She began her career as a clinical dietician at a New York hospital, where she worked with the nutritional values of food. In 1928, she married Charles F. Church, and they relocated to Boston while he pursued his medical degree at the Harvard Medical School. Like his wife, he was to become a respected public health specialist and would found, with nutritionist coeditor Anna de Planter Bowes, *Bowes and Church's Food Values of Portions Commonly Used*, first published in 1937. Bowes was a nutritionist "who first recognized that official nutrition tables listing the amounts of various vitamins and other nutrients in arbitrary laboratory portions of basic foods had little relevance to real world kitchen and dinner table conditions." Working closely with her husband and Miss Bowes, Helen Church was deeply involved in this nutritional project from the beginning and would become its editor after her husband's death in 1976.

While her husband was at Harvard Medical School, Helen Church was hired by Howard Deering Johnson as the dietician for the first restaurant in Quincy Square. Beginning in the summer of 1929, she worked with the founder to serve not just delicious but also highly nutritious foods that tasted as good as they looked. As Howard Johnson said, "The Howard

Johnson's Special Luncheons and Dinners are carefully planned by trained dieticians who never forget to make them tempting to the appetite as well as wholesome and nourishing." Among her first balanced-diet planned meals were simple chicken and meat pot pies, seafood and salads, but one wonders as a trained nutritionist what she thought of the double buttercream content of the twenty-eight flavors of ice cream. Although she was only with Howard Johnson's until her husband graduated from medical school, she made a lasting impression on the restaurant and would go on to have "the last word on the nutritional content of more than 8,000 popular foods" served in this country.

When her husband became chief medical officer at E.R. Squibb & Sons, they worked together to revise *Bowes and Church's*, "spending countless evenings on the screened side porch of their home...going over columns of figures." Although a nutritionist, she was also said to be an excellent cook and was not always content to serve her family precisely balanced meals. She also knew that most housewives didn't serve proper portions and often mixed foods that would be served as elaborate casseroles, but while she was employed at Howard Johnson's, she set a high standard for the nutritional value of the food served as well as the portion size.

Today, *Bowes and Church's* recently went to its nineteenth edition under Jean A. Pennington, who had served as editor with Helen Nichols Church prior to her death, and the book is said to "supply authoritative data on the nutritional value of foods in a form for quick and easy reference. The book's main table reflects the current food supply—listing more than 6,300 common foods—and contains data on the nutritional content of foods, organized by food groups."

Joseph A. Cicco

Joseph Anthony Cicco, AIA (1903–1986), was the vice-president of the architectural department for Howard Johnson's restaurants and started with the company in 1939 as the chief draftsman. It was his designs for the orange-roofed restaurants that became so familiar to the public.

Cicco was educated at the Wentworth Institute of Boston from 1920 to 1922 and the Boston Architectural Center, graduating in 1927. He served as a draftsman and designer with three prominent Boston architectural firms—Haven & Hoyt, Maginnis & Walsh and Desmond &

Lord—before joining the Howard D. Johnson Company in Wollaston as chief draftsman. He became head architect in 1944 and for the next two decades oversaw the architectural office with twenty-five architects that designed new restaurants and motor lodges being built throughout the United States. A resident of Merrymount in Quincy, he was married to Evelyn Daniels Cicco.

Cicco was a skilled architect, but he and Howard Deering Johnson worked on designs for restaurants to ensure that no two restaurants were exactly alike. Company architects, under the guidance of Cicco and the watchful gaze of Johnson, customized each restaurant to fit the size of its lot, the anticipated traffic volume, the size of the parking lot and the demanding whims of the individual franchisees. In 1968, Cicco said in *Landmark*, "I've seen the roof itself change. The first restaurants had asphalt shingles—which Mr. Johnson insisted always be brightly painted. After several coats of orange paint, the shingles curled. After many years and many coats of paint, the orange roof was a very leaky roof. We substituted a porcelain-finish metal tile and it has been standard ever since."

Joe Cicco said that "one thing he learned over the years is 'there's no such thing as an ultimate goal.' Style and taste change; new materials and new methods are constantly being developed. We can never let up. We're always designing prototype restaurants which are used for a few months or years, then changes are introduced. Our growth is so tremendous, we can't afford to stand still." In essence, as an architect, he thought that design must lead public taste, not follow it.

The Lynchburg, Virginia Howard Johnson's restaurant was owned by Joseph Cicco, chief architect for Howard Johnson's at the time. The Lynchburg "stand-alone" restaurant, which he personally designed, was opened in 1953 and was run by Lawrence and Muriel Cicco Holmes, his son-in-law and daughter. It remained a Howard Johnson's until 1986. He opened a second restaurant in 1956 in East Hartford, Connecticut.

Madeliene Dengeleski

Madeliene Dengeleski was a hand dipper in the Cole Chocolate plant in Boston and made delicious hand-dipped chocolates that were said to symbolize "the care and hand work that go into Howard Johnson's fine candies." These delectable candies were sold in the restaurants throughout the United States. She was said to represent a skill that's dying out: the art and craftsmanship of coating candies by hand. Her supervisor said, "Expertly, she covers the center and makes those little squiggles on top with the deft twist of the wrist."

Featured in the February 1966 "Landmark," Mrs. Dengeleski was quoted as saying:

> *Not many young people are going into this field…it isn't very glamorous. Howard Johnson's is one of the few companies still retaining hand dippers, and this company is the fussiest I've ever worked for. They have a high standard of quality, everything has to be just perfect. Of course, we use the finest ingredients and a high grade of chocolate. When I was only fourteen, I started to practice dipping at a summer job, and I wouldn't trade it for anything else. It's fascinating. It's steady work, and it gives me a good living. I love to make the designs on top. This is not just a job…it's an art, almost a lost one, and a skill.*

A hand dipper for more than fifty years, Mrs. Dengeleski had a steady and practiced hand that could make the unique squiggles on the tops of coated candies in a wide combination of coatings and various strings, bars, loops, scrolls, drops, knots and rings—to the seasoned eye, these actually reveal what is contained in the chocolate-dipped candy. She said, "For instance, when you select a 3-finger drop in a pink coating, you'll find a pineapple cream center. If the coating's green, however, you'll have a delicious black raspberry cream! Dark chocolate with a ring covers a cherry cordial. When you buy our Twenty-eight Flavors or Travelers' Choice assortment, you'll find these along with candies topped with strings."

Mrs. Dengeleski made a wide assortment of candies, but the squiggles on top are known as Chinese, S, E, R and plain strings, each indicating a different flavored center. A marshmallow cream was covered in delicious milk chocolate with a bowknot, expertly squiggled after five decades of practice. Proudly, she said, "When our boxes leave Cole, they have a freshness, gloss and sheen that's unbeatable. It takes care to make them the best available, and I just hope everybody takes care in storing them. I take pride in my work, and I like to think my candies are enjoyed at the peak of perfection."

Eugene J. Durgin, Esquire

Eugene J. Durgin (1916–1993) served as vice-chairman of the board of directors of the Howard D. Johnson Company and was not only a close business confidant of Howard Deering Johnson, the founder, but also a mentor to Howard Brennan Johnson, the son.

Eugene Durgin was the son of Eugene and Jane Fitzgerald Durgin and was born in Cambridge and raised in South Boston. He attended English High School in Boston and graduated in 1938 from Suffolk University Law School. Serving in the U.S. Navy during World War II, he was deployed to the Pacific Campaign. He married Dorothy A. Donovan and lived in Quincy until 1966, when he moved to Milton.

Mr. Durgin began his career with Howard Johnson's in Quincy in 1941 as an attorney. He became a close personal friend and trusted legal adviser

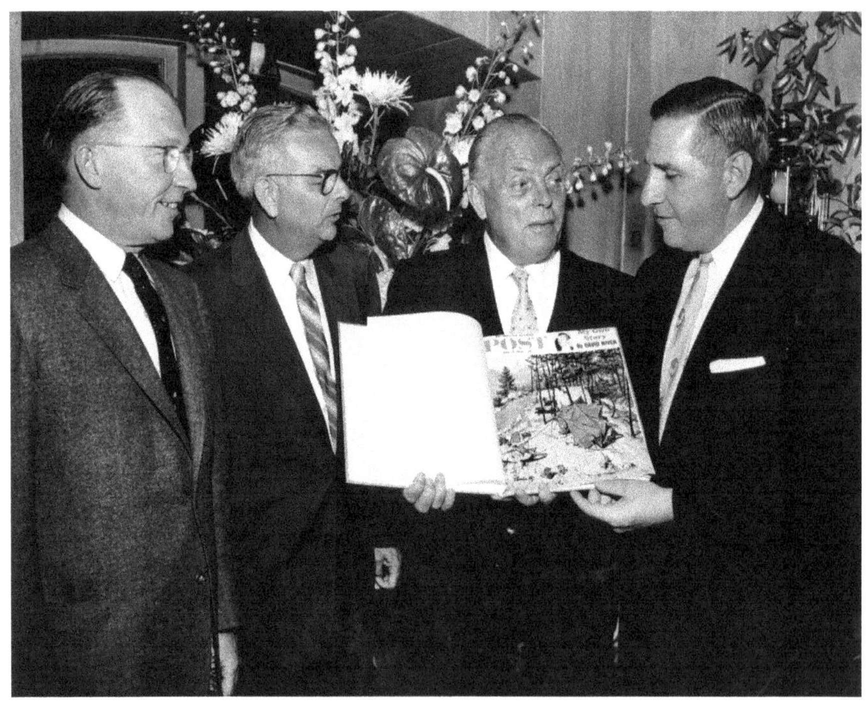

Howard Deering Johnson was featured in the *Saturday Evening Post* in a July 1958 article entitled "The Host of the Highways." A gala reception and dinner was held at the Red Coach Grill on Stanhope Street in Boston's Back Bay in honor of Johnson. *Left to right*: Robert Murphy, lieutenant governor of Massachusetts; G.B. McCombs, vice-president of Curtis Circulation; Howard Deering Johnson; and Foster Furcolo, governor of Massachusetts, who presents a bound copy of the magazine to the honoree.

to Howard Deering Johnson. In 1956, after fifteen years with the company, he became general counsel, and three years later, he served as vice-president and secretary of most of the Howard D. Johnson Company subsidiaries, as well as vice-chairman of the board of directors. In addition to having an office in Quincy, Durgin had a space at the Rockefeller Plaza offices in New York City and directed the activities of other legal department offices in New York, Miami and California.

When Imperial Group Limited bought the company, according to his son, Paul Durgin, it couldn't believe that Howard Brennan Johnson worked out of New York when his company was based in Boston. After his retirement, Eugene Durgin managed the Howard Johnson Foundation until his death.

Pierre Franey

Pierre Franey (1921–1996) was a well-known French chef and was probably best known for his popular *New York Times* column called the "60 Minute Gourmet" in which he simplified classic French cooking for busy home cooks.

Franey was raised in Tonnerre, in northern Burgundy, France, and had a natural love of cooking even as a child; his family referred to him as "Pierre le Gourmand." As a young man, he started as a pot scrubber in a Paris bistro and then worked at the highly regarded Restaurant Drouant, but he was soon hired to come to the United States, where he cooked in the French pavilion at the 1939 New York World's Fair. After two seasons, he and many others had to remain in New York rather than return to France, as during World War II it was occupied by the Nazis. This predicament caused many of those from Europe who had been working at the fair to be stranded. He reportedly turned down an offer to become the cook for General Douglas MacArthur, but he did serve in the United States Army as a machine gunner.

After the war, Henri Soule, who had operated the French pavilion's kitchen at the world's fair, opened a restaurant in New York and hired Pierre Franey as the executive chef of the new restaurant. The restaurant was called Le Pavillon and was patronized by prominent New Yorkers and gourmands visiting New York. It was immediately successful, and Franey lived up to his skill as one of the best French chefs in Manhattan.

In 1961, Howard Deering Johnson, a regular diner at Le Pavillon, hired Pierre Franey to work for him by developing new food lines for his chain of nationwide restaurants. Franey was hired as a vice-president and worked at the Queens, New York commissary alongside many well-known people including Jacques Pépin, a fellow chef at Le Pavillon who would later become famous for his books and television cooking shows. The two French chefs developed and perfected food that was frozen to be served to those patronizing Johnson's roadside restaurants throughout the United States.

In 1976, he and Craig Claiborne, another celebrated chef, gained nationwide publicity for an extravagant dinner they shared in Paris. At a Channel 13 fundraising auction in New York, Claiborne had won a dinner for two, with no set price limit, that had been donated by American Express. The two chefs went to the Paris restaurant Chez Denis and ordered a multicourse dinner with accompanying wines. The bill was said to be astronomical, and Claiborne's recounting of the story about the meal with Franey was printed on page one of the *New York Times*. It intrigued as many readers as it offended with its lavish details of the gastronomic feast. Franey said that the public "took us to task for such conspicuous consumption."

Franey retired from Howard Johnson's in 1977 but continued as a consultant to the company. He died in 1996 shortly after giving a shipboard cooking demonstration aboard the RMS *Queen Elizabeth II.*

Martha Hirsch

At Howard Johnson's Restaurant, Bellaire Boulevard, Houston, Texas, Martha Hirsh entertains children [dressed as a popular mouseketeer in Walt Disney's Mickey Mouse Club] at their parties. Now, this popular Johnson Girl is off to college with the help of scholarships she's won and money she's earned at Howard Johnson's.

One of 13 children, she was valedictorian at Houston's Marian High, an extra-curricular leader, a winner of many scholastic awards. Because she symbolizes all the admirable qualities of Howard Johnson's people, and because of her outstanding contribution to school and community, Martha Hirsch received the Howard Johnson's Spotlight Award. Howard Johnson's said, "We're proud of Martha—and all of our Johnson Girls. Some, like Martha, are helping out at home and earning money for further education. Many are wives of young professional men. Others are mothers with growing families, adding to the budget or sending a child through college."

Note: This section was taken directly from the Advertising in Life *booklet. Martha Hirsch was one of the employees who was recognized by the 1964 Howard Johnson's Spotlight Award Program, which appeared in* Life *magazine.*

Brenda Murphy Madden

Born at the old Carney Hospital on Telegraph Hill in South Boston and raised in Dorchester and later in Milton, Massachusetts, Brenda L. Murphy Madden was the daughter of Alice B. Murphy, who worked as a bookkeeper at the Walter Baker & Company in Dorchester Lower Mills, which was founded in 1765 and was the oldest manufacturer of chocolate in the United States.

A graduate of St. Agatha School in East Milton and St. Gregory's High School in Dorchester, she was hired by Garvey Custom Brokerage in Boston after graduation, working in its exports department. After a short time, she was hired by the Howard D. Johnson Company in 1970, where she worked in the real estate and legal department, which was located off Boston Street on the top floor of the Howard Johnson motor lodge in Dorchester, Massachusetts, where the New England Division's administrative personnel was located. She remembered that the "basement housed the

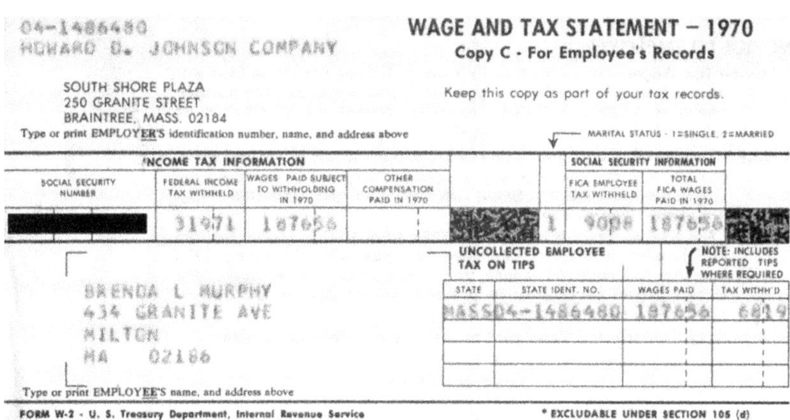

04-1486480
HOWARD D. JOHNSON COMPANY

SOUTH SHORE PLAZA
250 GRANITE STREET
BRAINTREE, MASS. 02184

Type or print EMPLOYER'S identification number, name, and address above

WAGE AND TAX STATEMENT – 1970
Copy C - For Employee's Records
Keep this copy as part of your tax records.

MARITAL STATUS - 1=SINGLE, 2=MARRIED

INCOME TAX INFORMATION						SOCIAL SECURITY INFORMATION	
SOCIAL SECURITY NUMBER	FEDERAL INCOME TAX WITHHELD	WAGES PAID SUBJECT TO WITHHOLDING IN 1970	OTHER COMPENSATION PAID IN 1970			FICA EMPLOYEE TAX WITHHELD	TOTAL FICA WAGES PAID IN 1970
[redacted]	31971	187656			1	9008	187656

UNCOLLECTED EMPLOYEE TAX ON TIPS

NOTE: INCLUDES REPORTED TIPS WHERE REQUIRED

BRENDA L MURPHY
434 GRANITE AVE
MILTON
MA 02186

Type or print EMPLOYEE'S name, and address above

STATE	STATE IDENT. NO.	WAGES PAID	TAX WITHH'D
MASS	04-1486480	187656	6819

FORM W-2 - U. S. Treasury Department, Internal Revenue Service

* EXCLUDABLE UNDER SECTION 105 (d)

The 1970 wage and tax statement of Brenda L. Murphy shows that the Howard D. Johnson Company payroll division was at the South Shore Plaza on Granite Street in Braintree, Massachusetts. Working in the real estate department in the Howard Johnson, she said of her time there, "You felt good when you went to Howard Johnson's." *Courtesy of Brenda Murphy Madden.*

offices for the Public Relations Department, consumer complaints, etc. They also did back ground checks on all employees for all the company owned restaurants. All the menus for all of the restaurants were produced from the basement offices as well." Although the job was not glamorous, the founder of the company and his son both had offices on the top floor of the building, and they were often there.

One thing that Brenda Madden remembered well is that there was an executive chef in the building who often tried new recipes requested by the Johnsons, and most of the office employees were encouraged to sample these new foods, which were served throughout the day on which they were prepared. She said, "You felt good when you went to Howard Johnson's" as well as to work. After a year, she returned to Garvey Custom Brokerage and eventually founded B&A Brokers, one of the leading import operations and customhouse brokerage companies in Boston, Massachusetts, where she currently serves as president.

Jacques Pépin

It may come as a surprise, but renowned television chef and author of numerous bestselling cookbooks Jacques Pépin worked for Howard Johnson's in a commissary in the Queens neighborhood of New York, where he is said to have perfected the delicious clam chowder that was served in every Howard Johnson's restaurant.

Jacques Pépin (born in 1935) is a popular French chef and author of numerous cookbooks in the United States, and for more than two decades, he appeared on both French and American television. Pépin was born in Bourg-en-Bresse, near Lyon, France, where his parents, Jeanne and Jean-Victor Pépin, owned Le Pelican, a restaurant where Pépin worked and learned the basics of French cooking. He went on to work in Paris, training under Lucien Diat at the Plaza Athénée.

In 1959, Pépin came to the United States to work as a sous chef at Le Pavillon, the leading French restaurant in Manhattan. Eight months later, Howard Deering Johnson, a regular diner at Le Pavillon, hired Pépin to work alongside fellow chef and former Le Pavillion employee Pierre Franey to develop and improve food lines in vast test kitchens for his nationwide chain of restaurants. In his book *The Apprentice: My Life in the Kitchen*, Pépin related that the job offer from Howard Johnson was accepted after considerable discussion, as it was a somewhat different course than that for which he had been trained. Pépin said that in Howard Johnson he had "found a second father figure. He was a charismatic, powerful, and yet soft-spoken man," but he was demanding and exacting. Toward his employees, he was "straightforward, candid, and always open to new ideas."

However, Pépin and Franey worked with others in the Queens Commissary as a team, trying to perfect recipes as well as learn what foods could and could not be frozen. Pépin said in an op-ed piece in the *New York Times* on April 28, 2005:

> *It was Mr. Johnson's contention that I should learn about the Howard Johnson Company from the ground up. I worked a few months as a line cook at one of the largest and busiest Howard Johnson's restaurants at the time, on Queens Boulevard in Rego Park. I flipped burgers, cooked hot dogs and learned about the specialties of the house, among them tender fried clams made from the tongues of enormous sea clams whose bodies were used as the base for the restaurants' famous clam chowder. Other specialties I became familiar with included macaroni and cheese, hash browns, ice cream sundaes, banana splits, and, certainly, apple pies... After working on a standard Howard Johnson's recipe in the test kitchen, Pierre and I would prepare it in progressively larger quantities, improving its taste by cutting down on margarine and replacing it with butter, using fresh onion instead of dehydrated onion, real potatoes instead of frozen ones. We made fresh stock in a quantity requiring 3,000 pounds of veal bones for each batch, and we daily boned 1,000 turkeys and made 10 tons of frankfurters.*

While working days at the Howard Johnson's commissary, Pépin attended Columbia University, receiving his BA degree from Columbia's School of General Studies in 1970 and, two years later, a master's degree in French literature. His obvious skill and adaptability as a chef served him well, as he said that his ten years with Howard Johnson's "changed my view of food along with my view of the world and of the restaurant business, a time in which I became immersed in the American lifestyle and came to understand American eating habits." It was his initial forays into television, though, that made his name well known. He was to co-star with the doyenne of French chefs, Julia Child, in the 1999 PBS series *Julia and Jacques Cooking at Home*, which was wildly popular as the two bantered in technique, style and presentation; the show was awarded a Daytime Emmy in 2001. His television show *Jacques Pépin: Fast Food*

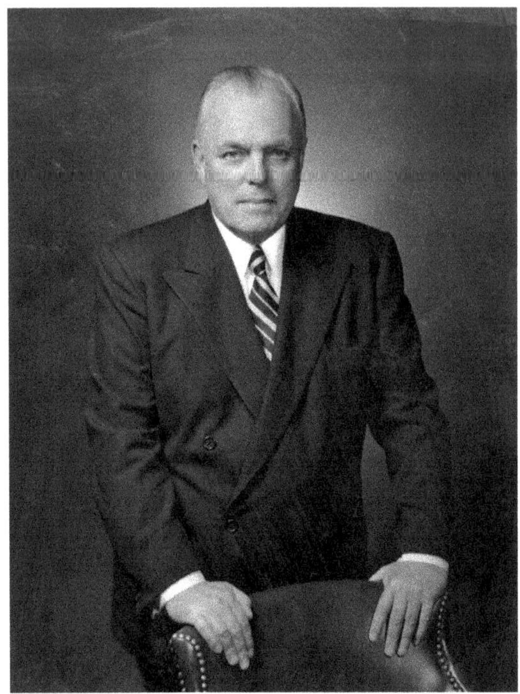

Left: Howard Deering Johnson, after he stepped down as president of the company in 1959, became chairman of the board and treasurer of the Howard D. Johnson Company until his retirement in 1964. His philanthropy would lead to the establishment of the Howard Johnson Foundation, which supports many charitable institutions throughout the United States.

Below: "A well groomed twosome" was photographed in evening clothes in 1955 at the Stork Club on East Fifty-third Street in Manhattan. Marjorie Smith Burgin Johnson and Howard Deering Johnson enjoy a cocktail and iced relish tray before dining at Sherman Billingsly's famous restaurant and nightclub.

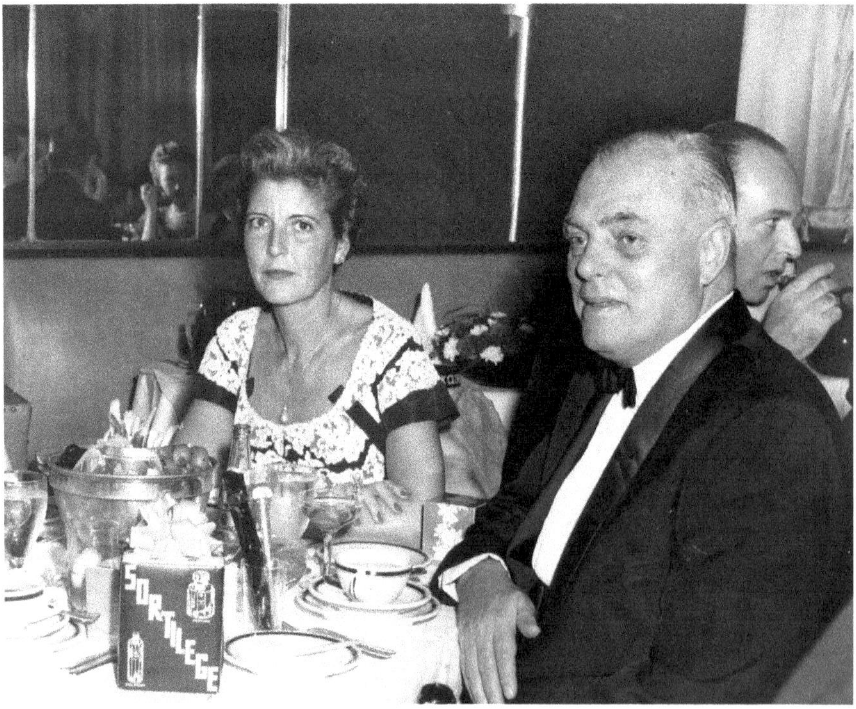

My Way also ran on PBS, and *Jacques Pépin: More Fast Food My Way* is currently being broadcast on the Create Channel.

Beginning with *Jacques Pépin: A French Chef Cooks at Home*, published in 1975, the chef wrote numerous bestselling cookbooks, including *Everyday Cooking with Jacques Pépin* in 1982, *The Apprentice: My Life in the Kitchen* in 2003 and *Essential Pépin* in 2011, in which Pépin brings modern touches to some of his favorite recipes from his illustrious career. His popular and direct approach to cooking has been embraced by the public, and he has received highly regarded awards, among them a Lifetime Achievement Award from the James Beard Foundation and the Chevalier de L'Ordre des Arts et des Lettres. Today, Jacques Pépin serves as dean of special programs at the International Culinary Center in New York City and is a contributor to the gastronomy department at Boston University, where he teaches a class on the cuisine and culture of France in association with Professor Kyri Claflin of Boston University's history department.

As he said in *The Apprentice*, he learned at Howard Johnson's that "Americans had extremely open palates compared to French diners. They were willing to try items that lay outside their normal range of tastes. If they liked the food, that was all that mattered."

Charles D. Polli

Charles Polli (1902–1994) started at Howard Johnson's in 1928 as a part-time worker at the original ice cream stand on Quincy Shore Drive opposite Wollaston Beach. He was quoted as saying:

> *I've seen a lot of changes and a lot of growth in my time. I helped to open summer* [ice cream] *stands and some of the first restaurants. In 1930 I went to the first store in Wollaston as a counter man and then got promoted to assistant manager when I began full-time work. After the war I was promoted again, and I managed that original news and drug store till it closed in 1954. The space was needed for offices. This is a wonderful company for personal advancement, you know. I went to the meat commissary in Quincy and stayed there for 10 years as sort of an all-round cutter. And then last May I was put in charge of the new employees retail store in Wollaston. It's a very interesting job, and I really enjoy it! Some people are amazed at the amount of business we do in a month! It's just like a little supermarket for all the wonderful Howard Johnson's take-home products.*

This store in Wollaston offered not just convenience but also delicious Howard Johnson's foods that were enjoyed by customers and employees alike. They could be purchased at a reduced cost to be enjoyed at home. The store sold a wide selection of prepared foods, but it was said in the "Landmark" that in this employee supermarket "Chocolate Chip is the most popular ice cream, Macaroni and Cheese is the favorite main dish, '28 Flavors' outsells all the other candy packages and these old New England standbys...Baked Beans and Clam Chowder...are tops in canned goods."

Charles Polli, who was said to always have a smile for everyone and was thought of as a happy man, remembered, "I've had chances to move, but the [Howard Johnson's] company and the South Shore have been very good to me. I've really got everything I want from life right here."

Everett Porter

Everett Eastman Porter (1895–1974) was featured in an article in the *Howard Johnson Scoop* as being "The man who turned the crank for the first batch of Howard Johnson's ice cream." Employed by Howard Johnson in April 1926, Porter was the first supervisor of newspaper routes that originated from Howard Johnson's store on Beale Street in Wollaston. As most of the seventy-five delivery boys did their paper routes by foot and by bicycle early in the morning before school, the newspapers had to be sorted, folded and dispatched so that the subscriber received his newspaper on a timely basis.

However, in 1927, after a year's reliable employment, Porter said that Howard Johnson made him an offer that was as delicious as it was hard to refuse. He remembered that "Mr. Johnson said he would make him the ice cream maker in his new venture," which had been started with Olive Belle Johnson's ice cream recipe and perfected by the techniques and freezing tips of William Hallbauer, a skilled ice cream maker, to ensure a smooth, creamy ice cream. He reminisced three decades after he started, "The first batch of ice cream was, of course, vanilla. They then branched out into chocolate, strawberry, and coffee—in that order. The ice cream was popular at once, and [he] recalls that Mr. Johnson had to buy a ten gallon freezer, then another, and still found it difficult to keep up with the enthusiastic demand for the ice cream. It became necessary to open the Wollaston Beach store to help distribute."

So popular had the premium double butterfat ice cream become that Everett Porter used to make trips in his automobile to deliver it to the ice cream stands locally as well as throughout the South Shore and, later, to Orleans on Cape Cod, until a Howard Johnson freezer truck was finally bought. Another of his myriad jobs was to take containers of new flavors of ice cream to the parks and playgrounds in Quincy to offer free samples to the youth of the community to seek their opinion.

Everett Porter, whose employment with Howard Johnson's would later continue in the maintenance department, said that he'd "done plenty of other jobs in my time...and learned something from everyone too! I've always found you can make the best of every situation...the experience gained will come in handy later. I went to Frigidaire night school in Boston to study refrigeration. In another field, after on-the-job training, I passed my exams for a stationary steam engineer's license."

Porter was recognized by Howard Johnson on his thirty-year anniversary of employment. He was "the proud recipient of a testimonial dinner, an automobile, and a trip to California. His [automobile] trip took 31 days and covered 8600 miles." Realizing that after thirty years he was indeed a fortunate and valued employee, he forthrightly said, "One of the things he likes best about the Company is that everyone is 'fair and square,' and all problems are cleared up to everyone's satisfaction."

Reminiscing in "Landmark" in October 1964 about his long employment at Howard Johnson's, he said that he "realized once more what a wonderful company we all work for. Life's been an education...I wouldn't want it any different than the way it's been. People are basically good...you treat them right and they'll treat you right. Cooperation is one of the biggest assets you can ever learn."

Patricia Rissmeyer

Patricia Rissmeyer began working at the Howard Johnson's restaurant on Route 22 in Somerville, New Jersey, in 1972. She was just sixteen years old but had worked at a waitress at a resort in the Catskills the summer before. Because of this previous experience, the hostess allowed her to forego the busgirl position that typically served as the apprentice job for first-time young employees. She recalled her time there with fondness.

At the time, waitresses at many restaurants were required to wear white oxford shoes with nylon stockings and the restaurant issued uniform. In 1972 the uniform was in a turquoise and white pattern tapered closely in the waist, with an apron. If I recall correctly the turquoise uniform was made of cotton and it was subsequently replaced by an orange and white polyester uniform. I am embarrassed to admit that although I held this grown-up waitress job, my mother laundered and ironed my uniforms and so I always met the high Howard Johnson standard. At the time there was a book titled something like "Being a Johnson Girl" that detailed those standards, and it also included specific requirements for undergarments like wearing the proper length slip. Although I could walk to the restaurant from my family's home, my father frequently transported me. This was particularly helpful when I was assigned the weekend breakfast shift which I seem to remember began at 5:30 AM. so for me, working at Howard Johnson's was a family affair! My younger sister Joyce was hired after securing her "working papers" a month after she turned 16. There were two other sisters Lucy and Annie who worked as waitresses and twin cooks Timmy and Tommy. Their brother Brian also worked in the kitchen.

Joyce and I have so many fond memories of working at Howard Johnson's. The work was physically demanding but there was a sense of camaraderie among the employees especially the waitresses. Joyce refers to it as "a real sisterhood across the ages; so many women sharing their stories with each one's life a unique experience." Joyce worked her way up through the organization and held positions of busgirl, waitress, cashier and hostess. She made many friends and recalls the surprise 18th birthday party that the entire staff threw her in the restaurant basement, as well as a Halloween when she and another young waitress dressed in matching costumes. In addition to the collegiality and the fun we had at work the tips were excellent. I seem to remember earning over $100 a week in tips. My grandmother once commented to my mother that Joyce and I were going to be challenged to beat that in any other line of work. I remember speaking to one waitress about the earnings and she disclosed that she had a master's degree in education but earned as much working at Howard Johnson's.

Because of our location on route 22 in New Jersey, our restaurant would attract many travelers. I seem to recall that singer and song writer Paul Simon would occasionally stop in on his way to New York and that we were instructed to treat him like any customer. If memory serves, he would sit in a booth, in a party of four which included a small child. Consistent with the Howard Johnson custom, we would conclude his child's meal with a complimentary ice cream scoop, shortbread cookie, lollipop and balloon. At our Howard Johnson's, even if you were famous, your child was the one to receive the attention!

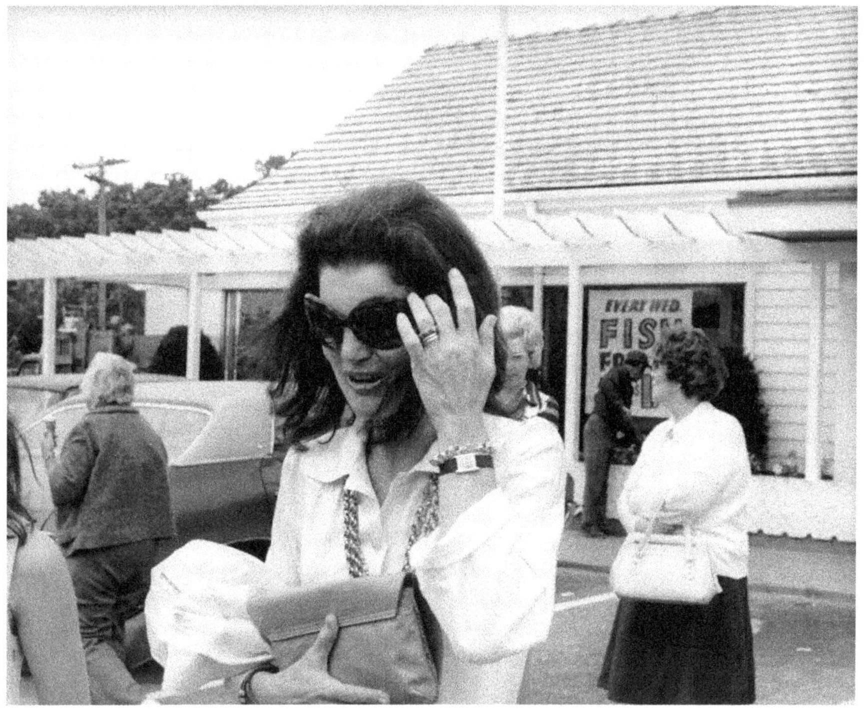

Jacqueline Kennedy Onassis is seen leaving the Hyannis restaurant on Cape Cod in 1971 after having dined under the orange roof. Howard Johnson's really did attract people from all walks of life with delicious foods and twenty-eight flavors of ice cream, as well as the fact that the diner knew that what they ordered would be as delicious and well prepared as the last time they enjoyed it.

Our restaurant had its regular customers, many of whom would request Lucy, Dottie or Annie, the older more experienced waitresses. Several of these customers were widowed or single men. They ordered their usual that may include a cup of coffee and a muffin at the counter or a Manhattan and dinner in the dining room. Speaking of Manhattans, our restaurant had a bar and once we turned 18 (the legal drinking age at the time). Gertie the hostess trained us to mix the drinks that were standard at the time—Manhattans, martinis, old fashions, sloe gin fizzes, tequila sun rises are a few that come to mind. Recently, I was in conversation with a work colleague about a two sided jigger and she was astonished to find that I knew that the small jigger was for vermouth and that I learned that as a bartender at Howard Johnson's at age 18!

The manager at the time was Jack Ambrose and although I did not have much interaction with him (Gertie was the supervisor), in my opinion, he ran a very good organization. We were trained and supervised to consistently deliver the Howard Johnson's standard that included well prepared food, accompanied by parsley garnish on every plate and underliners on every cup or bowl of soup or dish of ice cream. Employees were permitted to eat most items on the menu at no cost (however no steak, no sundaes except "the mistakes") which introduced me to unfamiliar foods. It was at Howard Johnson's that I acquired a taste for fried clams, rice pudding, pecan pie and corn bread—foods that my family did not prepare. I also acquired a taste for coffee although at that time, I drank it with lots of sugar! In 1974 I entered college in Connecticut and when I returned to New Jersey for school breaks, Gertie offered me some hours to work. I earned most of my college spending money at Howard Johnson's and certainly developed an appreciation for hard work and an understanding of how employees work together to deliver a quality experience for customers. To this day, I continue to have great respect for those in the restaurant industry. I would have considered entering that field myself although I did not want to commit to work that consistently required evening and weekend hours.

Finally, I am always excited to meet someone who worked for Howard Johnson's. One of my colleagues at work Mary Anne Murphy and one of my friends Marjorie Harrison worked at restaurants in the Boston area. Because of the consistency of the menu and the standardization of the work expectations, no matter the location there is always a common bond one shares with another Ho Jo waitress! Most of the people in my generation have very fond memories of Howard Johnson's either having eaten dinner out with their parents and siblings or shared a snack with their high school friends after a movie on a Friday or Saturday night. And of course, each person has their favorite of the 28 ice cream flavors! In my mind, Howard Johnson's is a very special place.

The Soffron Brothers

The Soffron Brothers Clam Company was established in 1932 by four brothers—Peter (1913–1984), George N. (1907–1990), Stephen N. (1919–1995) and Thomas N. Soffron (1907–2004)—whose family name was originally Soffranas. With their parents, the brothers and their sister, Virginia, had emigrated from Kalamata, a famous olive-growing area in the Peloponnese region of southern Greece, and settled on a farm in

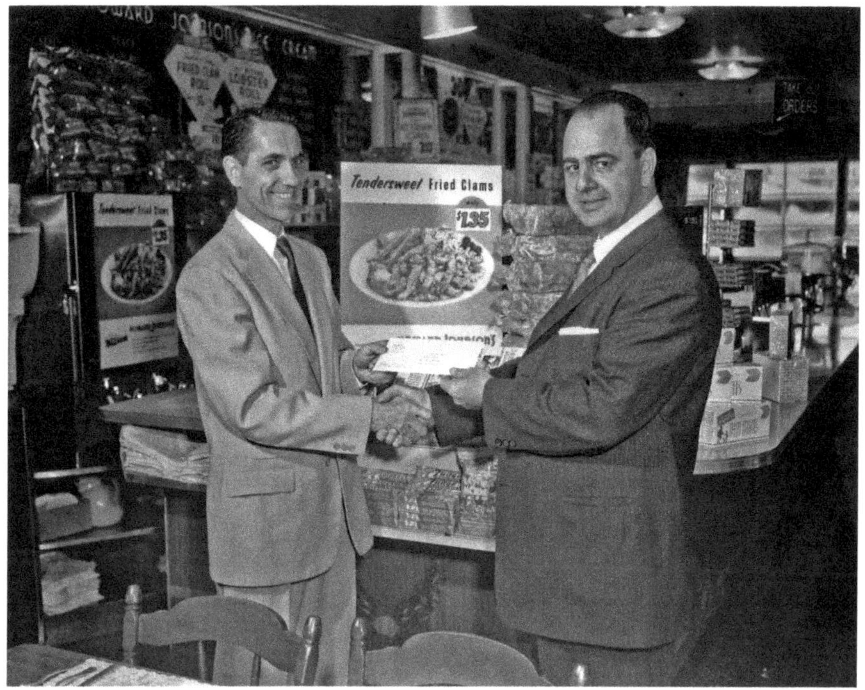

Posing in front of a "Tendersweet" fried clams poster are Howard Johnson's restaurant manager Robert Brindel and George N. Soffron, exchanging paperwork on the sale of the copyrighted term "Tendersweet" from the Soffron Brothers Clam Company to the Howard D. Johnson Company. *Courtesy of Peter Soffron.*

Ipswich, Massachusetts. Their parents worked in the textile mills that were the basis of the town's economy, but their sons struck out on their own after a few years.

According to a brief history of the company, the four Soffron brothers grew to dislike the idea of working in the same mills as their parents and instead found work digging and selling the local soft shell Ipswich clams. Prior to the 1930s, soft-shell clams were generally dug and purchased for use as fishing bait, but clams had become an attractive food source for consumption during the Depression years, along with the advent of the fried clam and the growing popularity of clam chowder. In 1932, the Soffrons took a bold step and purchased a building on Locus Road in Ipswich and converted it into a soft-shell clam shucking company.

The Soffron brothers arranged an exclusive deal to provide their clams and later clam strips to the Howard Johnson's restaurant chain that were sold under the trademarked name "Tendersweet" clams. Peter Soffron's obituary noted that he "was a picky eater and did not care for the clam's belly. He only ate the strip from the large clam, which he could sanitize." Some of us might agree with a finicky eater, but the clam strips were made from the "foot" of hard-shelled sea clams that were dredged from the ocean bottom offshore; they traveled better than did soft-shell clams that were dug by hand in areas closer to shore. So popular had the clam strips become that the four brothers eventually operated seven processing plants, from Maryland to Nova Scotia.

So, do you enjoy whole-belly clams or the "Tendersweet" clam strips?

Roy C. Stoke

As the Cuban crisis mounted, thousands of American troops were on the move. Designation: Florida. Hour after hour they rumbled southward in trucks, jammed together, tense from rumors that they could be in action tomorrow.

Late at night, just before closing time, two trucks from the 121st Signal Battalion swung into Howard Johnson's restaurant in Fort, Lauderdale. To manager Roy C. Stoke, a weary officer explained his convoy was ahead of schedule. His men had not eaten since noon, he said, and could expect nothing until morning unless Howard Johnson's would accommodate them. Without hesitation, Mr. Stoke invited the troops inside. Then he and the few remaining staff in the restaurant rolled up their sleeves and went to work.

As far as the travel-weary, hungry soldiers were concerned, a royal banquet could not have been more welcome. And when the crisis was over, Mr. Stoke invited the same convoy to Howard Johnson's for Thanksgiving dinner—on the house.

Note: This section was taken directly from the Advertising in Life *booklet. Roy Stoke was one of the employees who was recognized by the 1964 Howard Johnson's Spotlight Award Program, which appeared in* Life *magazine.*

CHAPTER 9

Howard Brennan Johnson, the Red Coach Grill and the Ground Round

Howard Deering Johnson's success derived from an uncanny ability to recombine current ideas into a new synthesis that unerringly appealed to a middle-class family on the road.
—*Chester Liebs*

Howard Brennan Johnson assumed the presidency of Howard Johnson's in 1959 when his father stepped down and became chairman of the board and treasurer, positions he held until 1964. The company in the 1960s saw tremendous competition with fast-food restaurants such as Kentucky Fried Chicken, McDonald's and Burger King, as fast food literally meant that one was served in a matter of minutes. However, even though the competition for customers continued, Howard Johnson's still did more business with its wide chain of restaurants than the three competitors combined in the mid-1960s.

With his education at Phillips Andover, Yale University and the Harvard Business School, Howard Brennan Johnson was equipped with the ability to manage the company, yet Howard Johnson's was still a popular restaurant; by the late 1950s, it had been patronized by two generations of Americans as the "Landmark for Hungry Americans." However, it was not just the orange-roofed restaurants that lined the highways of the United States that were serving the public. The Red Coach Grills and the Ground Round restaurants were also becoming part of the roadside empire. However, it seemed that the public's attitude had begun to change, and people were seeking something different than what their parents and grandparents had once found so appealing.

In the early 1960s, Howard Brennan Johnson tried a new concept for his father's company with the expansion of a restaurant chain called the Red Coach Grill, which had been started in 1938 and specialized in steak and lobster. These restaurants were said by the company to have distinctive character, as a "rustic, red-roofed building designed with fieldstone and California redwood. The red coach in front is a welcoming prelude to the delightful atmosphere and high-quality food which is offered to our guests." Red Coach Grills, in the 1960s, attracted upscale diners who enjoyed select cuts of meat, lobster, seafood and other choice entrées in a casual but relaxed atmosphere. From a menu in the late 1950s, the "Special Dinners" included baked sugar cured ham with Champagne sauce, roast duckling with giblet gravy, broiled swordfish with parsley butter and frog's legs sauté with white rice. These were not the typical entrées served at Howard Johnson's, and the Red Coach Grill offered a selection of appetizers, including Jack Larkin's famous clam chowder, and desserts, as well as its signature cocktail, the "Tally-Ho." Only a few of these restaurants were eventually opened in New England, but their distinctive charm was evident even though they were in stiff competition with the Hilltop Steak House and Valle's Steak House, two popular steakhouses throughout the Boston area.

The Ground Round, an American casual dining restaurant, was founded in 1969 by Howard Johnson's as a less formal restaurant than the Red Coach Grills, instead oriented more toward the young adults and their families; the first Ground Round opened in Illinois and proved to be a success, and though it was not a Howard Johnson's restaurant, the Ground Round chain of restaurants were company-owned and franchised. There was a limited menu at first, with only a dozen or so items being served, with burgers in a basket, delicious snacks, appetizers and pitchers of beer. The Ground Round was also well known for its children's parties, showing old-time silent movies and cartoons on a big screen, a mascot named "Bingo the Clown" and for passing out whole peanuts but not discouraging diners from throwing the shells on the floor, which became one of restaurant's more endearing qualities that attracted families with small children. The restaurant also offered diners popcorn with their dinner rather than bread. All of this strove to please a younger, hipper crowd of diners in a new era.

In the mid-1960s, Howard Brennan Johnson created a promotional contest among the Johnson Girls, the thousands of nationwide waitresses, to participate in the selection of a new waitress uniform. In 1961, Howard

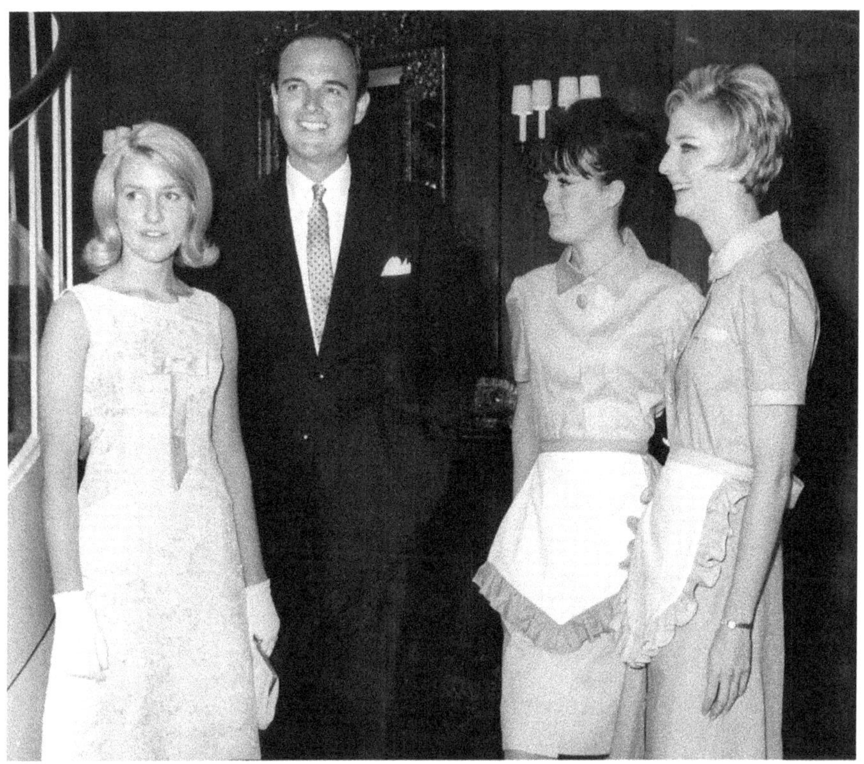

Howard Brennan Johnson commissioned the House of Dior to create four designs for a new waitress uniform in 1965. "Johnson Girls" from thirty-four states and the District of Columbia competed for a tour of Paris. Norma Farley, a Framingham, Massachusetts "Johnson Girl," and Howard B. Johnson pose with two Dior models on the right wearing two of the four designs that would be narrowed to one and ultimately worn by more than eight thousand waitresses in the company.

B. Johnson had an employee training picture (*The Johnson Girl—The Most Important Girl in the World*) produced that detailed the importance of the waitress as the point of contact between Howard Johnson's and the millions of guests. Promoting a new uniform, albeit a designer uniform, was in keeping with his ideas. According to the *Dispatch* of June 22, 1965, "The rumor whispered that for the first time in 20 years, there would be new uniforms for Howard Johnson's waitresses. The initial letter de Paris made this a fact and said that their uniforms would be replaced by a uniform based on a Dior design. The second letter contained a petite bouture de parfum 'Mme. Dior.'" This "letter de Paris" was sent to ten thousand Johnson Girls asking them to participate in the contest whereby six finalists would eventually be selected for an eight-day vacation in Paris.

In 1966, the new A-Line uniform was unveiled and featured in *Vogue* magazine. Of the four models featured by the House of Dior, the chosen uniform was a houndstooth check in aqua and white and worn with a white apron outlined in aqua. Howard Johnson Girls would now be wearing haute couture when they served guests at the restaurants.

The Red Coach Grills and the Ground Round restaurants seemed to stem the tide against fast-food competitors, but by the early 1970s, the public was seeking fast-food restaurants rather than Howard Johnson's restaurants, as the public perceived them as somewhat dated and old-fashioned. "Howard Johnson's had acquired a reputation for being overpriced, understaffed, and behind the times. The service, people complained, was s-l-o-o-o-w." Brian Miller, in his article "Howard Deering Johnson: The Man Under the Orange Roof," wrote, "The fall of the Howard Johnson's brand was faster than it took to build. When the reigns of the company were passed down from father to son, the son appeared to quickly lose control over the direction of the company. Without the persona of his father in his corner, the younger Johnson was leading a company that lacked the vision. Given the impressive growth of the organization in a relatively short period of time, the lines of supervision were not clearly drawn."

When Howard Brennan Johnson, son of the founder, got an offer in 1979 from a British conglomerate named Imperial Group Limited, he was happy to sell an empire that included just over one thousand restaurants as well as five hundred motor lodges for $630 million. But the deal did not bring lasting happiness to the Britons, and in 1985, they sold Howard Johnson's to the Marriott Corporation. The chain kept only about four hundred company-owned Howard Johnson's restaurants, which were swiftly turned into Bob's Big Boy restaurants, its signature eatery, and Marriott sold off the bulk of the empire to Prime Motor Inns Inc. Marriott had little interest in retaining Howard Johnson's traditions, naturally preferring its own traditions, as exemplified by the name of co-founder Alice Marriott, and began giving Bob's Big Boys in San Diego the new name of Allie's. "The intention, long term is to convert all Bob's Big Boys and Howard Johnson's to Allie's." While this was going on, some of the old-timers who had obtained their Howard Johnson's franchises from Howard Deering Johnson were concerned about being sold from conglomerate to conglomerate, and they hired Griffin Bell, a former United States attorney general, to legally represent them.

This never came to court but led instead to an agreement in which Marriott and Prime each put up $500,000 to enable as many as ninety old-timers to incorporate in 1986 as Franchise Associates Inc. A year later, fifty-four of the licensees actually bought stock in the new company. Franchise Associates Inc. then included individually owned Howard Johnson's restaurants in twenty-six states, and although they don't all have all twenty-eight flavors of Howard Johnson's ice cream, a Franchise Associates Inc. spokesman admits, they all have at least eighteen flavors, which indicates that if we can't preserve all the riches of the past in this forgetful and conglomerate age, we can, with a certain determination and a certain effort, preserve at least some of them.

Although Howard Brennan Johnson had publically professed no interest in selling the company that his father had founded and built, he accepted in September 1979 an offer obviously far too lucrative to pass up: an acquisition bid of $28 a share, or $630 million in all, from Imperial Group Limited of Great Britain, a conglomerate that included such businesses as tobacco, food, beer and packaging. For its money, Imperial Group received 1,040 restaurants (75 percent of which were company-owned) and 520 motor lodges (75 percent of which were franchised). Howard B. Johnson, who

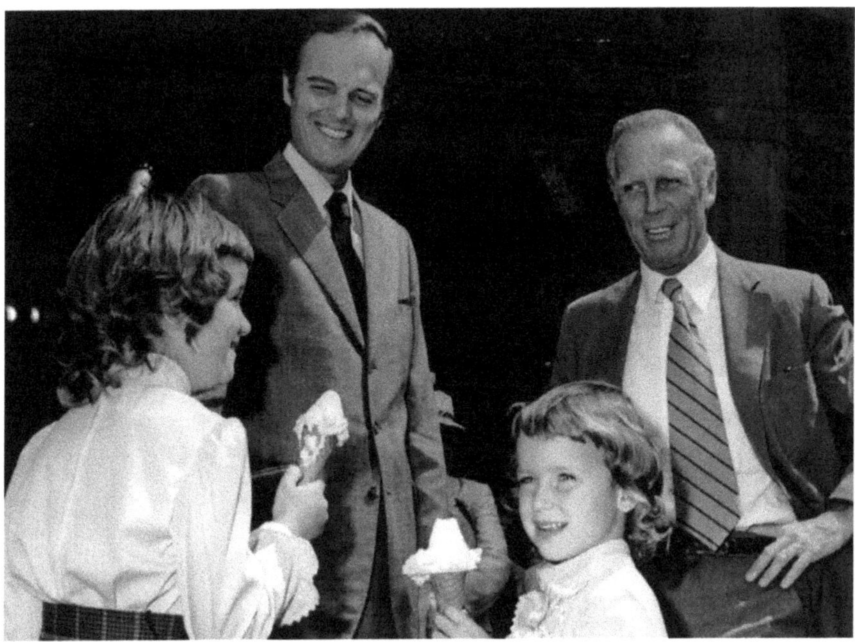

To celebrate the 150th anniversary of the city of Boston in 1972, Howard Johnson's declared the period between August 28 and September 28 to be "Howard Johnson Ice Cream Month" in Boston. Two young girls enjoy vanilla ice cream cones as Howard Brennan Johnson and Boston mayor Kevin Hagan White look on.

collected $35.2 million for his shares, resigned as chairman, president and chief executive officer of the company, and he was succeeded by G. Michael Hostage, a manager who had worked his way through business school and had been employed for fifteen years with the Marriott Corporation.

Hostage inherited a declining balance sheet, as Howard Johnson's was severely affected by competitors in the fast-food industry. In 1979, the company earned $34 million before taxes on sales of $588 million, but earnings dropped to only $14.7 million in 1980 and never fully recovered during the four succeeding years. Hostage vowed to integrate adjacent Howard Johnson's restaurants and motels, which were often under different ownership, by unifying their staffs and offering food-and-lodging package deals and to cut costs by allowing restaurant managers to buy food from a variety of sources rather than exclusively from the company as they had done for decades. The successful and popular Ground Round chain was expanded, growing to 210 units in 1985.

In order to lure business travelers to its motels, which trailed the industry average in occupancy rate and had fallen to sixth place among lodging chains, Howard Johnson's initiated corporate discounts and a new reservations system and raised the advertising budget. It gave licensees the choice of accepting low-interest loans to refurbish their properties by mid-1987 or losing their franchises. A new mid-priced Plaza Hotel chain for the business traveler was opened in 1983, with ninety or more planned over five years at an average cost of $20 million each. These units would include amenities that business people expected but were not receiving from the traditionally family-oriented Howard Johnson's restaurants: banquet and meeting rooms and lounges, as well as executive floors.

In September 1985, Imperial sold the Howard D. Johnson Company to Marriott Corporation for $314 million. Marriott kept the 418 company-owned restaurants but immediately sold the franchise system and the company-owned lodging units to Prime Motor Inns Inc. Prime also assumed Howard Johnson's debt. For its money, Prime received the Howard Johnson's trade name and trademark, 125 hotels and motor lodges operated by Howard Johnson's, 375 franchised lodges and 199 franchised restaurants. Imperial Group kept the Ground Round chain because Marriott was not interested in buying it.

Neither did Marriott have an interest in prolonging the life of a restaurant chain whose name was also held by a lodging operation in competition with its own. The corporation intended to convert these units to Big Boy and Saga restaurants, which would in turn be sold. By the

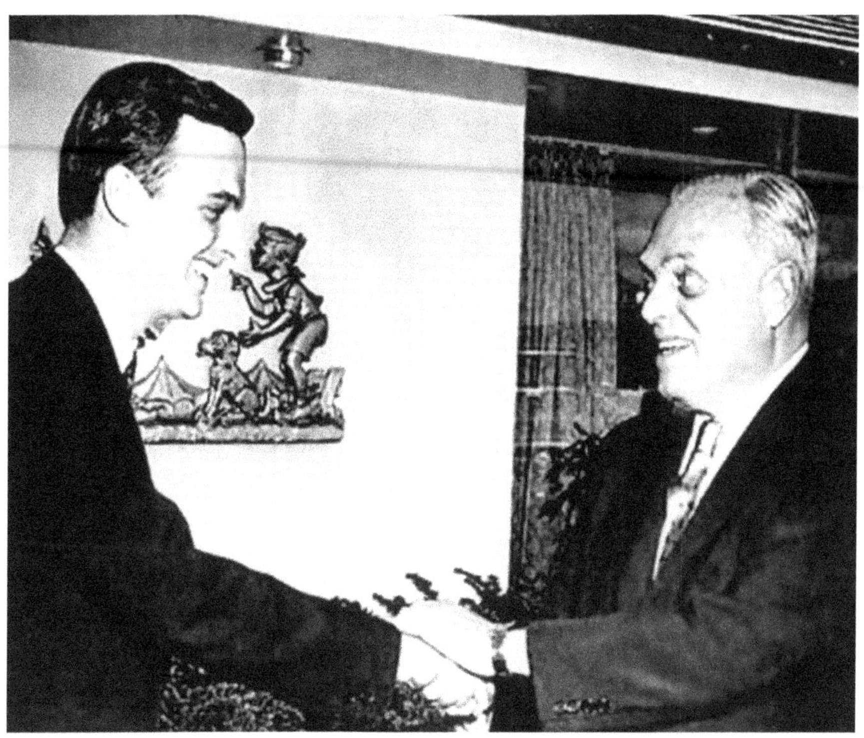

In 1959, Howard Brennan Johnson became president of Howard Johnson's, and his father became chairman of the board and treasurer. Shaking hands in front of a restaurant with the "Simple Simon and the Pieman" logo on the wall behind them, their company had become a famous nationwide restaurant chain that stretched from coast to coast, serving delicious foods and ice cream.

end of 1987, only ninety Marriott-owned Howard Johnson's restaurants remained and, by mid-1991, only fifty.

In direct result of the interests of the restaurant franchisees interests, Prime granted to Franchise Associates Inc., a company established by the franchisees, a perpetual exclusive license to the Howard Johnson's name in connection with the operation of Howard Johnson's restaurants in the United States, Panama and the Bahamas Islands, and granted Franchise Associates the exclusive right to use the Howard Johnson's name or license it to others for Howard Johnson Signature Food Products in these locations.

Franchise Associates bought seventeen of Marriott's Howard Johnson's restaurants in 1991. It had a prototype restaurant designed with a toned-down version of the orange roof and required all new franchisees to use the designated design. Oat bran muffins, salads and garden pizzas were among the health-conscious fare added to the familiar standbys in a new menu introduced in 1990. A stockholders' company of sixty-five franchisees, Franchise Associates owned and operated about two-thirds of the franchised Howard Johnson's restaurants in 1991.

Prime was described by a securities analyst as the fastest-growing company in the lodging industry with the highest profit margins. In 1988, it announced a joint venture to build twenty Howard Johnson suite hotels per year for the next five years at an annual construction cost of about $100 million. A Prime subsidiary was to supply the financing, while AAA Development Corporation would build the hotels. Suite hotels were a fast-growing segment of the lodging industry largely favored by business travelers, and Howard Johnson was planning to charge $55 to $90 per night. The following year, Howard Johnson initiated a $25 million marketing plan to present the chain as "home of the road warrior," the industry name for frequent travelers. Figures showed that 22 percent of U.S. business travelers were responsible for 56 percent of hotel stays.

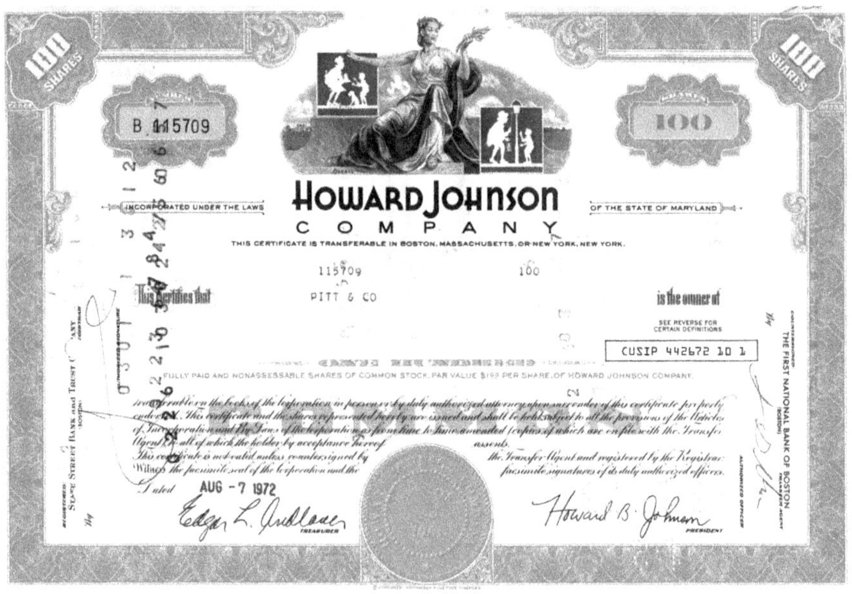

The Howard D. Johnson Company issued shares of stock that allowed the public to invest in the business. In 1961, the company became publicly owned, with its stock traded on the New York Stock Exchange. The stock certificates had an elegant allegorical woman holding laurel, with the logo of the restaurant and the logo of the motor lodges on either side.

In order to reduce its $280 million in bank debt, Prime, which had become the nation's second-largest hotel franchiser, sold its Howard Johnson and Ramada systems to Blackstone Capital Partners L.P. in 1990 for $170 million. A downturn in the lodging and real estate industries and problems in the high-yield, high-risk junk bond market had dried up financing sources for hotels and caused Prime's stock to lose 75 percent of its value in seven months. Blackstone Group, an investment banking firm, added the Days Inn chain and renamed the operation Hospitality Franchise Systems Inc. The company went public in 1992, but Blackstone retained 65 percent of the shares.

Hospitality Franchise Systems changed its name to HFS Inc. in 1995 and the name of its Howard Johnson Franchise Systems subsidiary to Howard Johnson International Inc. in 1996. In February 1996, HFS announced that it would require its Howard Johnson franchisees to upgrade their properties, including establishing a rating system designating properties as either full-service hotels or limited-service units and posting a new sign with a bright blue background. While conceding that the orange roof is "an American icon—as American as apple pie and Chevrolet," Howard Johnson president Eric Pfeffer said, "As we change with the times, we've got to show the newness." Pfeffer, who discontinued the franchises of thirty-seven Howard Johnson properties in 1995 for quality shortfalls, said that the company would be expanded worldwide.

Howard Johnson experienced changes in its ownership structure once again during the late 1990s. Known for his deal-making prowess, Henry Silverman orchestrated a $14.1 billion merger with CUC International Inc. in 1997. A February 2000 *Business Week* article explained Silverman's motivation for the deal, claiming, "The CUC merger was to have been Silverman's masterstroke. He saw CUC, a direct-marketing outfit that sold memberships in discount buying clubs such as Shoppers Advantage and Travelers Advantage, as the perfect partner. The idea was to feed the names of all the customers HFS channeled through its hotels and real estate brokerages into the CUC direct-marketing machine." The article went on to report that "CUC would then sell them memberships in its discount-buying clubs and, eventually, financial services such as insurance. Silverman also figured CUC's team, viewed as Internet gurus for creating the online shopping site Netmarket, could help extend his brands to the Web."

While Howard Johnson's parent worked to regain credibility with its shareholders, the hotel chain focused on expanding its presence in both international and domestic markets. Howard Johnson began to aggressively target business travelers. Known primarily in the hospitality industry as the place to stay for travelers on a budget, the hotel chain wanted to tap into a larger portion of the business traveler segment, and it launched in 1999 a new television marketing campaign with the tagline, "We've got a great name to live up to." The company also introduced Super Miles, a frequent-stay program designed to entice business travelers with future credits.

By the start of the beginning of the new century, Howard Johnson stood on solid ground. While a slowdown in travel after the September 11, 2001 terrorist attacks on the United States plagued the entire industry, the company remained focused on its continued growth. It had four different formats in its arsenal, including the full-service Howard Johnson Hotels and the Plaza Hotels; Howard Johnson Inns, which had restaurants but not room service; and limited-service Express Inns.

CHAPTER 10

The Rise of the Motel and the Johnson Legacy

I never played golf. I never played tennis. I never did anything after I left school. I ate, slept, and thought of nothing but the business.
—Howard Deering Johnson

Originally, a traveling motorist was said to be lucky to stumble upon a cabin with a bed, but increasingly, cabins were adorned with doilies, lamps and framed pictures. Many jumped at the idea of making a quick buck on the tourist trade. One could be self-employed and simply rent a cabin room, and motorists were said to be excited by the idea of real western gentlemanly hospitality. The cabin was easily accessed and free of tipping, formalities and other hotel snobberies. Many hard-pressed farmers jumped at the idea of renting out cottages that could be easily framed and built, and the mass production of goods was sparked in turn. Advertisers let their name be plastered all over a roadside dwelling. For the weary traveler, a "brand name you can trust" was more attractive than an empty-looking cottage.

Entrepreneurs envisioned more accommodations that they felt consumers would be willing to pay for. Indoor plumbing, stucco walls, kitchenettes, refrigerators, sofas and dinettes were added. The cabin would cost under $300 to build, while the "motor hotel" could cost well over $1,000. The first credited motel was built by entrepreneur James Vail in San Luis Obispo, California, and was known as the Motel Inn. It was very much like a hotel but accommodated the automobile. Oil companies envisioned national chains of "auto-havens" or "motor inns." By 1930, the scaffolding necessary

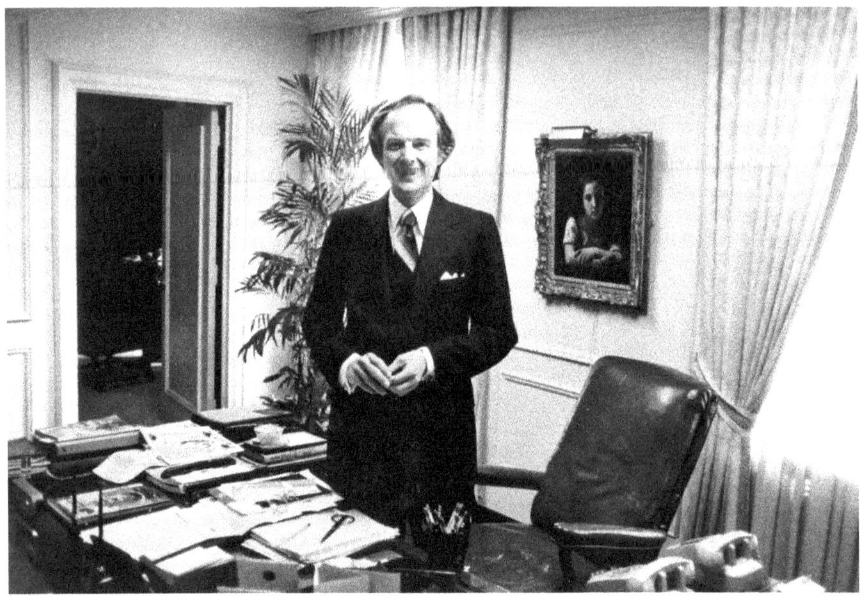

Howard Brennan Johnson, seen in his office at the Rockefeller Plaza in New York City, served as president of the Howard D. Johnson Company from 1959 until 1982 and as chairman from 1964 to 1982. The company was sold in June 1979 to Imperial Group Limited, a British conglomerate. Imperial Group had hundreds of pubs and hotels in the United Kingdom and acquired Howard Johnson's as it was thought that it would offer "long term prospects for growth and a favorable political and economic climate" in the United States.

for the Holiday Inn style was erected. These motels quickly threatened the livelihood of both hotels and camps. The motel and home decorating industries were quickly manifested in wall-to-wall carpeting, upholstery, televisions, air conditioning and Scandinavian furniture.

The motel was to embrace a very particular architectural style. Although the "strenuous life" poison may have been squeezed out of the motorists, the romance of the West remained. The colonial style was hugely important, and the Victorian styles were said to be outdated. Signs used the word "olde" to suggest that they embraced that old-fashioned hospitality the motorist desired. Silhouettes of covered wagons were used for storefronts, and visitors' centers and gasoline stations looked like Tudor cottages or Spanish missions. This period of historical renovation proved to be sustainable with examples such as Williamsburg, Virginia. This new age of motorists wanted a lot of atmosphere with a handful of accommodations.

The 1930s marked a different attitude for the automobile. Whereas in the days of auto camping, the traveler would simply throw a tent over the car and stay out all night, the modern traveler had more respect for the finish of the car. The polish and shine of the automobile meant a lot more. With "Pardon My Dust" long past extinction, the newer, cleaner look was desired. The difference perhaps was the psychological change in income derived from the car. In the day when the Model T was king, all cars were black and often muddy from long trips. However, consumers gained the sovereignty they never knew they deserved, and the ability to choose made a huge impact on the market. The supply-centered market switched drastically to a consumer-centered one. Demand decided production, not a company manager's choice. A different color or style of car was a piece of adornment that described the personality of the driver. The change of ideals perhaps led up to another addition for the motor camps: the garage.

The traveler tired of the mediocre food at rest stops and the pretentiousness of hotel food. Hotels not only had dress codes for dining and specific hours but also made it difficult to pronounce names of entrées with French or Italian words, and they were thought to be a mockery of the middle class. Eventually, restaurants found that serving well-known foods to a public that had become accustomed to the meals made for repeat customers. Because of pressure put on by motorists and by innovations of entrepreneurs, the food became unified. The traveler did not want to feel ignorant at dinner and refused to assimilate to new tastes overnight. Restaurants caught on, and where they didn't, a chain restaurant such as Howard Johnson's appeared. Roadside restaurants informally served predictable but well-prepared food.

What made Howard Johnson a success was his ability to incorporate the visions of the romantic wanderer with the realistic wants and needs of the motorist. He secured efficiency by eliminating variables and incorporating standards nationwide. The traveler, no matter where he stopped, would experience the predictability and uniformity as anywhere else. He made sufficient accommodations for the middle-class American family, including its newest member, the automobile. His colonial-style motor lodges were attractive to the nostalgic Americans, and the architecture style was not from any one place but rather a melting pot of New England architecture that triggered the "old-fashioned comfort" within the Americans. His architects combined the New England with the Virginia and added a little frontier for the design for the inn.

As W.L. Mann said in his *Howard Johnson History*, "HoJo's was a place that generations grew up on. A place where parents brought their kids to, and a place those kids eventually brought their kids to. The real truth now is there is a whole new generation that doesn't even know Howard Johnson's has

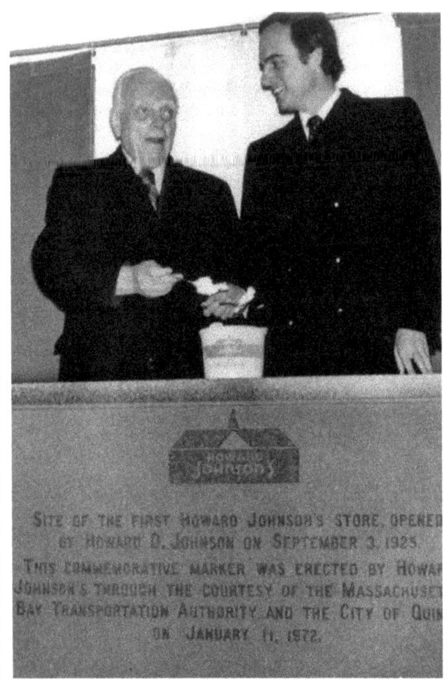

Howard Deering Johnson, seen enjoying some of his famous ice cream with his son, Howard Brennan Johnson.

At a dedication ceremony on January 11, 1972, marking the site of the first Howard Johnston's store on Beale Street in Wollaston, Massachusetts, Howard Deering Johnson said to the assembled friends and well-wishers, "I love Wollaston. Wollaston has been good to me."

A granite plaque marking the site of the store was unveiled at what is now the Beale Street side of the MBTA's Wollaston station parking lot. The store, the start of a system which now includes 871 restaurants and 438 motor lodges, was gutted by a fire in 1969 after it had been vacated for the Massachusetts Bay Transit Authority. Mr. Johnson recalled that he took over the store in 1925 with a borrowed $500, and started selling extra-rich ice cream which he made in the basement. His product caught on, and within a year he opened a stand at Wollaston Beach and in 1929 a restaurant in Quincy. Guests at the ceremony...included Mayor Walter J. Hannon, former Mayor James R. McIntyre, Rep. Joseph E. Brett, MBTA General Manager Joseph C. Kelly and MBTA Director Forrest I. Neal.

—newspaper clipping

anything to do with anything other than a place to sleep." Howard Deering Johnson created a "Landmark for Hungry Americans" that had provided a consistency of quality food and service that the public had come to expect.

In 1963, Howard Deering Johnson was appointed a trustee of St. Elizabeth Hospital in Brighton, Massachusetts, by Richard Cardinal Cushing, and he served as chairman of the 1962 fundraising drive of the Greater Boston Association for Retarded Children. He also generously provided a number of scholarships for students at the University of Massachusetts. He was awarded an honorary Doctor of Laws degree from the University of Massachusetts in 1958 and a Doctor of Civil Law degree from the University of King's College, Halifax, Nova Scotia, in 1962. In 1999, Johnson was inducted into the Hospitality Hall of Fame, which recognizes the world's most successful hospitality interests and the most recognizable brands in the United States.

Howard Johnson was buried at the Milton Cemetery in Lot 412-1 on Maple Avenue. His granite headstone has his name and that of his fourth wife, Marjorie C. Smith Johnson, as well as their birth and death dates. On the rear of the headstone is engraved the crest of the Clan Johnstone, from which he descended. The crest has the words *Nunquam non paratus*, which literally translates to "Never unprepared." Howard Johnson was never unprepared, and his contributions to the roadside restaurant empire have not gone unnoticed. He truly is one of the most famous self-made American men of the twentieth century.

Bibliography

Amory, Cleveland. *Who Killed Society?* New York: Harper & Brothers, 1960.

Bartlett, Apple Parish, and Susan Bartlett Crater. *Sister Parish: The Life of the Legendary American Interior Designer*. New York: St. Martin's Press, 2000.

Crandall, William Rick, Christopher Ziemnowicz and John A. Parnell. "The Growth and Demise of the Howard Johnson's Restaurant Chain: A Schumpeterian Perspective." Published in the *Proceedings of the Southern Management Association Meeting* newsletter, Charleston, SC, November 2005.

Feintuch, Burt, and David H. Watters, eds. *The Encyclopedia of New England*. New Haven, CT: Yale University of Press, 2005.

Fortune magazine, September 1940.

Friedrich, Otto. "Essay: Reflections on 28 Flavors." *Time*, May 1, 1989.

From Maine to Florida with Howard Johnson's. N.p.: Howard D. Johnson Company, 1939.

Liebs, Chester. *Main Street to Miracle Mile: American Roadside Architecture.* Boston: Little Brown, 1885.

Miller, Brian. "Howard Deering Johnson: The Man Under the Orange Roof." *International Council on Hotel, Restaurant and Institutional Education* 17, no. 4 (n.d.). Richmond, Virginia.

Milton, Massachusetts Public Library clippings.

Milton Record, 1930–72. Milton, Massachusetts Public Library.

Newsweek. "Business and Finance: Daddy's Boy." August 8, 1966.

New York Times.

Reader's Digest. "Who Is Howard Johnson?" July 1949. Condensed from *Pageant* article written by Blake Clark.

Sammarco, Anthony Mitchell. *Dorchester: A Compendium*. Charleston, SC: The History Press, 2011.

Saturday Evening Post, July 19, 1958. Curtis Publishing Company, Philadelphia, Pennsylvania.

Time. "Host of the Highways." September 5, 1960.

———. "Personalities." April 3, 1964.

Index

P

Q

R

S

T

U

W

Y

About the Author

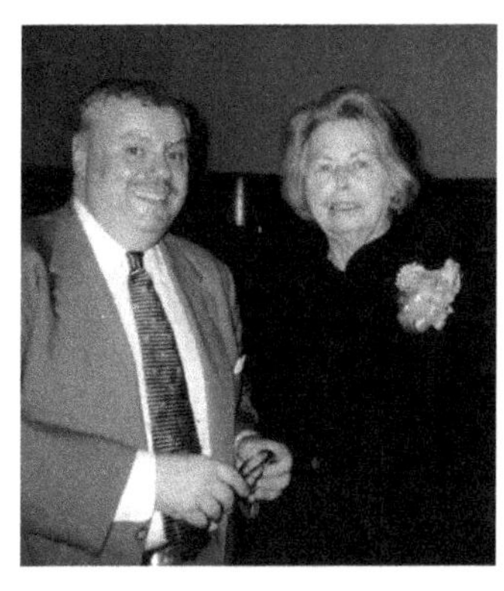

Anthony Mitchell Sammarco, seen here with Dorothy Johnson Henry, is a noted historian and author of more than sixty books on Boston, its neighborhoods and surrounding cities and towns, and he lectures widely on the history and development of his native city. He commenced writing in 1995, and his books *Dorchester* and *The Baker Chocolate Company: A Sweet History* have made the bestsellers list. *Boston's Back Bay in the Victorian Era*, *Dorchester: Volume II*, *Dorchester Then & Now*, *Boston's North End* (and its Italian-language version *Il North End di Boston*) and *The Great Boston Fire of 1872* are among his most popular books for both native Bostonians and tourists. He is currently writing *Lost Boston* for Anova Books in London.

Since 1997, Mr. Sammarco has taught history at the Urban College of Boston, where he was named Educator of the Year and where he serves on the Leadership Council. His course "Boston's Immigrants" was developed especially for the Urban College and its multicultural and diverse student base, and his book *Boston's Immigrants* was written to highlight the diversity of the city and is used in his course. Among the many awards for his historical work, he has received the Bulfinch Award from the Doric Dames of the Massachusetts State House and the Washington Medal from Freedom

Foundation, and he was named Dorchester town historian by Raymond L. Flynn, mayor of Boston, for his work in history. He was elected a fellow of the Massachusetts Historical Society, is a member of the Boston Author's Club and is a proprietor of the Boston Athenaeum. In his volunteer work, he is treasurer of the Victorian Society, New England Chapter, and a trustee of the Forest Hills Cemetery Educational Trust. He is also a former president of the Bay State Historical League.

He lives in Boston and in Osterville on Cape Cod.

www.ingramcontent.com/pod-product-compliance
Lightning Source LLC
LaVergne TN
LVHW052340100826
845147LV00021B/1130

* 9 7 8 1 6 0 9 4 9 4 2 8 5 *